Functional Aesthetics

for data visualization

Vidya Setlur
Bridget Cogley

WILEY

Published by John Wiley & Sons, Inc., Hoboken, New Jersey.
Published simultaneously in Canada and the United Kingdom.

978-1-119-81008-7
978-1-119-81010-0 (ebk.)
978-1-119-81007-0 (ebk.)

For general information on our other products and services or for technical support, please contact our Customer Care Department within the United States at (800) 762-2974, outside the United States at (317) 572-3993 or fax (317) 572-4002.

Wiley also publishes its books in a variety of electronic formats. Some content that appears in print may not be available in electronic formats. For more information about Wiley products, visit our web site at www.wiley.com.

Library of Congress Control Number: 2022930202

Cover images: The assets for the book cover are provided by Vidya Setlur and Bridget Cogley.
Cover design: Wiley

Printed in Great Britain by Bell and Bain Ltd, Glasgow

BB117043_120522

In memory of Kelly Martin, who knew true beauty and laughter.

(VS)
To Amod—my support and life partner
and
Naren and Narsim—whose unconditional love constantly helps me be a good mother and a better person

(BC)
To Mike—the ultimate dancer, driver, and super-spouse
and
Dominic—who gives me new eyes to the world and the freedom to play

Contents

Acknowledgments

This book would not have come together if it were not for the support and encouragement of so many people. We both would like to thank Patrick McCormick, Brandi Beals, and Madison and Milwaukee Tableau User Groups (TUGs) for your impeccable timing and brilliance for putting us in the right place at the right time. Without all of you and a famous blue Fiat, this book would never have happened.

We are also grateful to so many individuals who have helped with this project: October 22, 2020, to be precise, is when our book journey started after Jim Minatel, the associate publisher at Wiley, responded to our book proposal. We thank him for believing in us and being a good partner during the book-writing process. We'd like to thank our project manager, Brad Jones, for patiently doing all the content wrangling, keeping us honest with deadlines, and gently hustling us with his positivity. Also, thanks to Pete Gaughan, Barath Kumar Rajasekaran, and Melissa Burlock for helping with operations to move the content along to finish. Jock Mackinlay, our technical editor, has been an awesome sounding board, applying his vast experience in both academia and industry to enrich so many parts of this book. We thank Pat Hanrahan for graciously writing the foreword and inspiring us to think of how semantics with visual representation can help make sense of the world.

Vidya would like to thank her mother, Jayashree Raghavan, for basically taking over the kitchen during the writing process, texting her lunch and dinner menus so that she could emerge from her she-cave to eat. Her father-in-law, Rangaswamy Setlur, has been her personal cheerleader all these years, reading the manuscripts and providing kind notes of encouragement. She owes a great amount of gratitude to all her research colleagues for their wisdom and intellect and to her friends and neighbors, who have generously shared their joy and pride during the writing process. Finally, the long days just felt a little sweeter with Milo, her pandemic pup, with his playfulness and love.

Bridget would like to thank Mike Cogley for bringing tea and driving the Fiat where this all started and Dominic Cogley for the laughs and inventions while writing this book. The practitioner sections are stronger due to the extra eyes from Allen Hillery, Michelle Frayman, and Sarah Pallett. Bridget would be remiss if she didn't thank her mother, Sheree McKay, for teaching her to have a keen eye and to put things in the right place. Friends and family lent their support, even if it made no sense to them. The patience is much appreciated. Colleagues past and present made this process easier, providing much-needed motivation and encouragement. No book acknowledgment is complete without celebrating the cats that keep the laughs and fuzz coming: Fluffles, Minx, and Jaxx.

And we thank you, the reader, for giving these ideas a space to have this conversation.

About the Authors

Vidya Setlur is the Head of Research at Tableau Software. Prior to joining Tableau, she worked as a principal research scientist at the Nokia Research Center for seven years. She earned her doctorate in 2005 at Northwestern University. Her area of expertise is in natural language processing and computer graphics. The goal of her work is to develop new computer algorithms and user interfaces that enhance visual communication and understanding of the semantics of the underlying data. Since joining Tableau Research in 2012, Vidya has worked on various projects and prototypes ranging from semantic icon encodings to chatbot interfaces. She has also explored analytical conversation using principles of language pragmatics that led to Tableau's first natural language feature, Ask Data.

Bridget Cogley is the Chief Visualization Officer at Versalytix and long-time consultant in the data visualization space. As an interpreter turned analyst, she brings an interdisciplinary approach to data analytics. Her dynamic, engaging presentation style is paired with thought-provoking content, including ethics and data visualization linguistics. She has a deep interest in the nuances of communication, having been an American Sign Language interpreter for nine years. She is a Hall of Fame Tableau Visionary. Her work incorporates human-centric dashboard design, an anthropological take on design, ethics, and language. She extensively covers speech analytics and open text. Prior to consulting, Bridget managed an analytics department.

About the Technical Editor

Jock D. Mackinlay is the first Technical Fellow at Tableau Software, an expert in visual analytics and human-computer interaction. He believes that well-designed software can help a wide range of individuals and organizations to work effectively with data, which will improve the world. Jock joined Tableau in 2004 after being on the PhD dissertation committee of Chris Stolte, one of the cofounders of Tableau. Jock got a computer science PhD at Stanford University in 1986 and joined the research team at Xerox PARC that coined the term, "Information Visualization." In 2009, Jock received the IEEE Visualization Technical Achievement Award for his seminal technical work on automatic presentation tools and new visual metaphors for information visualization.

Foreword

Data is everywhere. Manipulating data is now considered an essential computer skill, along with searching for information, document editing, and slide making. Spreadsheets are no longer just number-crunching tools; by reading data into a tabular grid, they are now the gateway toward more sophisticated data analysis and graphing. Analyzing and graphing data is taught in high school along with experimental science and analytical reasoning. Solving almost any problem involves data. It is essential to understand your data, to be able to reason about it, and to draw out findings and conclusions. Data-based decision making is becoming a core doctrine of modern businesses and organizations.

How do people interact with data? The answer is obvious. They must be able to see it, as a list, table, map, time series, scatterplot—a visualization. The power of visualization leads naturally to the question of how to present data to people so they can best understand it. This book provides answers to this essential question.

The answers start with how to graph data. Obvious questions are how best to discern different magnitudes or compare values. Is a bar graph better than a pie chart? The next level is how to distinguish categories using color and shape. And how to perceive trends and other patterns. Even basic graphics can benefit from good graphic design. The techniques of graphical design show how to emphasize the most important information and deemphasize the less important. The answers to these questions require that we understand visual perception.

The more interesting questions arise when we think of visualizations as a form of communication. In this view, visualizations are a type of language—a visual language. Now new questions arise. How do we assign meaning to what we see? What do icons and colors mean, what do they represent and symbolize? These types of questions give us a deeper understanding of how visualizations work. A visualization is no longer a simple graph of data. A visualization contains a message; it tries to communicate information to us. We can use it as a form of rhetoric to spur people to action. At the next level, how do we interact with our data using visualizations? How can they be used to help us think? How can we have a dialog with our data?

This book by Vidya and Bridget takes you on this journey. It provides insight into how we see, interpret, understand, and reason about data. The book provides a summary of research findings and useful advice for the practitioner. It will enable you to use visualizations more effectively as you analyze data and communicate what you found to the people around you.

Pat Hanrahan

Introduction

You enter the restaurant, escaping quickly from the cold. The large glass windows minimize the distance between the brisk air outside and the warm air inside. The generous wooden beams lead you deeper into the hubbub of the restaurant, until you find your sweet spot, the highly coveted booth embedded in a tube similar to the one in Figure 0.1. The space is playful and inviting. The table is almost spartan, but the lighting, the slightly raised platform, and the delightful paradox between the openness of the window and the intimacy of the space draw you in. You and a few friends step eagerly into the booth, awaiting the dining experience you've read about.

FIGURE 0.1 A view into a restaurant space
Jon Tyson/Unsplash.com

You take in the aesthetics of the space as you wait for your server. The concrete around you forms a perfect circle. The wooden flooring supports your feet as you gently tap them in anticipation. The light above emits a warm glow, suspended from the top and allowing light to fill the whole chamber. It's surprisingly warm, the velveteen seat cushions softly supporting you. The architecture is open, but you're nestled comfortably away from the noise. You laugh, feeling both free and cozy.

The meal arrives, served in a beautifully arranged black-lacquered bento box similar to what is seen in Figure 0.2. One of the visceral pleasures of the lunch box is the arrangement. The intentionality of the food placement is juxtaposed with the sheer beauty of the delicacies. There is a state of delicate tension as each dish gets its space with a deliberate order that helps guide your culinary experience. The food is separated, no sauces mixing, and the wasabi and ginger are placed where they can easily be pinched with chopsticks and added to the sushi. The main dish occupies the largest container. A supporting dish of cooked vegetables sits with the pickled condiment. Salad and sides are placed in smaller containers acting as cheerful companions to the protagonists of the meal. The black framing neatly highlights the shape of each part and provides an implicit guideline for order and hierarchy. The meal is a delight, with each varied piece harmoniously playing an essential part that is functional *yet* aesthetic.

FIGURE 0.2 Arrangement of food in a bento box

These are the experiences we hope to provide our users, one that balances form with function and delight with efficiency. It's leveraging beauty to provide both a form and function that support an ideal. While crafting charts and dashboards to help people see and understand data, we often spend time trying to find the right balance between a functional design and an aesthetically pleasing design that breaks through the clutter and noise. Functionality is often thought to be obvious; graphics have a functional purpose, which is to make it easy for the reader to understand the patterns in the data. The aesthetic component is less obvious. How do we make charts visually delightful in a way that takes the process of visual analysis to a whole new level of joy? The aesthetics are seen instantly. The charts indicate that the visualization author is skilled. They hint that the design is also functional. The joy of the aesthetics also compensates for the daunting aspects of data work. This visceral feeling is something that we can actually relate to in our own lives through the sights, sounds, and smells of the world as we experience it. The challenge, of course, is that aesthetic design is hard to achieve, hence this book.

Imagine in our restaurant scenario, and you head to the restroom just before leaving. After washing your hands, you go to grab a paper towel. The paper towel dispenser is one of those automatic ones and you wave your hands to no avail. Finally, it spits out the tiniest bit of paper. It's not even sufficient to grab, and so you dry off your hands on your clothing.

The paper towel problem is common. It comes wrapped with the best of intentions, from reducing waste to eliminating the need to touch anything, yet it falls short. The intents compete—we want people to use *fewer* paper towels, but they still need to be accessible. Too often, inaccessibility wins and dysfunctional behavior ensues. We end up using more, not less, or none at all.

This experience happens with data visualization as well. We create charts and our users flail when the intentions of the chart and that of the user do not align. They struggle to navigate our carefully laid dashboards, tidy explanations, and lovely frames. In short, we've done everything right, but it's still landing wrong. Just as with paper towels, our charts can fall short in ways we don't anticipate. They include hidden barriers—often chosen more to preserve an aesthetic or meet a certain goal than to provide a function—making it far too easy to do or interpret the wrong thing.

This is not a design book about charts.

Rather, it's a book focused on how the intentionality of the data in the chart can be expressed through thoughtful design sensibilities. The book explores the interplay between what we see (perception), what information is encoded (semantics), and what we mean (intent).

Combined, this triad creates a powerful subsystem in the production of data-driven graphics. We call this concept *functional aesthetics* as a way of using beauty and form to guide and support function. Throughout this book, we'll highlight that charts are more than just visual artifacts; they come embedded with hidden linguistic components and interactivity that we can use to more clearly articulate our intent.

If you've picked up this book, we're assuming that beyond choosing effective charts, you're looking for ways to improve how your visualizations communicate. This could be presented as a traditional dashboard or as a data-driven app. It might be as an infographic or through data journalism. You might also be developing the next tool to help facilitate the making of data-driven graphics, as either a researcher or developer. Wherever you are using data to create an experience, we hope this book will help you move beyond literal chart making to semantically resonant data-centric creations. Legends, text, spacing, and so many hidden elements dictate how your work is read. This book is designed around that larger experience, so we're assuming you have a level of comfort with chart selection and statistically accurate data representation.

In this book, we'll center on the idea of data-driven experiences and how we can use functional aesthetics to both transport and cue our readers to the actions and insights we hope they'll take. We'll incorporate delight as a reasonable benchmark. Elegant design vanishes, becoming a backdrop in our memories and leaving us with a frictionless experience. We recognize it in physical spaces with a near-reverence for the place, as we saw with the restaurant example. Viscerally, we feel it, such as when we find a kitchen item stored just exactly where we'd put it, or a chair nestled in the perfect place to sit and enjoy the sunlight. Experiences delight and transcend the sum of the parts.

This book is also a conversation, one held between a researcher and a practitioner. We hope to challenge our own assumptions and to explore this subsystem deeper. Vidya Setlur, a researcher, has spent years investigating and integrating linguistics into her work, including Ask Data, a search engine within Tableau designed to display charts in semantically resonant ways. Bridget Cogley, a practitioner, has spent well over a decade working in data analysis and visualization. In addition to consulting experience centered on visualizations that captivate, she draws from her background interpreting American Sign Language to incorporate semantics in visualization. Our backgrounds form two sides of a coin:

what the research says about our ideas and how they can reasonably be incorporated into practice for better results.

A Fiat, Food, and Finding Commonality

Beyond Binaries:
A Conversation

It all started in a Fiat, headed to Milwaukee to attend a local TUG event.

Vidya sat tucked in the backseat, suitcase nearby. Bridget sat in the front passenger seat while her husband drove. Prior to this trip, Vidya and Bridget had spoken only briefly. They had finished delivering their presentations in Madison the day before and were preparing to repeat them again in Milwaukee. Vidya presented on color theory and semantics, while Bridget discussed the logic of dashboards. Together, these sessions represented two pieces of a puzzle—how semantics and visual aesthetics *together* help people see and understand their data.

One hundred twenty miles and a lunch later, a friendship started, and so did this book.

As we have this conversation, both with you and our-selves, we also want to expose where ideas in this book originate. Are they researched with specific points proven, a theory that's perhaps still evolving, or perhaps a common practice that stems from practitioner experi-ence or trend-following?

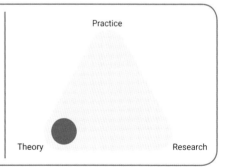

Some ideas tie back to a theory that we have or that's shared in academic or practitioner circles. For ideas solidly in the theory realm, we'll place the circle in the left corner.

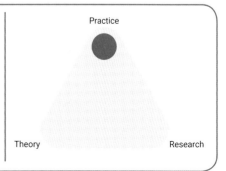

Other ideas are common in practice. It could be anecdotal—we find users at scale reject a specific chart or end up editing our work to specific charts quite frequently. Sometimes, charts in the real world inspire ours as a form of "data fashion."

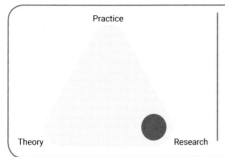

Research centers on answering specific questions, such as how users perceive certain graphics or interpret them. Many of these ideas originate from hypotheses, inquiry, and prototypes.

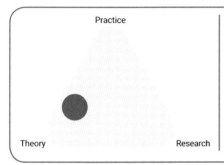

In this example, a particular idea is mostly a theory, with some use in practitioner circles. You will notice we are using location, and that the dot can land in a variety of spaces.

Throughout the book, we will use the following visuals to highlight where these ideas reside.

Through this visualization, we hope to make easier to understand what's explicitly researched, what's sometimes extrapolated from that research, and what's potentially thought but not fully proven scientifically. Here's how you'll see the triangles used in the book:

This book is a continuation of that conversation started in the car, a dialog between a researcher and a practitioner. It is a means to examine all the knowledge we have across a number of disciplines and find ways to integrate them holistically into a system of practice. Throughout this book, we will discuss research, current working theories, and how these concepts can be implemented in practice.

This Book at a Glance

This book isn't designed to be an introduction to data visualization. We assume that you have read various introductory books, have a plethora of chart choosers, and are looking to move to that next level in data visualization. Maybe you're struggling with endless feedback cycles or seeking novel ideas in how to approach unifying charts into a cohesive unit. You might be an analyst, a researcher, or a professional in a dedicated field comfortable with visualizing statistics. Maybe you're in marketing and looking to shift the paradigm in how infographics are designed. Beyond charts, we hope this book challenges you to look at data in a new light, a view where charts construct part of a data message and that perception, semantics, and intent inform how visuals are understood.

While many examples in this book are designed in Tableau, we intend that the principles presented can be used in any software or programming language. This book is not designed to walk you through code snippets or the making of a particular chart or dashboard. Instead, it's a conceptual challenge and a paradigm shift.

We hope this book is a dialog, one that introduces ideas and a philosophy to design.

Here's how this book is structured.

PART A: Visual Perception

Part A will focus on perception and common practice. As the dominant dialog in academic and practitioner circles most frequently centers on perception, we will cover this lightly and reference other resources. We will first discuss how the human visual system is extremely adept at process-ing visual information such as color, shape, and size. By encoding data in these visual attributes, visualization tools offload cognitive work to the perceptual system, enabling users to focus on answering questions about their data rather than reading and comparing data values. We will then delve into common practice, such as the creation of charts and dash-boards. We will also explore interaction patterns on the authoring side as well as for consumption.

PART B: Semantics

Semantics is the study of meaning. Language is a way of expressing and elucidating meaning in various ways; it makes use of a wide range of linguistic tools such as words, intonation, imagery, and gestures. In Part B, we explore how semantics can communicate visual expression through well-designed dashboards, effectively conveying the goals of the author to their audience as well as understanding the analytical goals of the user during data exploration. We will describe practitioner and researcher perspectives on how understanding the meaning of data and what it represents can in turn, help inform aesthetic yet useful ways of visualizing the data. In the next unit of the book, we will discuss in more detail what these analytical goals are, what we refer to as *intent*.

▦ **PART C:** Intent

A user expresses an information need as an intent when interacting with another human or with a computer system. Humans are particularly skilled at attempting to understand or seek clarification of an intent that is expressed. However, humans and computers have asymmetric and complementary skills, particularly in the areas of data, semantics, and aesthetics. Also, human-to-machine interaction can be particularly challenging as the human's and computer's mental models of what they would like to seek needs to be expressed and interpreted clearly. Part C will walk through various techniques for designing analytical conversations between data and the human in relation to their intent.

▦ **PART D:** Putting It All Together

As we step into the last section of the book, we will discuss how perception, semantics, and intent come together as a whole. Revisiting concepts from previous chapters, we provide key takeaways to help empower the reader, that's you.

Let's dig in.

Reader Support for This Book

Companion Files

As you read through this book, references are included for supporting material. You can find a bibliography of these references on the support page for this book at www.wiley.com/go/fafordataviz. Additional information about the book, including a glossary of terms, newsletters, and regular updates about the book can be found at www.functionalaestheticsbook.com.

How to Contact the Publisher

If you believe you've found a mistake in this book, please bring it to our attention. At John Wiley & Sons, we understand how important it is to provide our customers with accurate content, but even with our best efforts, an error may occur.

In order to submit your possible errata, please email it to our Customer Service Team at wileysupport@wiley.com with the subject line "Possible Book Errata Submission."

PART A

Perception

The description of a single visual memory highlights the way our senses are so important to how we experience the world.

As Ansel Adam says,

Yosemite Valley, to me, is always a sunrise, a glitter of green and golden wonder in a vast edifice of stone and space.

We are equipped with five senses—sight, hearing, smell, taste, and touch—to help understand the environment around us. Our senses have the uncanny ability to convert real-world information into electric and chemical signals that can be processed by the brain. Perception refers to the set of processes we use to make sense of these signals that we encounter every second, from the page of this book in front of you, to the smell of freshly brewed coffee emanating from your kitchen. Our perceptions are based on how we interpret all these different sensations, which are sensory impressions we get from the stimuli in the world around us.

Close your eyes. What do you remember about that restaurant where you dined? The color of the walls, the angle of the shadows, the smell of the food before you took that first bite? Whether or not we know it, we selectively attend to different things in our environment. Our brains simply don't have the capacity to attend to every single detail in the world around us. The first step of perception is the decision of what to attend to. Depending on the environment, and depending on us as individuals, we might focus on a familiar stimulus or something new. When we attend to one specific thing in our environment—whether it is a smell, a feeling, a sound, or something else entirely—it becomes the attended stimulus.

Once we've attended to a stimulus and our brains have received and organized the information, we interpret it in a way that makes sense using our existing knowledge of the world. Interpretation simply means that we take the information that we have sensed and organized and turn it into something that we can categorize. This happens unconsciously thousands of times a day.

The topic of perception is among the oldest and most important in psychology. Significant literature by leading experts explores this at far greater depths than we will explore in this book. However, an understanding of how the human visual system works will provide the necessary foundation in this book for unraveling the characteristics of what makes charts functionally aesthetic. In Part A, we will explore the various aspects of human perception and how they each play an important role in seeing and understanding data.

CHAPTER 1

The Science Behind Perception

The human visual system is quite intricate and remarkable. Cameras often serve as a common reference point when first starting to understand the mechanics of the eye itself. Like the lens on a camera, the cornea serves as the outermost lens and window to the world, protecting the viscous eye but letting light enter. The colorful iris acts as a shutter mechanism to control light. Similar to the camera metaphor, the eye can expand and contract to focus properly. While there are optical similarities between a camera and the eye in the way they capture an image, a camera does not have perceptual or cognitive abilities and the metaphor starts to break down when we get to how the brain interprets this information.

Seeing and Understanding Imagery

Beyond a picture that we perceive, our brains take this visual information and perform calculations on it. Think about it as you drive. You are analyzing in real time the placement of your car against the other cars as well as how fast the other cars are moving. When you buy a new car, your perception has to adjust from that vantage point: your new car might be smaller or larger, affecting all of your calculations and processes. Vision is an information processing phenomenon where neurons in our brain perform calculations on the signals so that we reason about what is in the imagery we see and how we act on it. In other words, it's not a simple picture or movie that we perceive.

Long before Isaac Newton discovered that colors were physical and quantifiable phenomena of light's spectrum, skilled artists figured out ways to trick our brain's circuitry. They often used color in clever ways to simulate illusions of the mind, whether it is creating the perception of depth on a flat surface or the sense of movement in a static object.

Claude Monet, an impressionist painter from the late 1800s, used unrealistic luminances in his masterpiece, *Impression, Sunrise*, which is shown in Figure 1.1. The scene deceptively looks rather simple; a few small rowboats at the port of Le Havre at sunrise in the foreground with the orange-red sun being the focal element. The layered hazy brushstrokes create the illusion of depth despite their imprecise details. Yet this piece is far more complex than it looks.

FIGURE 1.1 *Impression, Sunrise* by Claude Monet
Claude Monet/Wikimedia Commons

While it initially seems that the sun is the brightest spot in the painting, it turns out that it has the same luminance (i.e., the perceived brightness of a color) as that of the sky. Dr. Margaret Livingstone (2008), a neurophysiologist, showed that if you make a black-and-white copy of the painting as shown in Figure 1.2, the sun almost entirely disappears!

We can now barely see the shape of the sun. Rather than being drawn to the sun, the boats now stand out the most. Dr. Livingstone describes how the area of the visual cortex contains bands of cells that route signals coming in from the eye to specialized branches of neurons.

She presents a model of the neural processing of vision that argues that humans possess two distinct visual systems. The ventral stream (also known as the "what" pathway) leads to the temporal lobe and deals with visual identification and recognition through color and shape. The dorsal stream (also known as the "where" pathway) leads to the parietal lobe and concerns orientation and the location and movement of things in space. "We have all these modules in our brains for seeing things," Livingstone says. "They make us an expert at seeing those things."

FIGURE 1.2 *Impression, Sunrise* converted to black-and-white in GIMP. The sun blends into the sky.
Claude Monet/Wikimedia Commons

Since the "where" pathway can only discern orientation and movement, it is color-blind. Like our black-and-white painting, it processes the sun and the sky and does not register the presence of the sun. The "what" system discerns color and can find clear boundaries between the orange sun and the blue sky. This mishmash of neuron pathways results in a perceived sense of motion—the sun cuts through the blue-gray hues of the sky and *shimmers*.

An effective piece of art can convey an artist's message by bridging the biology of seeing with an emotional response in the viewer. A combination of carefully laid-out brush strokes can provide a harmonious combination of beauty and purpose for the painting. Early impressionists were considered radicals in their time because they did not follow the rules of academic painting from the Roman and Greek periods. Rather, these impressionists used the canvas to go beyond photo-realism to something that was imaginative and magical as they teased our human visual system.

Too often, charts can be intimidating. They can seem rather anonymous, flat, and so obscure. As a chart maker, how can we think about the intentionality of color, shape, and placement of marks in a chart? A simple chart is no more than a set of statistics made visible, showing what happened in the past and perhaps what might happen in the future. But it can do more than just being functional. It can engage the viewer by capturing their imagination. Nigel Holmes has pushed the boundaries of infographics by advancing charts into evocative illustrations with embellishments that serve as a visual metaphor to generate a strong visceral reaction, often making the takeaway from the chart memorable (Holmes, 1984). We will discuss more about how charts can (and should) intentionally engage with the reader through careful design, semantics, and even creative embellishments. And perhaps, your dashboard may evoke an emotional response similar to that of an art lover staring at a Matisse or a Renoir in a museum gallery.

Color Cognition

Color is a key visual aspect of how we observe and relate to objects around us. A *perceptual color space* (what we see as color) is defined from descriptions of attributes of perceptions of about 6 million different colors in the real world. A *cognitive color space* (i.e., what we understand as color) would refer to the internal representations of the colors and would also include semantic color representations, that is, names representing the colors mentally. In a box of Crayola colors, for example, the color names and color values need to match. To do otherwise would be very confusing, potentially creating cognitive interference.

Language has a long history of resources for describing color. Firstly, a word can have a strong association with color, especially when color is a salient feature of the concept it refers to—for example, *sky* (blue), *lemon* (yellow). Secondly, color names pertaining to pigments and dyes are often derived from the source, such as *indigo*, from the *Indigofera tinctoria* plant. Thirdly, many languages have morphological and syntactic processes that create complex color terms out of simple color terms (for example, *blue-green*, *yellowish*, and *pale pinkish-purple*). Finally, many linguistically simple terms that denote subtypes or "shades" of colors are denoted by other terms. For example, *scarlet*, *crimson*, *vermillion*, *puce*, *magenta*, *burgundy*, and *maroon* are among the more commonly named shades of red. This suggests that linguistic data sources that consider the semantics of color names might provide for better reference, selection, and retrieval of colors for various tasks, including for categorical palettes in data visualizations.

In dealing with color-naming data, internal consistency is usually good but there are high variations between people. In fact, Randall Munroe of xkcd (https://xkcd.com) comic fame asked 22,500 willing participants to take part in a color-naming survey. Munroe found some interesting disparities between how people name colors, with women providing more descriptive modifiers than men.

Now, why is all this important or even relevant to data visualization? From the literature on categorical color perception, we know that only a limited number of colors can be internally represented and absolutely identified across different cultures and during different tasks. Berlin and Kay (1969) conducted a study with native speakers coming from a diverse set of 98 languages to decrease the possibility of borrowed color terminology. They established that for English (and many similar European languages), there are 11 basic categorical color names: red, green, blue, yellow, orange, purple, pink, brown, black, white, and gray. Languages with fewer than the 11 basic color categories all followed a set of "restrictions" regardless of the language family. For example, they found that all languages have words for *black* and *white*.

For languages with just three terms, the third term is always *red*, and those with four terms have words for either *yellow* or *green*. In other words, the lack of randomness of color terms over the studied languages suggested a series of evolutionary stages in the development of color words. While Berlin and Kay's work has demonstrated how the evolution of language has influenced color names in its vocabulary, one must point out that speakers can also signify differences in color, not by separate terms, but by variations in syntax, morphology, tone, and inflection of the language in question.

In the 1950s, the US National Bureau of Standards created a color naming dictionary [ISCC] to both define a standard set of color names by partitioning the Munsell colors (1919) and create a dictionary of commercial color names, defined in terms of their Munsell specification and their standard name. While this standardization effort was not widely adopted, the use of color names to represent colors in commerce continues today. Go to any paint store, and the color samples are labeled with both a technical code for constructing the paint and a semantic name, designed for some combination of descriptiveness and memorability. The Sherwin-Williams red collection (2021) provides examples such as Positive Red, Eros Pink, Radish, Brick, and CoralBells. HTML 5 supplies 140 color names, from the basic blue and red to the exotic chartreuse and BurlyWood (W3Schools, 2021). The power of these names is not their accuracy but their memorability and ease of use.

What is fascinating is that the cognitive and representational aspects of color in categorical color perception have been found to be closely related to visual synthesis and spatial organization. This means that these color names are used to describe objects around us—the red and black lacquered bento box, the green pines in Yosemite, or that yellow New York cab.

The Stroop effect is perhaps one of the most striking phenomena illustrating the cognitive aspects of color. Let's do a little exercise. Look at each word in Figure 1.3 and say the color out loud, not the word itself. It's rather tricky, isn't it?

YELLOW BLUE ORANGE
BLACK RED GREEN
PURPLE YELLOW RED
ORANGE GREEN BLUE
BLUE RED PURPLE

FIGURE 1.3 Colors and the Stroop effect

This effect can be said to demonstrate a conflict between perceptual and semantic processing. When people are asked to name colors, they experience a conflict between the cognitive meaning of the word (yellow) and the perceived color (green). The Stroop effect also highlights a fundamental link between language and color cognition. This link demonstrates the importance of semantic coloring in the domain of the category.

Objects with strongly associated colors, like fruits, vegetables, political parties, and brands, also benefit from semantic coloring. Effective imagery must first determine the colorability of the objects in the category, then determine the appropriate coloring. Remember, we want to avoid that Stroop effect, which can trip up people. Semantic coloring is also defined by the context. For example, *apple* as a fruit is generally red, yellow, or green, but *apple* as a company brand is white or silver-gray. We will discuss how semantics plays a role in creating functionally aesthetic charts in Part B. Until then, Figure 1.4 is a teaser. After all, who doesn't love ice cream?!

Figure 1.4 is an example of a color palette automatically generated based on the ice cream flavor names in the data.

Coloring needs to be semantically relevant and is also defined by the context.

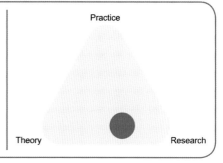

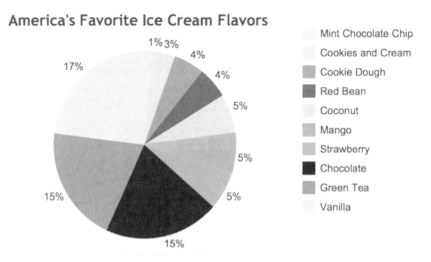

FIGURE 1.4 A semantically resonant color palette of ice cream flavors
Setlur & Stone,2016/with permission of IEEE

The lovely cream brings out the vanilla flavor from the graph, making one's mouth almost water. There is a balance of intentionally delicate hues with a certain playfulness in that pink strawberry, all while making it easier to identify the different flavors in the graph. As we better understand how the human visual system works, our charts can in turn be made more meaningful. Often, we are made to believe that it's form or function, especially when visualizing data; but one can have the cake (or rather ice cream) and eat it too!

Saccade and Directed Attention

In addition to color, contrast plays an important role in visual perception and allows us to effectively differentiate contours, depth, and shape. The human eye makes quick scans when viewing a scene or performing any activity. Referred to as saccades, it is estimated that the eye makes about three scanning movements per second and that these tend to occur unhindered during both focal and distributed attention. Saccades generally involve focal attention and are facilitated by a short-term memory system; but what catches the attention of a saccade? Several studies found that contrast, including strong light-dark contrast, color contrast, and movement, attracts saccades and draws focal attention.

The human eye tends to notice and focus on objects that are bright or feature movement. Called the fixational reflex, this occurs when a brightly contrasting or moving object is deemed significant. In visual design, strong contrasts in hue, saturation, and/or tonal value can create fixational reflex and are often used to draw attention to significant areas of text or imagery or create some significant level of differentiation. To illustrate with the example in Figure 1.5, poor contrast in the left image tends to impact negatively on legibility and the text is more difficult to read. Strong contrast in the right image allows the text to be read quickly and effortlessly.

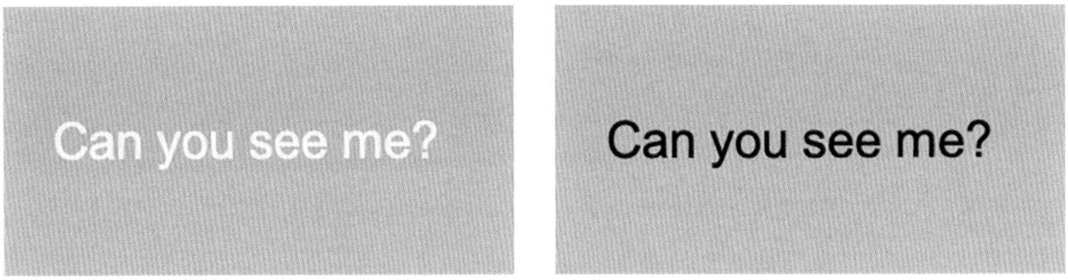

FIGURE 1.5 Illustrating the effect of contrast on legibility

Just as color plays an important role in human visual perception, visual contrast also has the capacity to discern structure, logic, and patterns; it helps us make sense of the world. As a result, color and contrast are frequently harnessed in the design of visual communication to draw attention to key elements such as headlines, text, or imagery.

The Notion of Space and Spatial Cognition

People conceive of spaces differently depending on the functions they serve. A dining table could very well function as a school project space with glue sticks, pencils, and cardboard while in the evening, it can transform into a cozy family gathering for dinner and conversation. The space of external representation of pictures, diagrams, maps, and charts serves as cognitive aids to memory and information processing. To serve those ends, graphics may generalize information suitable to the context and message they need to convey. In many useful diagrams, similar elements appear with similar abstract meanings; their interpretations are context-dependent, as for many word meanings, such as line or relation or area or field. In diagrams, notably maps and graphs, lines are one-dimensional paths that connect other entities suggesting that they are related. Crosses are intersections of paths. Blobs or circles are two-dimensional areas that depict how much space is occupied by an element. These elements schematize certain physical or semantic properties while omitting others.

In the 1920s a group of German psychologists—Max Wertheimer, Kurt Koffka, and Wolfgang Kohler—developed theories around how people perceive the world around them called Gestalt Principles, where *Gestalt* is German for a *unified whole*. These principles help reason why the human mind has the natural compulsion to find order in disorder. We group similar elements, recognize patterns, and simplify complex images when we perceive objects. In other words, the mind "informs" what the eye sees by perceiving a series of individual elements as a whole. Gestalt Principles are an essential part of visual design. There are more than 10 overlapping principles; 5 of the more prevalent ones are listed here:

FIGURE 1.6 Closure

Closure: We prefer complete shapes, so we automatically fill in gaps between elements to perceive a complete image. In Figure 1.6, we can interpret a cluster of black shapes set against a white background to reveal the familiar form of a soccer ball.

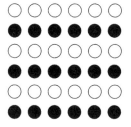

FIGURE 1.7 Common region

Common region: We group elements that are in the same closed region. Related objects are placed in the same closed area or boundary to show they stand apart from other groups. They are assumed to share some common characteristic or functionality. In the graphic in Figure 1.7, the black circles appear related and as part of the same group even though there is no explicit boundary drawn indicating so.

FIGURE 1.8 Figure and ground in Rubin's vase
iStock.com/ Ekaterina Chvileva

Figure and ground: We dislike uncertainty, so we look for solid, stable items, unless of course the image is ambiguous like the Rubin's vase in Figure 1.8. The visual effect generally presents the viewer with two shape interpretations, each of which is consistent with the retinal image, but only one of which can be maintained at a given moment. The brain begins "shaping" what it sees; the process involves higher-level cognitive pattern matching, in which the overall picture determines its mental interpretation rather than the individual effect of its constituents. We try to put together two distinct regions of the picture, that is, faces and a vase. Each makes sense in isolation, but when the brain tries to make sense of it, contradictions ensue and patterns must be discarded.

Proximity (Emergence): We group closer-together elements, separating them from those farther apart. So when we cluster individual elements like the pairs of vertical lines in the graphic in Figure 1.9, we recognize each line pair as one entity standing distinct from the other pairs.

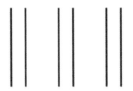

FIGURE 1.9 Proximity (Emergence)

Similarity: The principle of similarity states that when things appear to be similar to each other, we naturally group them together. We tend to attribute them to belong to the same functional category. For instance, in Figure 1.10, there appear to be two separate and distinct groups based on shape: the circles and the squares. The shapes are all equally spaced and are of the same size. Further, we also group them by color and categorize them into four groups, even though there's no rhyme or reason to their placement.

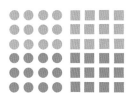

FIGURE 1.10 Similarity

The Gestalt Principles are vital in design. Users must be able to understand what they see—and find what they want—at a glance. The principles of proximity and common region are good examples. Colors and graphics divide the content into separate regions. Without this, users struggle to make associations between unrelated clustered-together items. Graphic designers commonly use these principles in their websites as a way to organize content with well-placed elements that catch the eye as larger, whole images. The result is a presentation that is aesthetically pleasing, yet easy to understand.

Diagramming the World

How do we want to share a message with the reader and what do we want to say? So far, we have revealed the design principles, guidelines behind how visual cognition works—the dots, lines, boxes of the world, each of which has meaning, in context. Just as *dough* in "I will make a batch of cookie dough" does not have the same meaning as *dough* in "After I get paid, I'll have enough dough to go buy a pair of shoes," a line on a map does not have the same meaning as a line on a bar chart. These forms need to be considered in the function with their meanings and inferences that they aim to promote. Appropriate colors, symbols, placement, and size are inherent to guidance, explanation, and storytelling.

Directing Attention Through Arrows and Signage

The visual environment around us generally contains more information than can be processed within a glance. We constantly look for signs around us to selectively focus on as we make sense of the world. As such, action and agency depend on mechanisms of selective visual attention for prioritizing an endless stream of sensory input. We rely on visual cues to help orient and give more weight to those objects, locations, or events that require immediate focus.

Our eyes and hands are our own arrows that we use for directing gaze and communication. The glances and eye contact you make with friends at a coffee shop or gesturing while providing directions to a stranger who needs help finding the nearest pharmacy are all ways of directing thought and attention. Arrows are specialized lines that depict paths, direction, and relation. Dr. Barbara Tversky (2019) describes the evidence of the arrow as an artifact in early cave paintings, with their depictions becoming a ubiquitous way of diagramming direction in the world. We see arrows as we get on an escalator or while driving a car on a one-way street, a means of establishing order and rules for our own safety.

Much of this book was conceived and written during the COVID-19 pandemic. Social distancing (or rather physical distancing) has become the new norm in these unprecedented times as we anxiously situate ourselves at a safe distance away from others, six feet away. We have grown accustomed to arrows to indicate the directionality of movement in an aisle of a grocery store as we plan not only our grocery shopping but our spatial plan of checking off items on our list through intentional movement. Businesses have placed markers on the floor to guide customers where to stand in line, often with additional creativity and branding to make the experience more personal. ZombieRunner Coffee is a local business that displays a marker with a cartoonized version of the owner holding his coffee cup and running. As shown in the example in

Figure 1.11, the markers help guide customers and perhaps instill a notion of safety and trust as they order their favorite cup of joe.

Arrows are an example of a broad class of techniques for directing attention. For example, user experience designers have the phrase Call to Action (CTA) for design techniques that direct attention. These techniques include layout, size, and color. The presence of arrows affects how we interpret diagrams. Arrows provide visual perception of causality and action. In the example in Figure 1.12, the arrow indicates the direction in which force is applied to the lever, and we can almost envision the rock being lifted up and the level of effort that would take. Actions such as push, lift, move come to mind, adding movement to a static diagram. We can begin to understand the effect of such force on the rock and the fulcrum that supports the lever in play. A physical phenomenon that would take a paragraph of prose to explain is depicted in a diagram with the simple addition of the humble yet mighty arrow.

FIGURE 1.11 Pandemic arrow markers and signage at ZombieRunner Coffee, a coffee shop in Palo Alto, California

Illustrations

While arrows provide a sense of movement in space, illustrations are static yet powerful images drawn from a single viewpoint presented on a non-stereo medium such as pen on paper. They can depict objects in the world and their meaning (i.e., semantics) that the human visual system will quickly understand. The illustration in Figure 1.12 defines *fulcrum* for a person who does not know that word. People will also go rapidly from the depicted instance to functional categories. A fulcrum can be more than a triangle—anything that allows the board to move freely in the direction of leverage. Think of illustration as yet another means of diagramming the physicalities of the world into a single image. An effective illustration determines *which* lines should be drawn to maximize the amount of

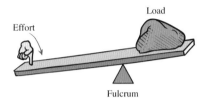

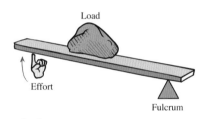

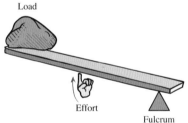

FIGURE 1.12 Physics leverage explained by mass and distance equation
iStock.com/corbac40

information conveyed while minimizing the total number of lines drawn. Edge lines consisting of surface boundaries, silhouettes, discontinuities, and creases to separate individual parts are used to suggest important features in the shape of each object. There are many line weight conventions from which the illustrator chooses based on the intent of the image. There are three common conventions for the use of lines in illustration:

- A single line weight used throughout the image

- Two line weights with the heavier one describing the outer edges

- Varying the line weight along a single line emphasizes the perspective of the drawing. Most illustrators use bold external lines, with thinner interior lines, which aid in the perception of spaces.

Continuing with the theme of coffee for a bit, Figure 1.13 is an illustration that explains the first design for the French press dated back to 1852 (Hoffman, 2014). Mayer and Delforge, two Frenchmen, describe their design in a patent showing the cutaway of the various labeled parts: the beaker, plunger, lid, base, and handle. It was a simple design that did not create a seal inside the carafe like the one you find today. Yet the illustration is functional and visually explains the components of the coffee brewer to the reader. The position of the labels shows the relative spatial relations of the parts across the two figures for cross-referencing. The outer edge lines are drawn thicker to accentuate the silhouette of the container. The thinner lines provide shading and contour information on the two-dimensional paper surface to indicate the curvature of the handle, plunger, and the beaker.

Maps

Similar to illustration, the map is another unique form of symbolic representation but is specialized for space. It depicts spatial relationships with objects in the geographic and physical landscape. By scaling down to a natural size conducive for reading, a map allows the viewer to see far

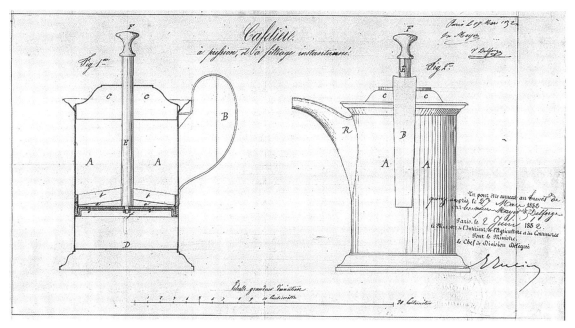

FIGURE 1.13 The first design for the French press
Henri-Otto MAYER/Jacques-Victor DELFORGE/Wikimedia Commons

more information in one glance than could ever be possible from ground level without the need for any pictorial realism. Creating a map involves integrating the 3D projection of landmarks and paths onto a flattened plane. While we may think that this translation is no ordinary feat, human-kind has been creating maps as far as history can go, starting with the intentional arrangements of stones to understand the movement of the sun to the earliest cave paintings perhaps depicting a hunting terrain for the cave people. In fact, some of the early maps have rather clever representa-tions of space and navigation.

Figure 1.14 presents one such example. Medieval mapmakers were aware of the Earth's sphericity, yet maps were schematic, as exemplified by the T and O map (or T-O map). It is a type of early world map that represents the physical world as first

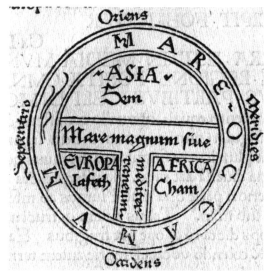

FIGURE 1.14 T and O map by Isidore of Seville
Isidore of Seville/Wikimedia Commons

described by the seventh-century scholar Isidore of Seville in his *De natura rerum*. The map is rendered with a stylized T-form of the major water bodies separating the continents and the O as the ocean surrounding the world. The orientation with east at the top of the map was often used.

Maps have inspired the early roots of information visualization by depicting information as a communication process (MacEachren, 2004). While details of these depictions vary, all maps share a basic structure with an information source identified by the cartographer who determines what and how to represent that information to the reader. Cartographers have come up with filters that information must pass through on its route from the real world to the map medium, and ultimately to the user. These filters consist of goals, knowledge, experience, and context that influence the abstraction process by which information is put into map form. Cartographers have found ways to make maps more legible and useful. They often simplify or eliminate less semantically important features, exaggerate more important ones, and resolve visual clutter to improve information quality. This is a process known as *generalization*.

To provide spatial lucidity and overview, there exist various generalization operators, including simplification, aggregation, and exaggeration. These operators are applied based on the intended purpose and context of the imagery and are particularly useful when maps need to be drawn at different scales (think of a mobile screen vs. large display). Lines, space, and color are used for integrating and segregating properties, providing structure and organization to the geospatial information presented.

FIGURE 1.15 Exaggeration

Exaggeration: As shown in Figure 1.15, spatial features are relatively enlarged so that the map's featured characteristics remain prominent at different scales or to draw the viewer's attention. This enlargement leads to a distortion in the representation of the object when compared to its true shape or size. An example of this is to make a small, slender spit of land larger in order to see its characteristics more clearly.

Simplification: As shown in Figure 1.16, shapes of retained features are altered to enhance visibility and reduce complexity or visual clutter. Often in a map, roads and region outlines are simplified, as seen in the image on the right. Small curves and points are removed to simplify lines and polygonal outlines.

FIGURE 1.16 Simplification

Aggregation: As shown in Figure 1.17, aggregation combines features of similar characteristics into a single feature of increased dimensionality that covers the spatial extent of the original features. Data aggregation is used for summarizing, partitioning, and simplifying data.

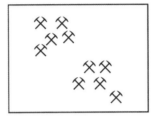

FIGURE 1.17 Aggregation

Typification: The typification operation refines the density of marks in a spatial area. A set of marks (i.e., points, lines, or polygons) is replaced with a smaller set of the identical marks to depict the same number of relative distributions between clusters of marks but reduce visual clutter, especially when the map is drawn at a smaller scale, as can be seen in Figure 1.18.

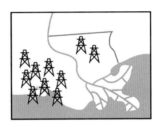

FIGURE 1.18 Typification

Merge: Merging takes multiple objects and combines them into a single feature, as can be seen in Figure 1.19. Features that are too small are grouped together and represented as a unified feature. Other examples include combining a bunch of proximal buildings in a university together and representing them as a single building in a campus map.

FIGURE 1.19 Merge

FIGURE 1.20 Label prominence

Label prominence: The label prominence operator emphasizes place labels based on their relative order of prominence. For example, as can be seen in Figure 1.20, large cities are made more prominent (e.g., larger labels in bold) than smaller cities; interstate highways are made more prominent (e.g., lines are thicker) than local streets.

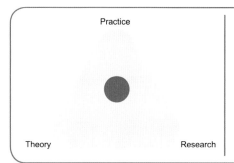

Emphasize the most important elements while still representing the view in the most faithful and recognizable way.

These elements must outweigh the insignificance of items that are deemphasized.

Route maps have succinctly applied various forms of generalization to effectively provide navigational direction. Generalization helps emphasize what is important and deemphasize the unimportant, showing points of interest, turns, and interactions such as pan and zoom. We will discuss more about maps and how they influenced the discipline of information visualization when we head to the next chapter.

Summary

The perceptual emphasis in this chapter sets the stage for discussion of how semantics and intent are linked to perceptual input in the interpretation of the use of charts. In the next chapter, we continue our journey of applying visual perception and cognitive processes to chart design and construction. These topics are critical to the design of functionally aesthetic charts to facilitate visual thinking, symbolization, and generalization.

CHAPTER 2

Perception in Charts

Maps are a type of chart that can convey relationships about space and relationships between objects that we relate to in the real world. Their effectiveness as a communication medium is strongly influenced by a host of factors: the nature of spatial data, the form and structure of representation, their intended purpose, the experience of the audience, and the context in the time and space in which the map is viewed. In other words, maps are a ubiquitous representation of spatial information that we can understand and relate to. Based on the geospatial task we have in mind, effective maps simply *work*. Take an example during your day when you use a map, subconsciously solving your problem without really giving it too much thought. You are running late to an appointment, but you park your car in the closest available parking spot. You whip out your phone and quickly punch in the address of the office you need to head to. The map application uses the context of your location, where you are standing in space, and assesses that given the proximity of where you are from the office, you are probably walking. Rather than a full-scale map, a walking map shows turn-by-turn directions with an estimated time of arrival that helps you determine your pace. It's a simple yet delightful functional representation that helps you reach your appointment on time.

Route maps, which depict a path from one location to another, are one of the most common forms of graphic communication. Before the mobile device became our digital napkin, these route maps were often created as quick drawings to direct someone to a particular location. Such handcrafted maps are usually simplified to make them reasonably intuitive to understand and follow. Mapmakers make explicit decisions about which aspects of the route are most relevant for a navigator to understand and follow. They use a variety of cartographic generalization techniques described in the previous chapter, to help improve the clarity of the map and emphasize only the most important information (Agrawala & Stolte, 2001). Cartographic generalization, performed either consciously or subconsciously, is prevalent in quickly sketched maps, as seen in Figure 2.1 where the artist, Mia Trachinger, sketched out the route to her wedding reception venue for the attendees.

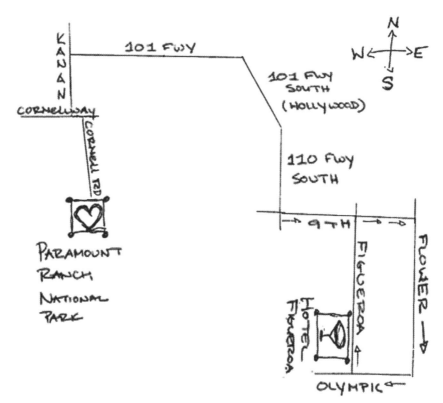

FIGURE 2.1 Hand-drawn route map
Mia Trachinger

From a practice standpoint, even this hand-drawn map embodies common practices. It includes only key information, dropping additional side streets that are not relevant to the task. The compass drawn above acts as a bit of a legend and clarifier: those with a sense of a direction or a compass can affirm they are headed in the right direction. The arrows also help guide the viewer.

Visualization and Task

While we can understand the utility of maps for spatial orientation and navigation tasks, what *exactly* a task comprises in visualization is rather a fuzzy topic. For instance, as Brehmer and Munzner (2013) point out, finding an extreme value is more concrete than exploring or integrating insights. Relating these task descriptions is difficult, though not impossible; however, visualization practitioners hardly have a shared vocabulary when describing these relations between levels of abstraction and application areas. In this book, we bring together both the researchers' and practitioners' perspectives to go beyond merely describing the use of visualization techniques in a specific application domain but rather abstract these tasks in order to realize an appropriate visualization design space.

In Parts B and C, we build upon existing visualization task taxonomies in this space (Munzner, 2015) to show how semantics and intentionality can make a chart or dashboard both informational and inspirational. This abstraction also enables practitioners to contribute back to the visualization research community, transferring their findings beyond a single domain.

Task can be classified by the actions one performs using verbs such as *identify*, *compare*, or *summarize*. These actions might be supported directly by how the data is encoded, arranged, and annotated, either in a static display or in conjunction with various forms of interaction. Descriptions of tasks also tend to include nouns such a *trend*, *correlation*, or *distribution*: abstract aspects of data observed during visual analysis. These nouns are the targets of corresponding actions, and throughout literature they alternatively appear in classifications of data facts, mental models of a dataset, and insights. Insights evoke qualities that go beyond the observation of data facts: they imply spontaneity and actionability; they must be a catalyst for self-reflection or hypothesis-based reasoning. Figure 2.2 shows an example of how line charts could be represented based on task target and actions.

Identify   Compare   Summarize

FIGURE 2.2 Examples of line charts for various task targets and actions

However, picking a chart type for a task is much more nuanced, and best depends on real-world phenomena, how the data is collected, and how that information is represented to meet the goal of the intended task.

Chart as an Informational Unit

Thinking of a chart as a unit of conveying information helps frame the use of perception as a means for regarding, understanding, or interpreting something, a mental impression. These charts encode information in the form of shape, color, position, and size. One of the basic aspects of learning the fundamentals of visualization is figuring out which chart can be most effective for a specific goal. There are some basic rules, but we will show during the course of the book how one can also challenge them.

Practice

Theory   Research

In practice, selecting charts may include effectiveness, user comfort, surrounding charts, text, software complexities of making the chart, how the data fits the chart, and what to expect if the chart continues to update on its own. Practitioners may choose a less-effective chart for a variety of reasons or may spread a task across several charts.

It's similar to learning how to cook. You start with the basics—understanding how to use your tools in the kitchen and the elementary flavors that make a functional meal. As you become more fluent with your cooking skills, you evolve from being a cook to being a chef, getting creative as you juxtapose flavors and presentation into something that is worthy of a Michelin star.

Researchers have conducted several perceptual studies to better under-stand what these basic rules are and how charts can provide effective visual cues for solving an analytical task. Most notable is Cleveland and McGill's seminal paper (1984). The paper has been foundational in providing a guideline for the link between data visuals and the human visual system. Cleveland and McGill hypothesized a set of elementary perceptual tasks, tasks carried out when people are trying to extract quantitative information from visualizations.

Figure 2.3 illustrates 10 elementary perceptual tasks that people use to extract quantitative information from graphs for making relative judg-ments. The findings from the studies showed that humans have a better judgment on dot position than they do on length, direction, angle, area, curvature, and volume.

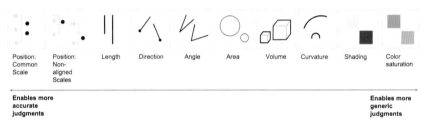

FIGURE 2.3 Ten elementary perceptual tasks and their efficacy for making relative judgments

Heer and Bostock's research (2010) performed an approximate replication of Cleveland and McGill's study while examining the viability of crowd-sourcing of perceptual experiments. They were able to confirm the relative rankings of the comparison tasks by using Amazon's Mechanical Turk (www.mturk.com) as an online platform for running graphical perception experiments. With its low cost and scalability, crowdsourcing presents an attractive option for evaluating the large design space of visualizations and replicating studies, which is important for research to be generaliz-able. Studies employing crowdsourcing pose challenges that include reduced control in the assessment of participants' background and training as well as ethical concerns around pay. Some studies, particularly those sensitive to factors such as color blindness or limited visual acuity, may not be well-suited for the Web. Nevertheless, crowdsourcing offers a scalable way to conduct a valuable range of graphical perception experiments, including four on bar charts (Talbot et al., 2014) that are relevant to the visualization community.

From these perception studies, key takeaways were made. For example, showing differences in a single line chart displaying the actual difference between values was recommended to be more useful than two lines showing the absolutes. On the topic of pie charts, there has been lots of discussion about the validity of pie and donut charts as a meaningful way to convey information that could accurately be interpreted. This is partly due to Cleveland and McGill's findings of the angle being evaluated at a low accuracy level. Skau and Kosara (2016) decided to focus their study on pie and donut charts with stimuli shown in Figure 2.4.

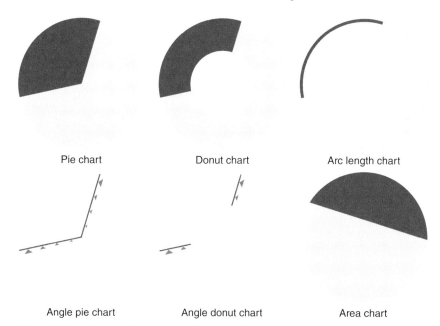

Pie chart	Donut chart	Arc length chart

Angle pie chart	Angle donut chart	Area chart

FIGURE 2.4 A sampling of charts used in the study of pie and donut chart encodings showing 33%
Adapted from Skau and Kosara (2016)

The results were quite interesting: the complete pie and donut charts did the best for reading accuracy, while the angle-only conditions (angle pie chart and angle donut chart) were the worst. People were surprisingly good with the area-only condition, which was completely unexpected. Arc-only was virtually identical with area-only.

The pie and donut charts encode with both angle and area. We speculate that redundant encoding and abstraction can support effective perception. We will explore these ideas deeper in semantics, but recognizable shapes help provide clues around measurement. For example, the pie charts, donut charts, and area charts tie back to items that are familiar in the real world, whereas the angles have fewer visual cues (no blue- or gray-filled areas), making them less likely to appear in the real world.

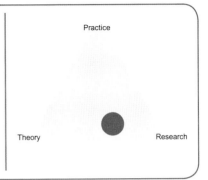

While these studies provide useful guidelines related to what kind of visualization to use, the findings are not meant to be prescriptive. As Cleveland and McGill note, "The ordering of the tasks does not result in a precise prescription for displaying data, but rather is a *framework* within which to work." Start with the visual fundamentals, but there is much more to what makes a visualization functionally aesthetic as we describe in the course of this book. You'll learn from practice how to get fancy with your visualizations and "break" some rules. And yes, sometimes pie charts may be the right choice.

We will explore how these individual charts form paragraphs that get woven into a narrative of sentences to convey a story or a certain point of view to the intended audience. Each chart plays its part, yet harmoniously coexists in its space with the others. The placement and natural sizing of these charts are thoughtful and intentional, similar to meaningful artifacts that we experience in the physical world.

Unboxing Functional Aesthetics in the Physical World

We first eat with our eyes. We scan our meal, the steam rising from parts, the colors contrasting in others. It's ritualistic; the experience of dining far exceeds satisfying an appetite. Multilayered and sensory, we see the food, smell the spices intersecting with one another and the heady steam carrying into our nose. Before we've eaten a bite, we're already taking in the flavor.

Arranging bento boxes is an art, but they aren't solely artistic renditions. They come packed with functions that are supported by their simple elegance. The red contrasts against the bright greens of the salad, the dark hues of the seaweed wrapping the sushi, and the brightness against the white of the rice. Our main dish, the largest piece, is the part most likely to have the least contrast. As we constrain space, details and nuance help guide us through the experience. The wasabi can go with the sides, but we may also mix it with our main. As it takes pride of place, we recognize that the small ingredient might just be the heart of our meal. It is one we can customize, taking in more or less heat and allowing the pickled ginger to provide a bit of an afterbite of sour.

As a perfect mix of form and function, traditional bento boxes combine the efficient use of space and arrangement and the beauty of food to cultivate joy. The Japanese aesthetic focuses on the beauty of simplicity and natural asymmetry, and what is considered to be appropriately tasteful. Both function and form embrace a rich, intertwined goal: concrete, multisensory, and visceral. The bento box is a paradigm we know well, even if it's not a direct experience we've had. We often turn to containers and frames to organize like with like.

Recursive Proportions

Architectural systems are founded on the same assumptions as the bento box. They always question the very premise of beauty. Is beauty in the eye of the beholder or does it come about through intrinsic properties of space? Probably both.

Three general principles—repetition, harmony, and variety—lie at the basis of beautiful design:

- **Repetition** is achieved by using a system that provides a set of proportions that are repeated in a design or building at different scales.

- **Harmony** is achieved through a system that provides a small set of lengths or modules with many additive properties, which enables the whole to be created as the sum of its parts while remaining entirely within the system.

- ▦ **Variety** is provided by a system that provides a sufficient degree of versatility in its ability to tile the plane with geometric figures.

Converting these principles into craft involves different issues regarding perception, physics, and dimensions. The generative approach to architectural design called "recursive proportions" (Corcuff, 2012) is the use of transformation rules, which often involve ratios. Recursive proportions guide the assemblage of parts subject to uniform established proportions, regulated by the premise that each part must perform, each distinguished by its proportions and characteristic profiles. Skilled builders are familiar with this order and hierarchy, and they typically don't get hung up on the small details. They take a step back and look at the intended work holistically.

Asher Benjamin, a prolific craftsman, published a clear system of proportion for designing a mantelpiece when he wrote in the *First American Architectural Handbook* (1797) with an illustration shown in Figure 2.5, "divide the width, or opening of the Chimney, into eight or nine parts; give one eighth, or one ninth to the breadth of the Architrave" (plate XVII). He started with a truly pleasing design, with an illustration describing the width and depth of the pilasters, the height of the entablature, and how far the cornice should extend. The result was also *scalable*. Builders have since taken this blueprint of proportional ratios and built mantelpieces of different sizes, yet with the same proportions of parts, keeping the aesthetics of the design intact.

George Walker (2013), a woodworker, describes how he learned to apply proportions to his woodwork: "I always had strong opinions about what looked right to my eye, but for many years I was unable to actually understand what I saw. I might have a feeling something looked clunky and might even be able to narrow it down to a single element being the culprit. What I could not do was make the connection and see that a leg might be too heavy for its height, or that a molding is too small for the form it's supposed to highlight. I had some knowledge of proportions but

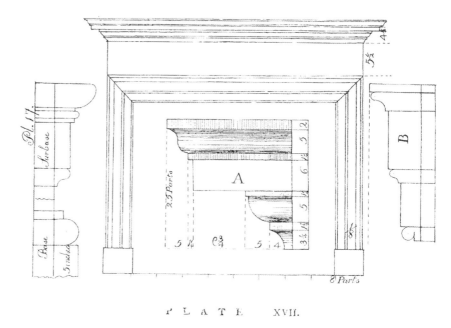

FROM Plate 17 to Plate 20, are defigns for Chimney Pieces, drawn one half an inch to a foot.——Plate 17, is a plain Chimney Piece, with its Cornice, Architrave, Bafe, and Surbafe, drawn half fize for practice ; divide the width, or opening of the Chimney, into eight or nine parts ; give one eighth, or one ninth to the breadth of the Architrave.

FIGURE 2.5 Mantelpiece design based on recursive proportions
Asher Benjamin 1797

was unable to think proportionally." He discovered that there is a big difference between just seeing the elements in a piece and really being able to see how they connect with other elements, and with the whole, a conscious practice that he even applies to tool assembly in his workshop, as seen in Figure 2.6.

These architectural constructs are beyond just guidelines. They provide a "visual grammar" that determines how each component fits in with a purpose. Thinking proportionally is not so much about finding answers. We may long for some quick cheat sheet approach that can unlock our design strengths, but it simply doesn't work that way. Instead of answers, we are looking for connections. The connections we have are with perception, art, architecture, and even the masterworks of furniture. Proportions are the essence that permeates a great design, and if we can somehow begin to grasp them, we open up a whole world of new expression.

FIGURE 2.6 George Walker's workshop

The Digitized Space: Creating Experiences on the Screen

As we move experiences from the physical realm to the digital one, some rules change. We lose a level of depth. We can certainly create it with illusions and graphics. Texture becomes visual—invoked—rather than physically felt. We rely on patterns to cue sensory perceptions: colors that create warmth with light rather than sunshine itself.

A traditional long-form website may try to fill the screen with a captivating image and use shadowing to push the image back or bring the text forward with contrast. Scrolling often leads to text, typically framed by white space. Somewhere below the text, smaller images may frame up pathways to further explore. The image creates the initial emotional resonance, while the text ideally builds on that image. Data visualization, however, is less straightforward. News organizations can take the long-form design and intersperse charts with text. The *New York Times* has made this an art form with its Upshot section, intermixing charts with paragraphs and often using animation to unfurl the experience. In one article, "You Draw It: How Family Income Predicts Children's College Chances" (Aisch et al., 2015), the reader is introduced to basic concepts around line charts and then must draw a line to get the rest of the text. While news organizations can certainly embrace a long-form design framed by a holistic narrative, dashboards and similar data-driven apps rely on less text and reduced scrolling. Like the bento box, space is typically constrained to a set size with various techniques used to expand, drill down, or otherwise expose further information.

To illustrate, take a look at the frame in Figure 2.7. If you want, sketch and think about the types of charts you would put in this frame. Do certain charts belong in certain boxes?

FIGURE 2.7 An example frame for charts

As you look at the framing, consider what types of charts you'd place within the frames. What rules do you feel about the space?

Now look at Figure 2.8. It, like Figure 2.7, has four boxes. Do you feel differently about this space? Beyond changing sizes, do you feel compelled to change charts entirely?

Like rooms, the containers start to inform use. We'll explore this more in later chapters.

FIGURE 2.8 An alternative frame for charts

In Figure 2.9, we can see how the container paradigm sets the tone. The large curvy title bar creates a backdrop and hugs the map. This element unifies the overall work and provides a bit of playfulness. A gray container sets the proportion for the high-level elements that drive most of the interaction. The design elements help users flow from the map down to the bars and the KPIs before rolling over to the shipping class details. The elements are interactive, highlighting and encouraging users to select a state to further filter the data.

FIGURE 2.9 A dashboard showing containers and proportions framing the various charts

Within the charts selected, the filled map shows geographic patterns of sales by state. Perceptually, it's not the best choice for this task, but it's a familiar paradigm that serves as a comfortable entry point for our end users. They instantly understand that a geographic field is encoded. The map uses color to do the overall comparison, calling out the comparison point in teal. The bar chart immediately below it accommodates the need for a more precise comparison; the teal from above is integrated as a dot to show the comparison point. KPI boxes within the frame provide the literal numbers, allowing end users a way to identify and describe counts. Within the body of the dashboard, we can compare trends both within a shipping class or as an average across groups. These two charts create shared groupings in their use of space and colors.

Summary

In this chapter, we proposed that perception, aesthetics, and function belong together: they are not separate parts. Conventional practitioner dialog often focuses on design being separate from chart making, most often framed in terms of "making it pretty" after the analysis is complete. Understanding the task at hand and how best the chart can draw a user's attention into a flow of analysis through thoughtful proportions and boxes is key. In line with Tableau Hall of Fame Visionary and blogger Kelly Martin, we believe that "beauty is meaningful design." The charts, the design, and the goals are one unit knitted together with functional aesthetics. The next chapter will explore how this premise can be practiced along with some history of data visualization.

CHAPTER 3

Charts in Use

Beyond getting all the charts right, bringing them together for the intended audience represents a challenge and is a large part of the learning curve for practitioners. As you saw in Chapter 2, the bento box provides a powerful paradigm for starting to lay out pieces and bringing them together. It provides constraints, helping us think about placement and tasks. When you consider widgets and legends to be views of data, most charts come under the bento box paradigm as they support the primary views. In building visualizations, we consider the task the chart represents and work with our end users to understand their world. Sometimes, it's easy. The charts fall into place, their purposes clear, and they work well together.

In 2019, a Vantage Partners survey found that over 77 percent of data initiatives failed to achieve reasonable adoption, per the executives polled. Sixty-five companies from a mix of Fortune 1000 companies participated. Data is supposed to bring forth insight when used, visualized, and deployed at scale. So why did these initiatives fail? It wasn't the technology, the executives said, but a breakdown around people and processes. Their efforts failed at the last mile, where users interacted with their solutions. Returning to the bathroom, this is back to where we stand with dripping wet hands, and a dispenser that refuses to release its wares. It's the paper towel problem, but with charts.

Paradigms on how to create meaning beyond a single chart vary widely. As we bring charts together, we hope to transport our users, to elevate the experience of fact finding to an endeavor that's successful and near-frictionless. Just as with the bento box, we want form to support the function in a way that delights while informing. Yet often, we struggle to build unity within the entire visualization.

Most data initiatives are hoping to move visualization beyond functionally providing paper towels to building an experience more like our restaurant visit. Beyond charts on a page, modern visualization paradigms push boundaries through interaction, expansion, and connection. These techniques provide us options but add more complexity as we look to interweave sundries of charts together.

Synthesizing data serves as a key function. Far from a niche component of certain jobs, data is a profession in its own right. In the early 2000s, we were awed by the terabytes of data we made. Today, we measure in zettabytes. Beyond creating this data, we have to understand it. A part of understanding lies in the research we've covered so far. The other part directly intersects with our history as a profession. So, how did we get here?

The First Charts

Throughout the long arc of history, humans have sought to make sense of their data visually. Numerous cave paintings often feature animals, but with interesting artifacts beyond what would be expected, such as the use of various symbols within a picture or seemingly systematic groupings and placements. Are these evidence of a hunt well done, documentation of dates, or annotations of star constellations? Research shows a number of these cave paintings may be the latter (Sweatman & Coombs, 2018). Patterns line up with where certain stars would be across a myriad of caves in ways too uncanny to just be portraits.

Beyond paintings, other artifacts shed light on how we visualize numbers. The Ishango bone in Figure 3.1, for example, has puzzled experts since its discovery in 1950. Is it a mathematical tool, a period tracker, or a lunar calendar of other sorts? The marks are grouped, their sizes different with a distinct pattern.

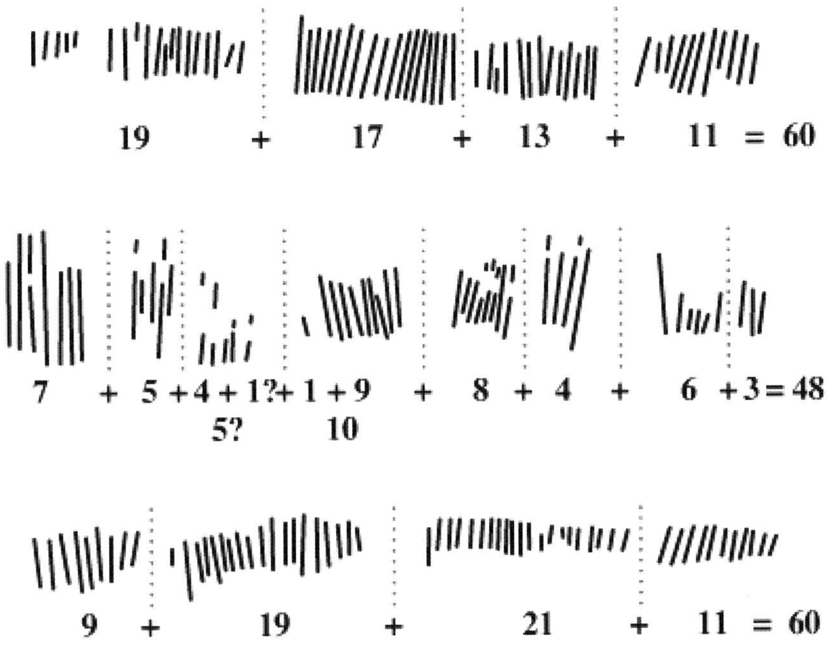

FIGURE 3.1 Ishango bone

As an early visualization, the bone itself creates spatial limitations. The marks are ticks, etched all around the bone using stone or another tool. Yet their groupings, sizes, and the patterns allude to a story, one for which we still have no definite answers. Like cave paintings, the bone provides us clues but not explicit details. Other items, like clay tablets, have preserved transactions and debts throughout a long span of time. Linguistics and mathematicians alike study these to understand how we've used numbers throughout the span of time to communicate and count but also recognize patterns.

Beyond tracking counts and stars, maps are prominent visualizations that document everything from ocean tides to geological changes to ever-changing land use patterns. The Turin Papyrus Map, dated back to 1150 BC, might be one of the oldest surviving maps. It served as both a topographic and a geologic map, identifying where materials were and routes for construction. It abstracted and systemized the types of stones available, using legends to clarify. The Marshall Islands stick chart shown in Figure 3.2 documents ocean wave patterns and currents using a variety of materials, including shells, sticks, and fiber. Individually created, they abstract information for sailing (Finney, 1998).

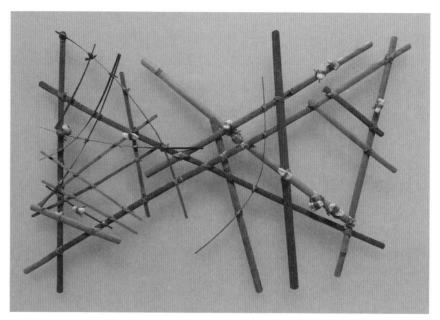

FIGURE 3.2 Marshall Islands stick chart photographed by Jim Heaphy
Cullen328/Wikimedia Commons/CC BY-SA 3.0

Bone, stone, clay, and other natural materials feature prominently in the early visualizations we have preserved. Modern data physicalization continues this tradition, using mediums such as knitting, Play-Doh, and clothing to share representations of data. Other experiments explore the sonification of data, allowing the patterns to be heard. Technology always played a role in how visualization was made and shared. Paper and papyrus served as key innovators in the greater proliferation and preservation of data. As lightweight mediums, they rolled and folded while allowing better preservation and transportation.

Advances in astrology, mathematics, and science leveraged paper as an innovation and abstraction to find patterns. Planetary rotations and motions could be tracked as curves and compared. Math concepts could start as doodles to think about a problem or pattern and evolve into paradigms we recognize today. During the Islamic Golden Age between the eighth and fourteenth centuries, innovations around cryptology, language, and algebra pushed the world in novel ways and have direct ties to the innovation of paper. As writing became cheaper to do and more broadly transportable, chart making further created a secondary documentation means around numbers and concepts, as seen in Figure 3.3. Advances in geometry, algebra, and trigonometry benefited by being able to sketch and test ideas.

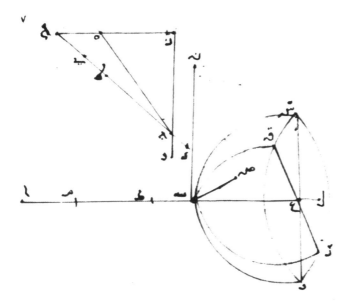

FIGURE 3.3 Re-creation of Ibn Sahl algebra graphics
Ibn Sahl/Wikimedia Commons

Advancements in mathematics furthered how societies tracked populations. Maps could capture growth but also changes in landmarks. Statistics matured from state-level tallies for taxation purposes to broader analysis techniques in the nineteenth century. Probability became more integrated in statistics, as various disciplines started leveraging both probability and analysis to predict future events based on existing patterns.

While data visualization has roots in the statistical presentation of data, it is not a neutral tool. In addition to supporting technical advances, statistics were used to further certain political agendas, such racist ideals fed by eugenics. Several statistical methods have direct ties to the eugenics movement, such as Fisher's T-Test. In addition to causing harm, visualization can help us make change.

Standardizing Visualization

William Playfair is widely recognized for inventing common charts, such as the line, bar, pie, and area charts. In Figure 3.4, you can see his time series chart on trade deficits. Note the annotations nestled in the lines. The first time he clarified the lines of imports and exports explicitly with "line of " preceding each and repeated what it stands for after the lines cross. The areas between the lines are colored in and labeled. The gridlines go from 0 to 200 in intervals of 10. One hundred is clearly called out as the midpoint with a more prominent line. The title clarifies what is being measured (imports and exports) with what filters (from Denmark and Norway) over a given time period (1700 to 1780). The axis is on the right. The years are marked below with additional annotations clarifying units of measurement.

These charts are a turning point in visualization. They take trends and abstract them into a visual system of communication—an idea we will explore in depth in later chapters. The gridlines on this chart likely serve two purposes: they provide the anchors in which to map the points but also reference points for consumers to understand the message.

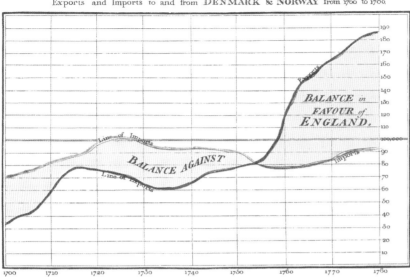

FIGURE 3.4 William Playfair's time series chart

Other turning point visualizations include John Snow's cholera map and Florence Nightingale's coxcomb chart, shown in Figure 3.5. In the era of COVID-19, both of these visualizations are particularly striking. In the summer of 1854, a mysterious illness gripped a part of London. Within a week, 10 percent of the people in the area had died from the illness. At the time, most people and doctors assumed it was related to miasma, or bad pockets of air. Snow, already an esteemed medical doctor, began mapping out the data as he had a hunch it was not miasma, but the water. Snow's map and accompanying papers helped shift the tide by encouraging people to boil their water to rid it of exposures to cholera.

Only four years later, Florence Nightingale created her famous coxcomb chart. Included in her 800-page book that she also sent to Queen Victoria, the diagrams clearly highlight the role sanitation plays in avoiding deaths. The coxcomb chart showing the number of soldiers who died using the areas of the circle segments clearly shows the early excess deaths. Better sanitation in later months reduces those losses. Nursing the war-injured

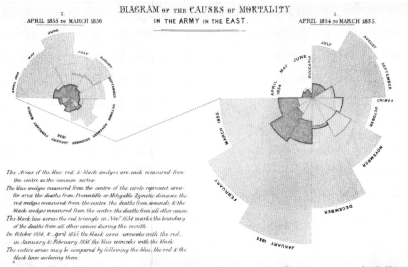

FIGURE 3.5 Cholera map and coxcomb charts
Florence Nightingale/Wikimedia Commons

and ill with few supplies and resources, Nightingale sought to highlight the burden while also showing where improvements were made. Using data proficiently was critical to Nightingale's success and pivotal to nursing.

By 1900, American sociologist W. E. B. Du Bois brought data to life at the World's Fair in Paris, show-casing data sketches alongside portraits and articles around how Black Americans lived in the United States. The color line he

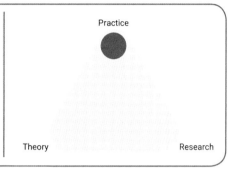

Sociologists, psychologists, and other social science majors make heavy use of data. As seen so far in this chapter, it was domain experts that pioneered a number of methods we use today.

discussed in his work was on vivid display in France. The charts were large, framed, and meant to be turned and pursued. Hoping to use sociology to create change, the data clearly showed the broad-ranging effects of slavery and racism.

Du Bois and his team used a variety of charts to showcase his findings, some of which are shown in Figure 3.6. Light lines sketched between bolder colors helped annotate trends. Photos humanized the data, putting faces and stories juxtaposed with the data.

By 1915, engineer and statistician Willard Cope Brinton published the first textbook on data visualization, *Graphic Methods for Presenting Facts* (1915). Brinton's work is a departure, as it is focused on making charts accessible to the masses. It discusses examples of graphics, their purposes, and how to re-create them. It covered a wide array of chart types and started cataloguing them in ways that would feel quite familiar. We can credit Brinton for shaping the path toward broad use of charts, regardless of industry.

The Shifting Role of Data Visualization

In *A Whole New Mind,* Daniel Pink (2006) highlights the drastic shift in our economy since the information age. "We are moving from an economy

FIGURE 3.6a Composite of a few Du Bois charts
The Library of Congress

and a society built on the logical, linear, computer-like capabilities of the Information Age to an economy and society built on the inventive, empathetic, big-picture capabilities of what's rising in its place, the Conceptual Age," he writes. Within the Conceptual Age, we are inundated with technology, abundance, and a globalized workforce.

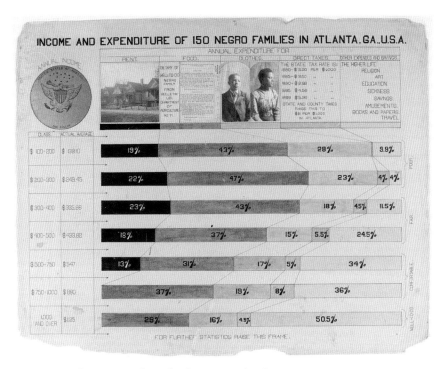

FIGURE 3.6b Composite of a few Du Bois charts
The Library of Congress

Data visualization plays a critical role. As limitations around data storage drop, parsing out meaning grows even more difficult. Moreover, working with smaller, disparate sets of data fails to yield the types of findings companies seek. Data itself has become lower-grained over the years, moving from vague aggregates of groups to incredibly personal and tracked down to small minute actions of an individual. While data science leverages these findings for predictions, visualizations serve as a means to communicate and build trust in these models.

Where visualization has existed as a task in a number of domains, recent years have shifted it to a profession in its own right. Those visualizing data don several titles:

- Analyst
- Data scientist
- Designer

- Developer

- Data journalist

- Informaticist

These titles often intersect with specific tools or programming languages. It is common to see titles like *D3 designer* or *tableau developer* listed as defined positions within a company. Many roles require a level of data management and transformation in addition to the ability to present information. Others may specifically focus only on front-end creation, dedicating greater focus to user experience and user interface design. Some roles may specifically only focus on training end users to become more proficient in consuming data visualizations or working with executives to formulate a cultural shift to one that is data-informed.

Organizations like Data & Society and the Data Visualization Society seek to further elevate and professionalize the work. As these groups identify members, follow-up initiatives expand to include understanding the work, building standard practices, and ultimately shaping the discourse and vision for the work. These organizations are starting to build surveys, chat groups, and content. Beyond establishing terminology, these groups must also begin supporting professionals with training opportunities and pushing standards. Emerging practice professions rely on these types of networks not only to build on fundamentals but to formalize by building broadly centered certifications that go beyond use of a tool, establishing codes of ethics, and working to shift legislation to protect practitioners and the broader population.

This paradigm shift within visualization is essential. Historically, those working within visualization made charts from smaller, disparate datasets with limited impact. Most modern datasets, however, capture the human experience at a deeper scope than ever before. With today's data, we can understand what makes us think, believe, and act in unprecedented ways. Beyond just seeing patterns, visualization can be used to further shape how we behave. Our challenges are less about finding information and more about identifying meaning amid all the data we have available.

This paradigm shift in data requires us to think more broadly about the impacts of what we visualize. The COVID-19 pandemic also corresponded with an infodemic. Beyond the abundance of charts in certain geographical areas, political agendas interacted heavily in impacting *how* the data was interpreted. Skeptics leveraged open data to spin the interpretation against masks and other precautions, creating a subculture that propagated misinformation by way of self-analysis over expert interpretation of the data.

Kate Starbird (2020), sociologist and researcher of crisis informatics, also noted the risks of public sensemaking. As the public engages in "collective sensemaking," rumors form and proliferate, further skewing and fracturing understanding of an event. With COVID-19, this has meant wide variances around interpreting the effectiveness of various precautions and how to handle them. As Starbird writes, "In the connected era, the problem isn't a lack of information but an overabundance of information and the challenge of figuring out which information we should trust and which information we shouldn't trust."

We saw this collective sensemaking play out in the proliferation of visualizations created around COVID-19. Tableau Public, a free platform for visual analysis, allows users to quickly and easily explore data. By March 9, 2020, there were over 931 visualizations containing the terms *COVID* and *Coronavirus* in total, shown in Figure 3.7. They contained a heavy mix of case data, as well as other explorations. Attempting to isolate down to just case data by using terms like *case*, *death*, and *infection* dropped the number a little, with the record high being 143 different visualizations posted on just March 31, 2020. These numbers are still an undercount and represent the "work only on one platform", using terms in English.

Additional analysis showed notable declines in sensemaking as governmental policy started informing lockdowns, mask usage, and other practices (see Figure 3.8). By late May of 2020, individually made case tracking dashboards shifted down to a steady cadence with a focus moving to peripheral topics and personal stories.

Clear Cut Case Visualizations

Pulled from Tableau Public API using terms "COVID" and "Coronavirus" and filtered to include terms that highlight cases.

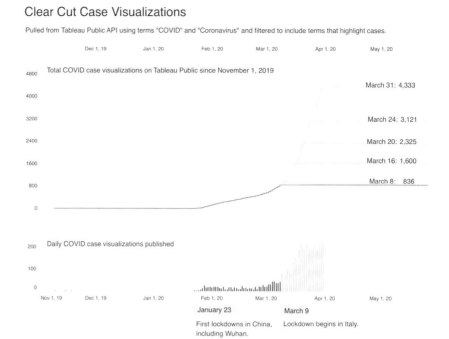

FIGURE 3.7 Showing collective sensemaking around case data

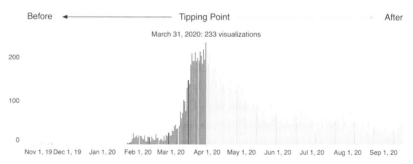

FIGURE 3.8 Timelines and publish dates

The COVID-19 infodemic is an important turning point for visualization practitioners. Beyond making charts to support a story, visualization often is the story in its own right and plays a key role in communicating and understanding the world. We find more charts integrated within the news, particularly as more news moves online, where charts can be embedded interactively within the story. The *New York Times*, the *Guardian*, *Financial*

Times, and a number of other organizations have dedicated data journalist teams. Additionally, Twitter, Reddit, and other platforms allow citizen analysts to also share and present data. Yet by themselves, charts widen the possibilities of interpretation. Later chapters will explore how and why by exploring data literacy but also how we create abstraction systems.

COVID-19 visualizations also highlighted the divergences within the visualization practitioner community. Some felt it was their duty to get the information out there, while others called for pause and direction. These dialogs will start to inform and normalize values within the profession. Visualization as a domain, intersects with so many industries and verticals. While practices and skills may center on a common core, ethics will have to consider how topics are handled. These events serve as cultural flashpoints.

Maturity within the Profession

So many of us learn to make charts on the job or through statistics courses. Process improvement paradigms like Six Sigma are a powerful way to see charts drive action. Visualization courses exist under the guise of several names, such as data journalism, analytics, informatics, and numerous others. As an evolving profession, academic majors dedicated to data visualization are growing but still limited.

Most practitioners learn on the job and through community ties. Yet growth trajectories often share a common thread and arc. Much as with learning a language, there are clear stages. These paradigms also mirror the broader evolution of the profession itself. We'll introduce them lightly here but revisit the concepts in later chapters.

Pictorial Representation

In these early stages, charts are abstract representations of data. Their encoded meanings are still fuzzy, and the selection of proper charts still feels ambiguous at best. Surveys from organizations like the Data Visualization Society highlight how newer professionals feel the load of attempting to learn the language of charts and balance in aesthetics for effective communication.

At this stage, practitioners are attempting to learn how to gather requirements, explore data, and present it so others can use it. They are attempting to match charts to tasks and nouns by translating requirements, deciphering descriptions and needs to the chart tasks we showed in Chapter 2. Sometimes, user needs for charts are explicitly stated: they want a map, trend, and maybe some pie charts to allow for quick categorical comparison. Most common are requirements that are loosely defined and highly ambiguous. Newer analysts are left wondering if the comparative task is best served by line charts, stacked bars, or even heat maps. They may favor charts that allow a variety of tasks to perceivably be performed, such as grouped bar displays or stacked items. The nuance of how and when to use specific charts is still evolving, often leading to compositions that fail to guide end users enough on tasks.

Beyond selecting charts, tying them together is an intimidating task. Early works may look like Figure 3.9. In this example, the practitioner knows the end user of the report needs to encourage donors to increase donation amounts, frequencies, or ideally both. Additionally, within the build specification, brand colors of red, yellow, teal, and lilac must be used on the company's midnight-gray and black standard. The users want a map so that they can localize their pitch, and they need to understand the composition of how users map to the newly rolled-out campaigns. Lastly, they must be able to access information about the individual donor.

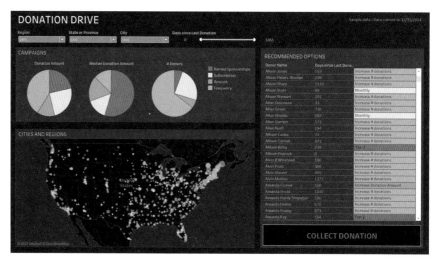

FIGURE 3.9 Sample pictorial-style dashboard

Within this example, we can see an allusion to the bento box, framing to constrain the charts in place but also to differentiate them. The color requirement adds complexity but is quite common in the field. The pie charts start to allude to the power of how the campaigns are organized: we can see that most donors fall in the frequency program and, despite smaller amounts, drive close to half of all donations. The map shows donations, but the colors obscure some of the pattern finding. The table serves as a bridge, sharing information about the last donation date and what campaign a possible donor matches. Tooltips may show additional information. Depending on complexity, more text may be used to guide the user. A large part of the interaction relies on the drop-down filters.

Perceptually, we recognize that this work is hard to navigate. The colors overwhelm and the button at the bottom manages to be both visually distracting and hard to see simultaneously. The colors themselves obscure meaning, particularly in this arrangement. The weights from the charts affect how the colors are seen: the pie charts are large, the table is filled with a wall of color, while the map has smaller, lighter splotches everywhere. Both the table and the pies feel complete, while the map gets lost in the shuffle, feeding a type of reading pattern that feels more like a boomerang.

The charts are literal matches to most of the requests: we can see composition with the pies, we have a map, and there is a table at the donor level. In this state, practitioners rely so much on tools like chart choosers to select the individual charts. Structured frameworks help organize charts by size or importance. It is frustrating for the practitioner attempting to translate loose requirements to abstract charts and equally challenging for consumers attempting to navigate a dashboard like this. Yet a vast number of data visualizations land in this category. It is a key reason that most data initiatives, books, and training courses address this level of maturity. Experienced practitioners can easily pick out opportunities to reduce the signal. Color needs to drop drastically. We should revisit chart selections. We might even consider dropping the literal frame.

The pictorial stage is about embracing the feeling of being overwhelmed. It is understood that visualizing data requires more nuance than initially seen from early exposure points. Communities, training, and mentors serve as powerful guides at this stage. A number of communities have training initiatives both publicly and privately to train on more automatic chart selection as well as reducing visual complexity. Most growth trajectories at this stage move toward minimalism and refining work toward what we know from perceptual research discussed in earlier chapters.

Perceptual Refinement

Beyond basic charts, practitioners must also learn to compose visualizations together elegantly. The perceptual stage focuses on making the literal charts more precise as well as working to de-emphasize the entire piece. Design choices start to consider distractions, reducing visual clutter and centering on the message. Minimalism is espoused as a core value with an emphasis on shifting toward precision as accuracy. This is the most common next step for practitioners.

Minimalism is also a key stage in maturation. It is experimentation at one extreme that helps practitioners distill down to core, shared practices. As with other professions, it focuses on using a smaller set of tools better and more precisely. As a visual medium, the library of possible charts starts wide and quite ambiguously—minimalism reduces this to a core vocabulary that covers a wide swath of most visualization practice. Consider these charts to be like the tables and chairs of restaurants. For dine-in service, you need a place to sit. Bar charts are one of the most basic and precise ways to communicate data. Learning to use and present data well with bars, lines, and scatterplots covers a wide library of common charts used in practice.

If we revisit the donations dashboard at the perceptual stage, we will notice wide and extreme shifts, as shown in Figure 3.10. We have dropped down to a monochromatic view, selecting the color with the greatest contrast against our midnight-gray: the lilac. In addition, we dropped the explicit bento box framing and moved to more figurative ones. The charts are significantly changed. The story of our donor profile is more explicit: we can clearly see the outsized donation amount that named sponsorships provide while also realizing that those in our frequency campaign cover most of our donations with the juxtaposed bar. The scatterplot acts as a bridge to individual donors, allowing us to interact and get far more details about donors within the clearly delineated donor profile while being far more targeted about the choices we have in selecting possible donors. Do we want to prioritize those we haven't heard from in a while yet still maximize possible dollar amounts? The scatterplot makes this decision quite efficient.

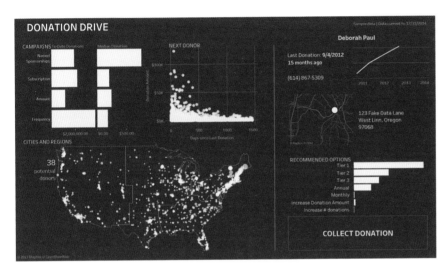

FIGURE 3.10 The perceptual dashboard

Moreover, this dashboard adheres to common practices of removing ink, minimizing color, and mostly following a logical reading pattern. A light line highlights the profile pane as a separate entity, allowing it to be read apart from the left side of the dashboard. It is functional and tidy. The information within the pane is greatly expanded with the path to action far clearer. We want to collect certain donations and these explicit options exist.

Yet the work itself is not the only thing that changes at this stage. It is also at this stage that practitioners start embracing the jargon associated with their work. Charlotte Baker-Shenk and Dennis Cokely (1991) provide a cultural paradigm that gives us powerful insight into how language, sociopolitical dynamics, and identity intersect, as shown in Figure 3.11. Role provides a pivotal context: are you part of IT, marketing, or a distinct visualization group? The politics within the org chart would also affect identity: is visualization centered closer to IT, marketing, or communication, or is it wholly independent? Socialization includes common or valued education paths as well as celebrated heroes. Who does data visualization "right" and what counts as a mistake? The language developed, using shared context, becomes harder to crack from the outside.

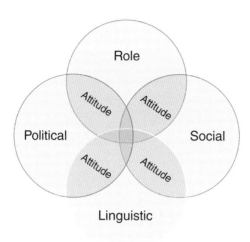

FIGURE 3.11 Adapted from Baker-Shenk and Cokely

Within cultural groups, charts take on even more nuanced naming conventions, such as a column versus a bar chart, with the direction of the axis being the lone differentiator. Naming conventions may also be tool-dependent. Tableau, for example, provides a smart drag-and-drop interface for chart building. Practitioners introduced to visualization by way of GUI tools like Tableau may talk about "columnar bars" or "bars on columns" rather than "column charts." The nuances align practitioners to their tool communities and serve as cross-community shaming vessels. These activities serve to acculturate the practitioner to norms associated with their preferred tools, work community, and even job title.

Beyond terms, maligning charts that are commonly not used well reduces the load in selecting charts but also demarcates the move from casually producing charts to becoming fluent in data visualization. It is a separator, a line that clearly defines "us" versus "them" around educated chart use and a clear, strong pendulum shift from the pictorial stage. "Pie charts are bad" in particular serves as a hallmark of and rally cry between the general population and educated chart use.

Emerging practice professions rely on these extreme shifts. They serve to identify in- and out-group members by way of attitude as you saw with the norms of chart practice above, and allow greater formalization of the work. As visualization moves from a task done by anyone to a distinct trade and skill set, taboos and attitudes create explicit boundaries. Charts that are heavily misused or presented incorrectly—out of either misunder- standing around their use or seemingly endless relatability—drop out entirely. The identification against something else pushes members toward the professional group. It becomes a principle to present data as precisely as possible.

Computers have shifted us from printing static visualizations (with considerable effort and cost) to interactive visualizations (at much lower effort and cost). We are rather early in this shift with many practices and skills still mostly in the printing of static visualization work. However, the reduction of effort and cost, thanks to computation, gives us more capacity to focus on the semantic aspects of data—by both authors and their audiences.

These shifts alone aren't enough. Beyond perception, other factors influence how our compositions are read and understood. We see broader patterns and influences as practitioners and researchers look to neighbor- ing disciplines, such as user experience, design, and cognition.

Building Subsystems

The perceptual stage is all about learning to build functional visualiza- tions. It is core to learning how to define what a chart should do and achieving it in an efficient manner. As one end of the spectrum, it is not enough. The end users are begging for more. At this point, practitioners start pushing boundaries and testing theories—are pie charts really that bad? Is there a way to reduce precision but remain true to the message?

Figure 3.12 illustrates this shift. Unlike the diametric relationship from pictographic to perceptual, later stages that we propose in this book seek to preserve the lessons learned while expanding to meet a broader range of users. They build from and wrap around the lessons we have learned while seeking to solve problems in new ways.

FIGURE 3.12 Functional aesthetics paradigm at a glance

Summary

This chapter closes out Part A and our brief look at perception. From this point, we are going to assume that you're comfortable with why certain charts are chosen from a perceptual lens and dig deeper into the semantics within the visualization in our next section. There, we will dive into semantics and further clarify and define semantics. We'll also explore how chart types range between more concrete and abstract representations of the data and what data literacy really encompasses. Where we briefly showed the influence of maps on visualization tasks, we will zoom into the parameters that drive that discussion and how those concepts affect other graphs.

PART B

Semantics

Journalist Flora Lewis once wrote,

Learning another language is not only learning different words for the same things, but learning another way to think about things.

n the late 1970s, Nicaragua established its first Deaf schools. While the schools originally focused on teaching speech and reading, the students did something not seen or easily traceable in modern times: they spontaneously created a new language. By 1986, Dr. Judy Shepard-Kegl, an American Sign Language linguist, and her team of researchers observed the children, noting the clear distinctions between the first generation of signers and the second. Beyond communication, the children matured a sophisticated language within one generation. For many linguists, Nicaraguan Sign Language proved not only our innate desire to communicate but our abilities to create grammar and semantics to further nuance meaning.

This part focuses on how we harness that ability to create and share meaning: semantics. Beyond our abilities to communicate in real time, we are able to pass down knowledge through generations using both oral memorizations and written passages. This knowledge has transformed our trajectory and understanding of the world, just like the ability to

create fire. Writing, in particular, allows us to build on knowledge in new and novel ways. It has transformed how we think and communicate, including how we visualize numbers and patterns.

Throughout the next chapters. we'll explore how semantics affects charts in isolation as well as together. We'll clarify a number of concepts that factor into linguistics and the semantic properties of what exactly charts express. Beyond charts as individual units, we'll also explore what happens when we combine them, including the grammatical constructs we impose while we design visualizations.

As we segue from perception to semantics, this section begins our journey to learn not only new names for things, but a whole new way to think about data visualization. Beyond perception, we'll look at how our brain finds patterns and systemizes them for meaning. The presentation of charts has matured to a new level of sophistication. Let's explore how the semantics of charts provides new light.

Coming to Terms

As humans, we are innately curious creatures. We seek meaning, connection, certainty, and clarification in the world around us—whether it's looking at signs as we drive or finding a vegetarian meal to order by scanning a menu marked with icons or trying to understand the pointed gestures of our friend showing directions. Beyond pattern finding, we seek to find meaning in the world around us. To find meaning, we must establish a connection and come to reasonable terms, just as the Deaf children in Nicaragua did, as described in the Part B opening.

While meaning and understanding the various relationships and patterns in the world is second nature to us, describing it in a way that can be formalized is rather difficult and abstract. This is where *semantics* comes into play. *Semantics is the study of how we draw meaning in communication* (Cann et al., 2019). With semantics, we can explore how words or signs combine to convey a concept, why icons denote specific ideas, or which gestures effectively support a message. We can take these interactions—between ourselves or machines—and abstract them to find common patterns across different languages, cultures, and experiences. We can use a variety of cues to affirm our message, or we can send signals that conflict, making it hard for others to understand the message.

In data visualization, incorporating semantic elements can be as simple as including an icon showing people where to click or how to interact. A known graphic is a specific "click" arrow that we have seen thousands of times, placed in proximity to a chart. Close your eyes and you'll probably even have a specific arrow in mind. This task is done without long explanations or training. This is semantics at work. We've taken a visual abstraction, agreed on its meaning, and put it to use as a shared symbol.

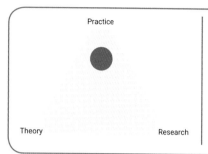

Using symbols is one common way of applying semantics to help make sense of the world. Symbols provide clues to understanding experiences by conveying recognizable meanings that are shared by societies.

Sports uniforms, company logos, and traffic signs are symbols. In some cultures, a gold ring is a symbol of marriage. Placing your hands into the shape of a heart is also a symbol, one we can playfully toss to a friend across a variety of contexts. Other symbols are highly functional: stop signs, for instance, provide useful instruction for traffic flow. They are a ubiquitous form of what functional aesthetics provides, serving as pictographic representations of intent or purpose.

Figure 4.1 shows a variety of symbols. Which ones are meaningful to you?

These icons come in a variety of styles. When you see these out in the world, they are easy to spot, making them visually distinguishable. As you scan them, you can see the differences between all of these graphics. A symbol is perceptually distinguishable and semantically meaningful if you are part of the group that uses it. Even though we can most likely describe an abstract figure without understanding its goal, for these symbols to work, they must have semantic resonance in our lives.

Statistical Graphics Are Inherently Abstract

Charts abstract information. They make it easier to see patterns at a distance, compare, and extrapolate. Icon encodings are graphical elements that are often used to visually represent the semantic meaning of marks for categorical data. Assigning meaningful icons to display elements helps the user perceive and interpret the visualization easier. These encodings can be effective in enabling visual analysis because they are often rapidly and efficiently processed by the preattentive visual system (Setlur & Mackinlay, 2014). The human visual system spatially categorizes

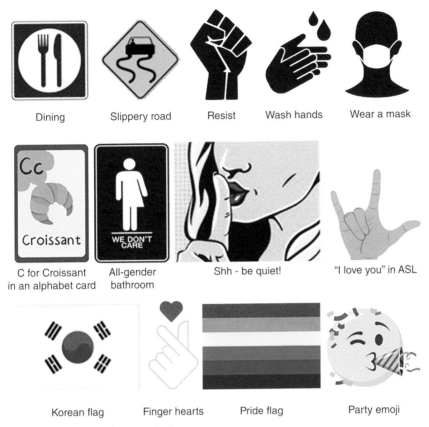

Dining   Slippery road   Resist   Wash hands   Wear a mask

C for Croissant   All-gender   Shh - be quiet!   "I love you" in ASL
in an alphabet card   bathroom

Korean flag   Finger hearts   Pride flag   Party emoji

FIGURE 4.1 Popular symbols

these icons in order to create a meaningful understanding of the visualization.

In his book *The Dragons of Eden* (1977), Carl Sagan showed a chart with the brain-to-body-mass ratios plotted for various animals, as seen in Figure 4.2. In order to make sense of this visualization, your eyes need to follow the dots and the labels to figure out a pattern.

Both label and icon indicate the semantics of the marks. However, the labels make it harder to see the centers of the dots, which makes it harder to see the correlation between body and brain masses. The icons, on the other hand, show the semantics of the marks while also helping the person to see the correlation. By associating each animal with a semantically meaningful icon (Figure 4.3), suddenly, the chart becomes more useful to understand and follow.

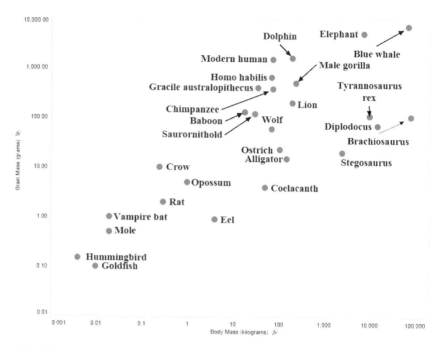

FIGURE 4.2 Carl Sagan's scatterplot
Adapted from Carl Sagan 1977

FIGURE 4.3 Carl Sagan's plot with icons

These mecha-
nisms are far
from perfect.
While we can
detect pat-
terns, we don't
always see or
interpret the
same things.

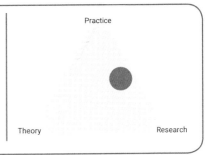

The effective depiction of an icon often depends on how semantically resonant the image is to the information it represents. The use of icons in charts depends on various factors, including task, how representative they are of the underlying data, and their general recognizability.

Some of this goes back to our minds which will fill in patterns to better align with what we expect. Charts that ask you to draw your assumptions are powerful tools to combat some of these cognitive jumps. They force us to see what we expect compared to what the data shows.

As we abstract forms, we rely on shared semantic understandings of what is encoded in the chart. The COVID-19 pandemic led to a prolifera-tion of visualizations: analysts showed daily counts, rolling averages, and accumulated totals over time and a myriad of ratios in a variety of ways. Yet, we didn't take away the same understanding of the data, and a small network leveraged this ambiguity to create more confusion.

Flattening the Curve

In 2007, researchers examined the impacts of non-pharmaceutical interventions within a pandemic (Hatchet et al., 2007). A single chart highlighted the differences between two cities: Philadelphia and St. Louis. These two lines are marked with a legend and two different styles, one solid and the other dotted (Figure 4.4, left). The paper highlighted the need for early intervention—mitigating the spread of endemic outbreaks by curbing interactions and using masks. In 2020, this paper fed one of the most iconic visuals of the COVID-19 pandemic: the graph showcasing our ability to "flatten the curve" with specific social interventions.

"Flatten the curve" is an abstraction. It takes curves seen from the cities and smooths them to two clearly distinct curves. One is a fast and high peak, while the other stretches across a longer span (Figure 4.4, right). It generalizes a fact and feeds our need for story: we can choose our path. Additional layers of annotation can highlight what feeds the spike: hospi-tal capacity, our willingness to partake in social interventions, and the introduction of vaccines. Variations of "Flatten the curve" morphed to part of the visual vocabulary of 2020.

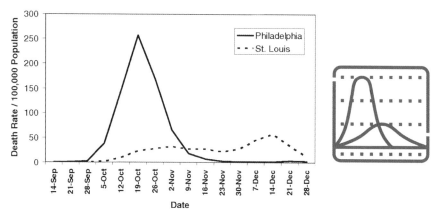

FIGURE 4.4 The original chart (left) and the derivative showing an iconic visual (right)

This symbol extracted a proven pattern beyond a literal example to that of a rally cry. We could use it to highlight healthcare system limits and the goal of delaying cases—we knew they would come—to perhaps when we had more capacity and more pharmaceutical options. Its ambiguity allowed its broad use but relied on clarification of what it showed. Explainers from *Vox* (Barclay et al., 2020), the *Spinoff* with Dr. Siouxsie Wiles (Morris & Wiles, 2020), and others used interactivity, showing tangible examples of each in isolation before showing both curves together. They highlighted the behaviors, leveraging comic-style graphics and pithy quotes to give an idea of attitudes that fed each curve.

Beyond "flatten the curve" graphics, reporters visualized case data in a number of ways. John Burn-Murdoch of the *Financial Times* shared his insights both through the news site and Twitter (https://twitter.com/jburnmurdoch), his charts highly annotated to help readers navigate the graphics. He featured a number of line charts generated across a variety of calculations to highlight his findings. Twitter provided a testing ground, a way to converse and derive a better understanding of how to annotate displays and showcase patterns.

As news organizations visualized COVID-19 data, they had to overcome hurdles associated with displaying ambiguous data. Case report dates varied, with weekend data delayed until the following Monday for reporting. This affected the visual pattern. Defining a case varied across geopolitical lines, deaths were not always directly listed as COVID related, and the delayed relationships between onset and death needed clarification for public understanding. Aggregated data hid location clusters and stratification-based discrepancies such as race, gender, and sexuality in outcomes. Spikes in data could be reporting-related, delayed by holidays, and are often smoothed out by rolling aggregations. These calculations needed to be exposed fully and explained to the broader public.

Along with what news organizations provided, analysts and other data workers took to chart making to find and highlight patterns. Sites crowd-sourced and shared a variety of data points. As you saw in Chapter 3, the COVID-19 pandemic coincided with an infodemic. It wasn't just the onslaught of information, but the types of information. Skeptics leveraged the ambiguous nature of charts, pushing untrained individuals to do their own analysis on tabular data (Lee et al., 2021). This ambiguity feeds into data literacy discussions, which we'll explore in Chapter 6, and the blurry lines around how charts are interpreted.

Toward Meaningful Depictions

Symbolic representations manifest in various ways for effectively communicating a specific concept, as we have seen in the various examples so far. However, we know that communication is richer and more nuanced than that. Creativity is often seen as the ability to create novel ideas by making connections between existing concepts. It is the basis of how language has evolved and how we use graphics to share meaning. It plays an important role in graphic design not only in conceiving new concepts but also in visually representing them. As far as the visual representation of concepts is concerned, humans have been doing it since more than 77,000 years ago, starting with cave paintings (Relethford, 2008). These representations vary from being completely pictorial to more abstract.

The link between the visual representation and the conceptual connections behind it can be observed. Examples of this can be seen by looking at Chinese characters, more specifically at the ones categorized as ideogrammic compounds (Tung & Hopkins, 2012). These characters can be decomposed into others whose concepts are semantically related, belonging to the same (or at least similar) conceptual space. Figure 4.5 shows Chinese characters for *root*, *tree*, *woods*, and *forest* (left to right). Root can be obtained by adding a line to the tree character; the woods character can be obtained by using two tree characters; the forest can be obtained by using three tree characters.

本　木　林　森

FIGURE 4.5 Chinese characters for *root*, *tree*, *woods*, and *forest* (left to right)

These visual alterations are also how we mature semantics broadly in language. Deaf children in Nicaragua used similar paradigms to expand meaning in their newly birthed language, expanding, changing placements, and multiplying to enrich meaning (Senghas & Coppola, 2001). Spoken Korean is rich in vocabulary words that tie back to characters like these being combined to make new concepts. We will revisit some of these ideas in Chapter 6 with literacy. Beyond language, this creative response also flows into icons.

Some authors were inspired by this relationship between concepts to their visual representations. One of them was Charles Bliss, who developed a communication system composed of several hundred ideographs that can be combined to make new ones, called Blissymbols (1965), with various examples shown in Figure 4.6.

Several interesting things can be observed by looking at Blissymbols, such as variation in the degree of abstraction in the symbols. By *combining* symbols, new meanings are obtained (examples in Figure 4.6: pen + man = writer, mouth + ear = language); by using the same symbols in a *different position*, new meanings are obtained, as seen in symbols for water, rain, steam, and stream.

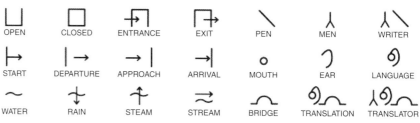

FIGURE 4.6 Blissymbols

These systems work because of how we draw meaning with semantics: we create visual allegories to our intent by building up to the concept. These examples can be found in languages and other pictorial systems quite frequently. Researcher Neil Cohn (2014) has found a semantic lens in drawing. For him, drawing parallels between language fluency and "I can't draw" highlights a lack of *semantic fluency*.

We can help others draw meaning in charts as well. We can layer them, break lines and boundaries, and expand concepts to create new clusters of meaning. Figure 4.7 shows an example that intentionally blurs lines between the proportional brushing of the bar chart into the axes of the area charts. Proportional brushing is a technique where a proportion of the selected data is shown in relation to all the values rather than just filtering to the selection. Shared color helps obscure the boundaries.

PROFIT BY CATEGORY

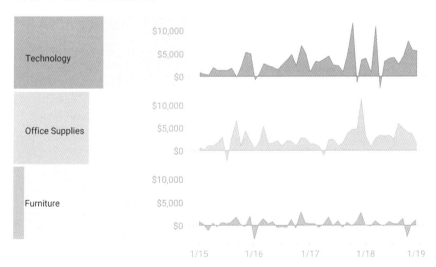

FIGURE 4.7 Profit by Category showing proportional brushing in bar charts with an area trend

This example highlights another tactic for creating meaning. By combining disparate charts into one that visually becomes more like one unit, we leverage semantics to expand our repertoire. In this case, we use color to provide a bit more clarification about the part-to-whole relationship.

Situating with Semiotics

When dealing with meaningful visual representation, aspects of a representation's meaning can be altered by modifying its visual characteristics; these characteristics are extensively explored in *semiotics*, the study of signs and symbols and their use or interpretation. Changing an aspect ratio changes meaning (Chandler, 2002). In Figure 4.8, Tableau Hall of Fame Visionary Kelly Martin analyzes animal strikes. Within the visualization, she embeds aspects of semiotics masterfully and deeply.

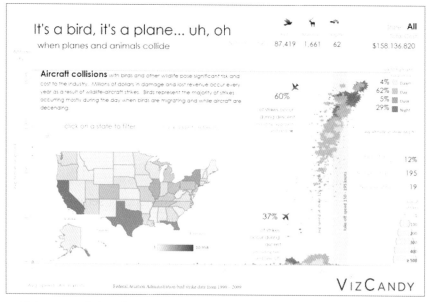

FIGURE 4.8 Bird Strikes by Kelly Martin

Deconstructing the dashboard highlights the three semiotic properties commonly applied to visually express meaning:

One semiotic aspect, *position*, can be seen in the various positions and directions of the plane. When the image is flipped, our eyes and brain envision the movement that these visual representations convey, giving us "departure" and "arrival." The descending plane is higher, while the ascending plane is lower, also supporting and enriching meaning.

Shape is another aspect. The jarring shape affirms the topic of collisions, one leveraged in comics to highlight violent contact. Beyond comic design, an experiment to map shape and sound (Ramachandran & Hubbard, 2001) showed that we tend to associate sharp shapes with sharp, high-pitched sounds and smoother, organic shapes with softer sounds.

The last semiotic aspect is *color*. The shapes are colored by time of day, leveraging a bright yellow for dawn, darkening to orange for day, and shifting to blues for the evening. At a glance, they align with the shifting natural light we experience.

The result is a delightful form of creative expression that cleverly blends the semantics of data with the effective use of color, shape, and space. The graphics in her view, are used to encode data values and show how those data values are connected to the world. Her shapes are particularly clever because the size of shape is used to encode the number of strikes, while the form of the shape connects to the violence of the event. It's visually striking, thoughtfully crafted, and visceral. We'll explore other elements within this visualization to further expose its craft. Semiotics is a useful tool for effectively depicting data in the form of semantic concepts in visualizations. The process of creating functionally aesthetic visualizations deals specifically with understanding the forms and functions of individual charts and skillfully compositing them into an effective representation.

Summary

Our knowledge of the world helps us understand the semantics of representation. It is a fundamental component of how we reason and make sense of everything around us. Our understanding of meaning is based upon a blend of perceptual, cognitive, and affective states arising from our direct sensory experience, familiarity, and understanding as seen with the various examples described in this chapter. While the world may be best measured and represented as concrete quantifiable entities such as meters and Fahrenheit, the way we interpret information is more loosely defined. We often use words like *tall* and *warm* as a way of describing concepts. The next chapter will explore language and its impreciseness and how to represent data as concepts that may be fuzzy around the edges.

CHAPTER 5

Vagueness and Ambiguity

In the previous chapter, we discussed how the role of semantics informs graphical presentation, making information easier to understand. Functionally aesthetic charts take categories, place, time, and numbers, weaving patterns and stories in creative ways. Data often loses precision when interacting in the real world. Most of the things around us have boundaries that are only vaguely defined; a *tall person* means different things to different people, for example.

So why is all this relevant to visual analysis and the data driving the analysis? Understanding language goes hand in hand with the ability to integrate complex contextual information into an effective visualization and being able to *converse* with the data interactively, a term we call *analytical conversation*. It also helps us think about ways to create artifacts that support and manage how we converse with machines as we see and understand data. We will circle back to this during the course of the book, especially as we go into intent in Part C.

How Tall Is Tall?

Language can be vague, as its interpretation depends on the context and our inability to precisely determine the boundaries of vaguely defined concepts (Kessler & Kuhn, 2014). One of the most prevalent kinds of vague language involves the use of adjectives. These vague concepts that include adjectives appear throughout language and are expressed on a spectrum of concreteness, from "tallest" to "cheap" to "safe," as illustrated in Figure 5.1. Research from linguistics says that people deliberately use imprecise language as a way to better communicate (van Deemter, 2010). They do this for many reasons—to avoid error, because of the absence of a mutually understood metric, to reduce cognitive effort, or because precision may not be relevant.

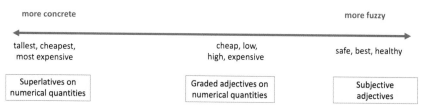

FIGURE 5.1 Vague concepts can be interpreted along a spectrum from concrete to fuzzy.

Let's take the concept of "tall." What counts as a tall basketball player is different from what counts as a tall kindergarten student, which differs again from what counts as a tall glass. Some humans are definitely not tall, like actor Danny DeVito, who stands at 4'10", while Serbian professional basketball player Boban Marjanović is definitely tall at 7'4". A height of 5'10" is almost definitely tall for a woman in the United States but might be a borderline case for men. "Tall" is not the sort of quality for which there are definite criteria that sort the world into "tall" things and "not tall" things. In other words, "tall" is vague.

This fuzziness in language permeates into how we ask questions about our data. Studies from cognitive linguistics (Schmidt et al., 2009; Solt & Gotzner, 2012; Qinq & Franke, 2014) show that human judgments of these vague adjectives vary depending on the data distribution of a set of presented data items. In these studies, crowd worker participants were shown bars of differing heights, presented in random order. They were asked to mark which items were considered "tall." Viewers were quite sensitive to the distribution of the relative sizes of the items, how many appear in plateaus adjacent to one another, and if the relative values formed a convex or a concave shape when placed in sorted order.

A study by Hearst et al. (2019) wanted to probe further into the boundaries of what an appropriate visualization would be for responding to queries that contain these vague, imprecise concepts. The study showed the participants different visualization views for the question "Which of my grocery expenses" followed by one of the following: "*is the highest* this month?" or "*are the highest* this month?" or "*are high* this month?" Figure 5.2 shows the three data shapes used in the study with multiple top *k* bars highlighted.

- Shape 1: A roughly exponential drop-off. The first three items were marked as tall by nearly all participants, with the rest marked not-tall.

- Shape 2: A roughly inverse exponential curve. No clear visual markers as to where to distinguish between tall and not-tall.

- Shape 3: Plateaus. A first plateau of items followed by an 80% drop to a second plateau of items, followed by a 65% drop.

Participants showed a strong preference to highlight the top *k* bars in the charts as opposed to filtering to those top bars. They also chose multiple highlighted bars for the superlative questions, i.e., "are the highest" and "is the highest."

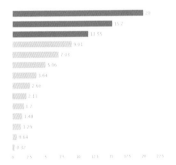
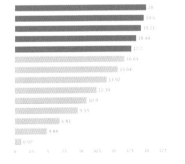
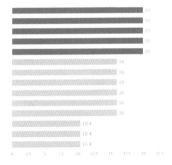

Shape 1: Exponential drop-off   Shape 2: Inverse exponential   Shape 3: Plateaus

FIGURE 5.2 The stimuli shapes used in understanding how to represent vague concepts for visual analysis

Other vague forms of analytical questions occur when people talk about *place*. Places may be referred to using colloquial or local names (e.g., "in the city" versus the surrounding suburbs) or cultural nicknames (e.g., "the Big Apple" for New York City). Once these places are disambiguated, there is still the issue that people often think in terms of vague spatial concepts rather than absolutes. It is more natural to use fuzzy spatial terms, such as "restaurants *near* me" as opposed to "restaurants within 1.5 miles."

Natural language interface tools for visual analysis need to constantly address these vague questions that people type or say to them. Eviza (Setlur et al., 2016) was a research prototype that supported vague queries in the context of a visualization. Figure 5.3 shows a map of earthquake data in the United States. Here, the map shows marks selected in response to the user's query "Find *large* earthquakes *near* California." Eviza finds two ambiguities in the query: "large" and "near,'" which are fuzzy terms for size and distance. The system semantically associates the size descriptor "large" to an attribute, and "magnitude" with values 5 and more, while "near" is a 100-mile radius around the border of California. Now you may ask, "Hmm, earthquakes are scary, and I prefer associating *large* to be 4 or more." To handle this subjectivity, two ambiguity widgets are added to the interface to allow the user to modify these settings. We will discuss more about repair and refinement as a natural part of language and communication a bit later in this chapter.

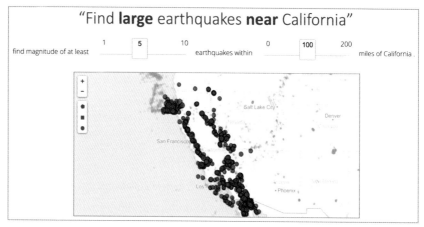

FIGURE 5.3 Eviza's interface shows a map of earthquake data in the United States.

The semantics of place is a common notion prevalent during information seeking activities with queries such as "show me the best coffee places around *here*" or "what is the cost of living in the *midwest*?"

Research in geographic information science (Goodchild, 2011; Gao et al., 2017; McKenzie & Hu, 2017; Adams & McKenzie, 2012) discusses how people form regions in their minds, reflecting informal ways to identify and organize places like "Midwest." These places can be subjective and allude to different meanings for different people, often depending on the context and the nature of the inquiry.

Hopefully by now you are starting to appreciate that ambiguity is present at many levels and in many forms. Visual analysis tools such as Tableau create visualizations automatically based on the data attributes of interest, allowing users to ask questions interactively through the visualizations. However, the user's mental model may not operate at the same level as the tool. Let's take an example: say I'm in Sales and I'm interested in looking at the revenue for San Francisco and Seattle in 2020. How should we answer this question? Should we show the total San Francisco revenue over all years versus Seattle in 2020 or the more likely comparison of both cities in 2020? Even if we ignore the potential ambiguity of the language, there are several possible ambiguous visual representations:

■ A bar chart with aggregate information

■ A stacked bar chart

■ Two bar charts, one for each city

■ A multi-line chart with a line for each city

■ Two separate line charts, one for each city

Each representation has its pros and cons and will depend on the task and message. As you mull over these multiple possibilities, we've started to get into the language and design space of concepts that are ambiguous. Let's explore that crossroad.

Spicy or Hot—What's the Difference?

A concept, term, or phrase is *ambiguous* if it has more than one meaning. Take "hot," for example. One meaning of "hot" has to do with temperature, and in this sense, "hot" can be associated with other temperature-related concepts such as "warm" and "cold." If you've been to an Indian or Thai restaurant, "hot" is a term used to indicate the level of spiciness when ordering food. Figure 5.4 shows an assortment of dishes that are part of an Indian thali. Another meaning of "hot" has to do with fashion and social attractiveness. And there are other senses of hot as well, as in "his hot temper prevents him from making any progress in a very pressured situation."

FIGURE 5.4 An Indian thali of dishes that can be both "spicy hot" and "temperature hot"
Joe Gough/Adobe Stock

In a particular context, the meaning of an ambiguous term may become clear. Knowing the semantics of your data helps with sensible data transformations. Take the column of date string birthdays on the left in Figure 5.5. At first glance, they look like dates. But hold on—what is the date format for these strings? The United States uses a date format in which the month goes first, then the day, followed by the year. Since the month is the middle-sized unit in the date, this format is called *middle-*

endian. The vast majority of European countries, on the other hand, format dates with day, followed by month, and then year, called the *little-endian* method. The term *endianness* came from Jonathan Swift's famous book *Gulliver's Travels*. One of the stories involves a political faction called Big Endians, people who liked to crack their eggs at the large end. The Lilliputian king considered this method too primitive and required his subjects, the Little Endians, to break their eggs at the small end. But the Big Endians rebelled. And, somehow, some way, this is how we got the names for date formats; the system, itself, being called endianness.

Now, back to the example—how do we know the endianness of the date strings? If you look carefully, the second row has the value 4-15-08. We know that there are no months beyond 12, so this is a middle-endian format (mm-dd-yyyy). Rather than looking at one single row, looking at the entire column as context can help resolve ambiguity in the date formats.

| Name | Birthday | Gold Stars | | Name | Birthday | Gold Stars |
Abc	Abc	#		Abc	🗓	#
Claire	1-3-07	18		Claire	1/3/2007	18
Donny	4-15-08	9		Donny	4/15/2008	9
Sam	10-3-07	22		Sam	10/3/2007	22
Trent	7-11-07	25		Trent	7/11/2007	25
Agatha	8-3-08	11		Agatha	8/3/2008	11
Geraldine	2-7-09	3		Geraldine	2/7/2009	3

FIGURE 5.5 Transforming ambiguous birthday strings into precise date types

The simple premise of using context to help clarify and come up with reasonable assumptions has also found its way into automation and sensible defaults in visual analysis tools, such as Tableau (Wesley et al., 2018). Another example is around place ambiguity for geocoding place strings. Take a look at the cities in Table 5.1. Where would you think Paris is located based on the domain of the data?

And in case you are wondering about Table 5.1, there indeed happens to be a Paris in Texas.

TABLE 5.1 A sample data table. Where in the world is Paris?

City	Sales
Austin	$912,791
Dallas	$1,281,047
Houston	$1,568,974
Paris	$645,335
San Antonio	$1,426,697

Clarification, Repair, and Refinement

"Context is king" as we navigate this complex and often confusing world of information vagueness and ambiguity. Beyond context, we do use other tools to engage as we converse with people. We *clarify* by asking follow-up questions if we do not understand what someone is saying. We *repair* and *refine* what we just said to make ourselves clearer and more articulate. We *point* at objects, gesturing toward things to make the conversation more enriching.

Understanding the context and the domain of the data is important to help disambiguate concepts. While reasonable defaults can be used to create a visualization, there should be no dead ends. Provide affordances for a user to understand, repair, and refine.

Practice

Theory

Research

The next time you visit a coffee shop, just observe human communication in action as people chat over cups of coffee.

Conversational repair is the process people use to detect and resolve problems in communicating, receiving, and understanding. Through repair, participants in social interaction display how they establish and maintain communication and mutual understanding. Language interpretation formalizes multiple levels of repair, from monitoring and evaluating various benchmarks of accuracy to proper ways to intervene and seek clarification.

The Colonomos model (2015) for simultaneous interpretation takes into account the mood, intent, setting, and register of the speaker. It analyzes the source message against these factors and others as the production message starts getting built. Remember, this planning is happening while the source is still speaking or signing. Interpreting isn't about word for word but meaning for meaning with sensitivity to other factors such as register and setting that would affect the message. A 5-year-old child would present very differently than a 79-year-old in register, tone, word choice, and mood. In fact, a computer also presents differently. As interpreters construct the message, they are continuously evaluating what they have produced versus what the source states. Some repairs are added on within the interpretation, adding nuance a language may seek throughout the arc of the rendition, or stopping the process and intervening. Repair is critical to providing an effective interpretation. We argue that repair provides a crucial theoretical interface as we explore diverse approaches to enabling *analytical* conversation between people and data.

Pointing is a common gesture used to clarify or repair a message. Yet not all pointing is the same. Pronouns in signed languages rely on a sophisticated system of pointing. There are grammatical rules about where signed pronouns, or *referents*, can be placed and how verbs and deictic references must agree. In a study of pointing (Fenlon et al., 2019), formation features of signed points from British Sign Language (BSL) favored the 1-handshape and a single hand, while spoken language gestures tended to use both hands to create full-hand (B-handshape) references. Durations of points were shorter for signers and far more systematic. The grammar around pointing made the signed points far less vague.

With vagueness and ambiguity prevalent in language and communication, understanding and interpreting what someone means is always a challenging problem. When constructing interactive charts and dashboards, it is important to make thoughtful defaults and assumptions about the intended message to the reader. Similar to human language, it is equally important to make provisions for repair and refinement during the interaction experience. Some of these provisions are showing filter controls and widgets, as we saw in Figure 5.3, for a user to tweak and make adjustments to the visualization as they make sense of the data. Other scaffolds are clicking on marks, similar to deictic gestures from American Sign Language (ASL) and other forms of human communication to set the context for clarification.

Iconicity of Representation

In linguistics, iconicity is used when the form has direct ties to meaning or clear motivations in origin (Sandler & Lillo-Martin, 2006). In spoken language, onomatopoeia is an iconic representation of a sound, such as the *whoosh* of the wind or the *cluck* of a chicken. ASL uses space and the body rather than phonemes to create meaning, so iconicity is visual. Take a look at Figure 5.6. The three graphics illustrate two signs. On the left, the signer uses a 1-handshape against the palm of an open hand and moves the 1 up. On the right two frames, the signer uses a bent-handshape with an eye gaze and mouth morpheme "cha" to convey a concept. . What do you think these signs mean?

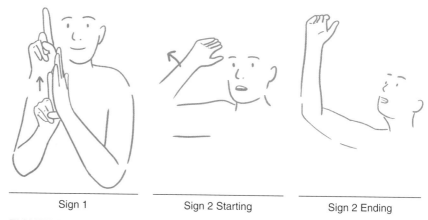

| Sign 1 | Sign 2 Starting | Sign 2 Ending |

FIGURE 5.6 ASL signs drawn by Deaf graphic artist Brittany Castle

Both signs are used for "tall." The first sign is fairly vague about how tall a person is. The second sign removes vagueness because of the additional grammatical elements that support it: eye gaze and lean are governed by grammar and the mouth morpheme affirms a *very* tall person. It's the myriad of elements, combined with the transparency of the sign. that reduces vagueness.

Communicating data through functionally aesthetic charts is not only about perception and precision but also understanding. The International System of Typographic Picture Education (ISOTYPE) was developed to bridge the gap between showing data in a way that's easy to read and at the same time easier to understand than abstract charts (Neurath, 2010).

The ISOTYPE includes two ideas that nicely complement each other: a visual language for creating icons and the idea of using multiples to represent quantitative data (Haroz et al., 2015). By converting abstract information into something more concrete, ISOTYPES, when used effectively, is one way to engage with the reader and tell stories with data. Figure 5.7 shows the change in employment during the industrial revolution in England.

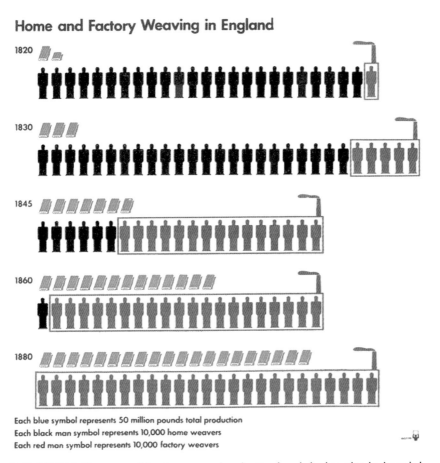

Each blue symbol represents 50 million pounds total production
Each black man symbol represents 10,000 home weavers
Each red man symbol represents 10,000 factory weavers

FIGURE 5.7 Home and factory weaving in England during the industrial revolution

In Figure 5.7, each figure stands for a multiple, in this case 10,000 workers, and each bale of textiles represents 50 million pounds of product. Notice how the red factories (with the little smokestacks) are swallowing up the home weavers over the course of time. What is interesting is that the net total number of workers (home and factory) stays roughly the same, while the amount of production (blue symbols) increases dramatically.

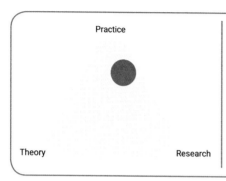

Iconicity supports familiarity and better chart understanding, especially when the visual treatment is semantically meaningful. By making the patterns in the representation surface more meaningful to the reader, the chart becomes less abstract.

Charts also draw on iconicity to facilitate understanding and reduce vagueness depending on the task. As they grow more abstract, we rely more on inherent systems to clarify. The ISOTYPES use color and outline to call out the differences between weavers and shape and size to note differences in production and workers. These semantic elements, along with the text, reduce vagueness.

The Art of Chart

Let's look at purchasing books as an example, as shown in Table 5.2. In January, a customer bought 22 books; in February, they bought 4; in March, they bought 16; and then in April, they returned 3.

TABLE 5.2 Number of books purchased over the first four months

Month	Books Purchased
January	22
February	4
March	16
April	−3

Table 5.2 relies on literacy and numeracy to provide a sense of purchase. While we know that the first column has the names of months, we don't know that the numbers in the second column, such as 22, are the number

of books purchased just by viewing the numbers alone. We need to know the domain from where the numbers came. The column heading "Books Purchased" provides the required semantics for us to understand these numbers better. The number −3, however, adds complexity, which we'll see play out in the example representations.

We can visualize this in several ways, including leveraging ISOTYPES. In Figure 5.8, we can see the books organized by groups of 10, allowing easier tracking of numbers, much like tick marks. April's books are lighter and below the line, using both position and color to highlight a negative number.

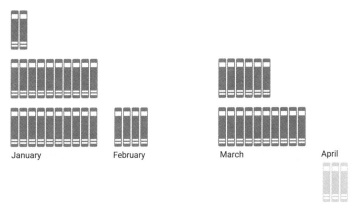

January   February   March   April

FIGURE 5.8 A graphic similar to the ISOTYPE charts

Stacking in groups allows us to clearly see the 22 the customer purchased in January, the 4 in February, and the 3 they returned in April. March requires us to work a bit more to determine that we have 16. We could further subgroup in 5s to make this task easier. Instead, we start pivoting from representations that favor numeracy and literacy to those that rely on seeing the larger visual pattern. We build stacks this time, which almost perfectly mirrors a bar chart. We get a better sense visually of the differing quantities of books purchased. The bar is fairly iconic as a representation of the data. We can easily see that there is a positive aesthetic quality to this visual representation that is connected to a literal stack of books, as demonstrated by Figure 5.9.

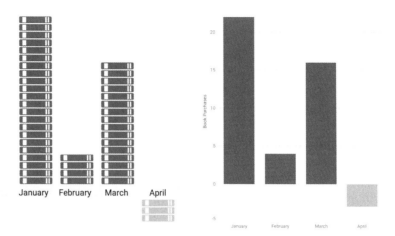

FIGURE 5.9 An iconic representation of stacked books and a bar chart

We start shifting the focus from the clearly defined groups of bars to the trend shown in Figure 5.10. First, we preserve the anchor to zero while shifting the focus of the representation to the pattern over time by using an area chart. The points represent the counts, and the shaded area helps draw attention to the pattern. We then further abstract the area chart into a line graph.

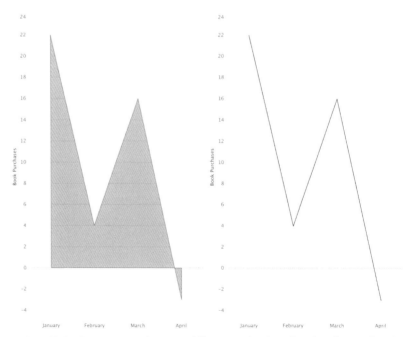

FIGURE 5.10 An area chart and line graph showing book purchasing trends

When we look at these charts in succession, we can see how the bar provides tangible stacks, the area turns into a mountain with points that climb and dive, and the line directs the most attention to the lightning bolt style pattern of purchases. The line is the most abstract representation of this data. Without a filled anchor to 0, the eye is drawn to the flow of the lines rather than the literal values. We can break the illusion by adding the books back into the picture, as shown in Figure 5.11.

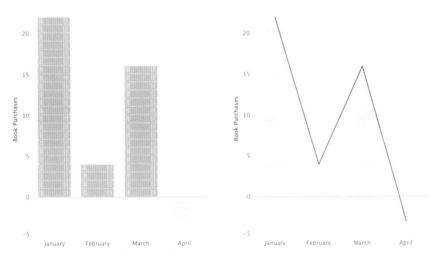

FIGURE 5.11 Breaking the illusion

Summary

The way charts are designed plays a large role in how they are later interpreted by others. Bar and line charts are often comfortable entry points in practice because they are tangible for newer chart readers. For example, vertical bars relate to our perception of physical objects standing adjacent on flat ground, while ropes, and seaweed floating in the ocean, relate to line charts. Refinement tools such as interactivity, tooltips, annotations, and icons help further reduce vagueness while allowing readers to better understand chart types. We explore how vagueness and abstraction intersect to affect data literacy in the next chapter.

CHAPTER 6

Data Literacy

We've seen the roles abstraction and iconicity play with both language and charts. Literacy is a further abstraction, a system for representing words and ideas to preserve thoughts over time. Yet literacy isn't one thing; it's many. The online version of *Merriam-Webster's Dictionary* defines being *literate* in several ways, including as follows (n.d.):

1a: educated or cultured

1b: able to read and write, such as population literacy rates

2c. Having knowledge or competency, "computer literate"

When we intersect these definitions with *data* literacy, discussions tend to center somewhere around 1b ("reading and writing") and 2c ("competency within a specific skill"). For a bit of added spice, some definitions come with a flavor of 1a ("cultured") added. These slight variations create some confusion. In community discourse, we sometimes try to fold *reading and writing* (1b) and *competence* (2c) into the same idea without distinguishing between the terms.

These paradigms affect how we design, deploy, and use visualizations as well as our discourse around data visualization as a profession. Charts are a written language for data. Is data literacy about how to train ourselves and users on the language of charts (1b), or is it a broader paradigm that encompasses the entire ecosystem of data (1a and 2c)? The first represents an individual effort, one we'll call *graphicacy* in line with Alberto Cairo's (2019) definition of reading and creating charts. Graphicacy plays a key role in data literacy but represents a small part of the overall process.

When we look at the broader paradigm, data literacy becomes less about a specific task and more about navigating a system like health literacy. This process, shown in Figure 6.1, encompasses the following elements:

Inputs: How the data came to be in the first place

Storage: Whether it is generated in a flat (spreadsheet), relational (database), or array format (JSON)

Modelling and prep: The changes in shape and aggregation to allow for analysis

Defining: The meanings and limitations of the fields and individual members of data

Analyzing: The process of understanding the data in visual and aggregated formats

Output: The means in which the interpretation is shared, such as in visualizations, dashboards, or other data-informed composition

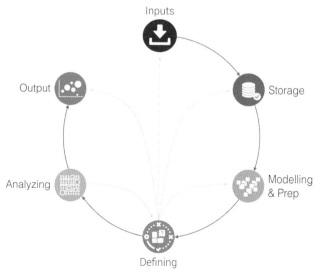

FIGURE 6.1 Data literacy circle

Inputs decide how the data is collected. Can users type in a field, select single variables, or check multiples in response to a question? For example, COVID cases may be reported as a date of onset, as a test result, or by presumption. This data is then stored in a spreadsheet, in a database where it's modelled dimensionally, or as a JSON file. A case may be defined by country or state: some may allow reporting based on symptoms or require a test. Graphicacy comes into play with analyzing. We're making charts and exploring relationships. Lastly, the final analysis is shared to some type of output, whether as a digital composition or printed to paper.

Navigating Data Literacy

A broader definition significantly affects how we disperse data literacy skills and to what levels. It spells out what we, as a society, expect people to know to navigate a modern and highly abstracted world. Both computers and writing transformed how we navigate the world, with one change being within the last few decades and the other centuries ago. With COVID-19, we've seen that data visualization is becoming a *primary means* of understanding the world.

At the beginning of the pandemic, news organizations started reporting on a novel coronavirus in China. The virus quickly spread, with various Centers for Disease Control (CDC) departments and the World Health Organization (WHO) struggling to keep pace with reporting. Johns Hopkins University (JHU) also began tracking the numbers separately and showed markedly higher numbers (Dong et al., 2020). The JHU dashboard, in addition to the pandemic, also marked a turning point for data literacy.

Even the pandemic's early rally cry—"Flatten the curve"—relies on a data-literate culture. Understanding the curve formed by cases over time relies on recognizing the pattern of data and what it represents: a longer, flatter hill means fewer cases over a wider span of time. Data visualization is a primary means of understanding the COVID-19 pandemic.

The dashboard itself served as the backbone for news organizations reporting on the pandemic. If sites did not directly use the images, they rewrapped the visuals in a variety of formats and styles with JHU data as the source. Charts, more than words, told the story of the COVID-19 pandemic. Health departments have since made their own iterations of dashboards, expanding from the original focus of cases, deaths, and positivity rates to include vaccination data and other relevant information and calls to action (Patino, 2021).

This shift is no accident. The rise of graphicacy and broader data literacy intersects with the technology that makes it possible and the critical need to understand information in ways current literacies fail. Like reading and writing, data literacy must become mainstream to fully democratize information access. To understand the role graphicacy plays in data literacy, let's look at the impact of reading and writing.

The Impact of Writing

In the fifteenth century, Koreans exclusively used Hanja, Chinese characters repurposed for Korean sounds. While the *yangban*, or aristocratic elites, mastered the numerous borrowed ideographs to read and write, literacy remained out of reach to most social classes. Faced with a population where only the richest could read, King Sejong, the ruler of Joseon (now modern-day Korea), faced a challenge: How do you make a language accessible to the masses?

Sejong knew he needed to capture the sounds of the Korean language. Alphabets are tricky. They attempt to codify the smallest units of sound—phonemes—and allow them to build up to syllables and words. Precision and utility are key. Hangul artistically combines the higher-level syllables and the lower-level phonemes, or individual sounds.

FIGURE 6.2 *Hangul* written to highlight letter and syllable features

Enter Hangul, a written language most sources attribute directly to the king that epitomizes functional aesthetics (Kim & diRende, 2014). It is an alphabet with distinct letters for individual phonemes. Unlike most alphabets, Hangul isn't written linearly. Rather, sounds are grouped into syllable blocks systematically, much like a syllabary. The larger units of sound can be scanned and memorized quickly. Figure 6.2 highlights this dual nature: the word *Hangul* is written with initial consonants (*h, g*) in dark green, vowels in light maroon (a, u), and ending consonants in blue (n, l). Note how the vowels affect the shape.

Hangul is a lesson in functional aesthetics. The script contains featural elements with iconic roots—certain letters mirror key shapes in the mouth, shown on the right in Figure 6.3. These consonants use triangles, squares, and circles as base elements to formulate their design. Letter families use the same placement in the mouth but alter whether the sound is voiced, aspirated, or tensed in that position. For example, *t* and *d* have the same placement but differ in voicing. Hangul preserves these relationships and marks them with additive line changes. Figure 6.4 shows how the original consonants build from each other in design with obsolete letters marked in yellow. These basic letters expand systematically by adding a line for aspiration or by duplicating the base letter for tenseness (selected letter families shown in Figure 6.5).

Vowels have their own philosophy and harmony rules, using aggregation and yin and yang groupings (shown in Figure 6.6). These rules may help with spelling. Despite its simplicity—or maybe even because of it—the aristocratic class objected, labeling it with contempt toward the people most likely to use it: peasants and women. Yet Hangul precariously survived and is celebrated in South Korea with a holiday.

As a writing system, Hangul is elegant. It supports reading by grouping sound families, systemizing letter creation, and clearly defining syllable boundaries. It works to make the task of reading sounds as transparent and efficient as possible. As we broaden our lens from writing to visualization, we hope to capture Hangul's balance of form and function.

Like King Sejong, we can work to make graphicacy attainable and legible, in addition to supporting the broader cycle of data literacy by clarifying inputs and definitions. Many of the debates we have today around data literacy share a common theme with historical discussions around the value of literacy. With visualization, we worry about who needs to learn to make graphics, how end users will understand what we present, and what levels of data literacy skills to disperse.

Visualizations are abstractions, relying on primary graphicacy skills to fully understand the composition. Dashboards, infographics, and data-driven news articles are rapidly maturing in exposition styles. They too are making the shift from where charts were an auxiliary part of communicating information to where they can drive the composition.

FIGURE 6.3 Featural elements

$$ㆆ$$
$$ㅇ$$
$$ㄹ ㄷ ㄴ ㅁ ㅇ ㄱ ㅋ ㅂ ㅍ$$
$$ㅅ$$
$$ㅿ$$
$$ㅈ$$
$$ㅊ$$

FIGURE 6.4 Additive design
From Pae (2018)

FIGURE 6.5 Selected letters (base, aspirated, tense)

FIGURE 6.6 Korean vowel harmony
Kim, Y., and diRende, S. (2014), Korean Hangeul: A New Kind of Beauty. Ecobook

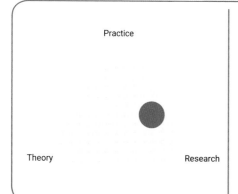

Practice

Theory

Research

Research explores the fallacies of misconstrued information. Approaches involve assisting analysts to help them tackle questions they couldn't ask before but do so responsibly in a way that promotes safe, ethical, and well-supported conclusions from the data (Correll, 2019).

Data Orality

Orality exists in spaces before literature takes hold. The culture and cognitive tools center around using conversation and verbal expositions to learn. *Data* orality is where the use of charts serves as supplemental to the exposition of data. Charts are not intuitively read. Instead, consumers rely on outside narration, expanded supplemental text, and numeracy to navigate what the visualization shows.

Literacy changes both the brain and culture. The brain recycles areas for common tasks into networked reading zones (Wolf & Stoodley, 2008). Areas dedicated to shape awareness also take on the task of recognizing the written word as notable and reading as a dedicated process. The process of learning to read takes years, requiring skills that go beyond recognizing the words on the page to understanding the broader concepts presented by the author (Wolf & Stoodley, 2008). For literate societies, reading eventually becomes a primary means of learning. Books not only educate but create a cultural backdrop and shorthand.

Socrates, the famed Greek philosopher, distrusted the idea of reading for learning (Plato, 1952). Rather, he found memorization and dialog pivotal for understanding, hence the Socratic method commonly used in schools. Writing may supplement, but the primary means of understanding relies on discourse, or *orality*. Orality isn't about the individual but the broader culture.

The societal impacts of literacy profoundly change exposition styles. Walter Ong (2012) studied the differences between cultures not exposed to writing in contrast to those with literacy as a bedrock institution. Cultures centered around orality—like the ebbing Greek oratory that Socrates cherished—rely on the ability to recall at hand. Works like Homer's *Odyssey* carry evidence of orality like meter, tempo, and proverbs rarely found after literacy took hold in Greek society. These systems allow recitation of the same story in slightly different patterns. An arc may be exposed slightly early, or a person's thoughts may be phrased differently depending on recitation, without impacting the overall work.

Figure 6.7 shows an exposition style favored by orality. Details form the crux of the exposition. Socrates himself often started his dialogs with an example and then proceeded to expand that example into themes, going back to details to create the setup for the next theme. Each theme added nuance to the story. Themes are drawn to a close to establish both rapport and context (the latter represented with light gray boxes in the figure).

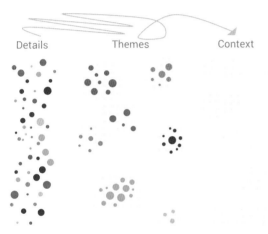

FIGURE 6.7 Orality exposition style

As we look at methods of presenting data, we see patterns that mirror the shift from orality to literacy as a primary means for comprehension. Early data compositions rely on other methods to explain the information shown in charts. Just as the printing press expanded access to literacy (Wolf & Stoodley, 2008), digital advancements have transformed data literacy. Interactivity, animation, and customization options enable a new way of exploring and understanding visualization. Just as early written compositions had oral residue, data visualizations indicate cultures centered around data orality.

Tables as details and experiences: Tables provide granular details and allow consumers to build trust through their own direct experiences.

Figure 6.8 shows a tabular version of antibiotic data visualized by designer Will Burtin. The lowest number indicates the most effective antibiotic. Can you find the pattern? Try highlighting.

Burtin's Antibiotic Data
Minimum Inhibitory Concentration (MIC)

Bacteria	Gram Staining	Penicillin	Neomycin	Streptomycin
Aerobacter aerogenes	negative	870.0	1.6	1.0
Brucella abortus	negative	1.0	0.0	2.0
Brucella anthracis	positive	0.0	0.0	0.0
Diplococcus pneumoniae	positive	0.0	10.0	11.0
Escherichia coli	negative	100.0	0.1	0.4
Klebsiella pneumoniae	negative	850.0	1.0	1.2
Mycobacterium tuberculosis	negative	800.0	2.0	5.0
Proteus vulgaris	negative	3.0	0.1	0.1
Pseudomonas aeruginosa	negative	850.0	0.4	2.0
Salmonella (Eberthella) typ..	negative	1.0	0.0	0.4
Salmonella schottmuelleri	negative	10.0	0.1	0.8
Staphylococcus albus	positive	0.0	0.0	0.1
Staphylococcus aureus	positive	0.0	0.0	0.0
Streptococcus fecalis	positive	1.0	0.1	1.0
Streptococcus hemolyticus	positive	0.0	10.0	14.0
Streptococcus viridans	positive	0.0	40.0	10.0

Penicillin, Neomycin and Streptomycin broken down by Bacteria and Gram Staining.

FIGURE 6.8 Burtin's antibiotic data

As with Socrates, oral data cultures are not yet ready to trust charts as a *primary means* of sensing patterns. Rather, finding these patterns by seeing the data and manually highlighting and reordering it, allows the insight to be trusted. Tables such as the one in Figure 6.8 provide the example first and set the tone for understanding any auxiliary charts. Medium also plays a role: static visualizations historically required an exposition more in line with oral styles. We see this trend changing with more newspapers including charts as the primary driver of a story and using text, rather than tables, to clarify.

Outside guidance for themes and context: Works such as Homer's *Odyssey* and religious texts are often hard for literature societies to navigate as they contain oral residue. Their exposition styles and pacing are unfamiliar. Oral data cultures design with the visualization serving as a supplement.

These compositions may provide a variety of graphics on a dashboard or only a single visualization. Ensembles supplement a greater whole that exists outside the dashboard rather than serving as cohesive compositions. Figure 6.9 shows an example of data orality within a dashboard.

FIGURE 6.9 Dashboard with residues of data orality

There are four parts to the dashboard shown in Figure 6.9. Each part can exist independent of the others. Someone using this dashboard can easily cut segments and put them into external presentations and documents. Rather than this dashboard being used as a whole unit, the exposition can be rearranged and trimmed with minimal impact to its greater context and meaning.

Technologies like paper and the printing press democratized writing access and literacy (Wolf & Stoodley, 2008). Data visualization software shifted from specialized departments and IT to broader business and academic users. Online tools like Datawrapper allow nearly anyone to create charts rapidly and easily. New mediums require different exposition styles.

Changing Exposition Styles

COVID-19 is rapidly altering how we read and interpret charts. We expect charts to work together, clarify one another, and align to a particular thesis. Essays provide a powerful metaphor for understanding current expectations around data visualizations. Like essay writing, visualizations require anticipating questions and exposing information in a clear manner.

Figure 6.10 shows how literate cultures expose information. Framing context at the beginning concisely prepares consumers for what to expect (shown in light rectangles). Themes are explored at a high level and then exposed in a stair-step manner, with details used as supports; it is the inverse of what orality prizes.

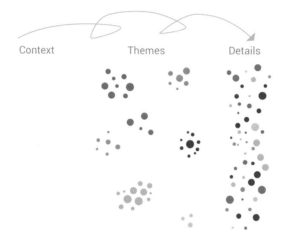

FIGURE 6.10 Literate culture exposition

As we look at Figure 6.10, it mirrors essay writing that gets taught as early as elementary school. Written expositions aren't refined through conversation with others, but with ourselves. A literate culture relies on the reader to personalize the information and the author to provide enough information and clarity to do so. It's a different thought process, one that rewards unique phrasings and the ability to create clearly resonant themes in advance. We bring these models to other literacy paradigms.

Literacy and numeracy work together. Numbers were the first thing we documented, using tallies on various clay tokens and stones to track quantities (Pae, 2020). As these accounting systems matured, they started to incorporate pictures in addition to tallies. These tracking systems set the stage for early literacy development. Interpreting and creating charts relies on both numeracy (the first tier) and literacy (the second tier) to fully grasp what the chart represents. Figure 6.11 shows how graphicacy is a third-tier skill, after numeracy and literacy.

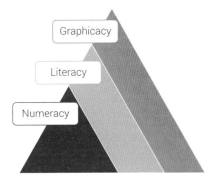

FIGURE 6.11 Graphicacy as a third-tier skill

Data Literacy Democratization

Moving from orality to literacy requires democratizing access, much like Hangul made reading Korean easier. Charts, too, are an abstraction designed to be read. It's a cultural shift, one that creates shared expectations. Essay writing follows a formula, and it's one that children learn as early as third grade in the United States. Graphicacy has progressed and matured, initially starting with more annotation and progressively reducing it as comfort increased. Look at some of the historical charts in Chapter 3 and you'll see more annotation and lines than we typically provide now.

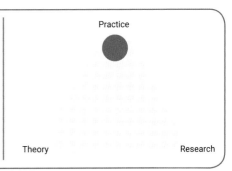

Schools are progressively teaching students to read charts and figures early. There's a new generation of data-literate students who can make data-driven decisions to think critically while solving problems of the world.

Democratizing access to visualization requires both an individual shift in abilities (learning to read and write charts) and a sociological shift in communication patterns (from orality to literacy). Practitioner, writer, and Columbia University teacher Allen Hillery (2020) is one of many voices calling for apprenticeships to make data proficiency far more equitable. Underserved communities are often left without resources for advancement. College degree attainment has a direct correlation with parent income—those at the lowest income face a vast number of navigational issues in addition to cost. Hillery also shows how making access more equitable helps the final product: they're more likely to address the needs of a wider user base.

Sarah Nell-Rodriguez, an educator and founder of Be Data Lit (https://bedatalit.com/educating-organizations-on-data-literacy/), takes a similar approach with an emphasis on reskilling. In the aftermath of COVID-19, workers faced immense challenges in an economy where so much has moved online. Nell-Rodriguez proposed a modified version of Bloom's theory when it comes to data literacy. Within this paradigm, literacy can be measured as a quantifiable skill. Credentialing of both practitioners and end users serves as a powerful means for pushing the group as a whole. Users have more comfort with more charts and practitioners gain more freedom in the range of charts that can be used.

Numerous software platforms have signed onto this view to data literacy. Qlik has partnered with various entities to create and sponsor the Data Literacy Project (https://thedataliteracyproject.org), featuring leaders across toolsets. It focuses on providing training on visualization with some data shaping skills. Tableau incorporates "data culture" into its literacy approach as a means of democratizing access and knitting data into decision making. Everyone from the top down at a company is encouraged to use data. Most of these approaches overlap with the idea of data literacy as chart-reading and creation, or the reading and writing definition of literacy (1b, per *Merriam-Webster*). Some embed ideas of ideas of being cultured (1a) in addition to composition.

True democratization of data literacy takes into account the entire ecosystem of data. It recognizes the proliferation of charts in our daily lives and works to make them intelligible broadly. Interactive pieces can build in additional clarifiers through details on demand or by teaching the end user how to read the chart.

Defining data literacy beyond graphicacy means it's up to us, the practitioners, to build tools that keep our users from falling off a cliff. It requires understanding our user's culture and proficiencies in charts and working to meet them where they are, while providing tools to understand novel ideas. Beyond training the users, we act as interpreters and provide both linguistic and cultural clarification around the entire cycle of data. It means we can bring a literary craft to our work when the time calls but that we must also be sensitive to users who seek a CliffsNotes guide to our work. The systemic paradigm pushes visualization toward the role of a profession, one that encompasses taking ownership of the message we present with data and acculturating into shared norms.

Summary

Technology and COVID-19 rapidly accelerated the need to understand the abstract language of charts. Yet, data literacy doesn't stop at reading and writing charts but encompasses a broader ecosystem. Data orality exists before data literacy. Without established graphicacy skills, consumers rely on tools beyond the chart to parse the information. Democratizing access relies on recognizing the fundamental need to make data literacy accessible and culturally transformative.

As Steve Jobs said, "When you're a carpenter making a beautiful chest of drawers, you're not going to use a piece of plywood on the back, even though it faces the wall and nobody will ever see it. You'll know it's there, so you're going to use a beautiful piece of wood on the back. For you to sleep well at night, the aesthetic, the quality, has to be carried all the way through." The next chapter explores how we carry data literacy through data preparation, a task that is often viewed as "behind-the-scenes."

Data Preparation

So far, we have seen semantics utilized within visualizations. These depictions rely on data that is ready to analyze. Drawing from the data literacy circle in the previous chapter (Figure 6.1), data preparation is a meaning-centered exercise to prepare, clean, and curate data. As we clean, we think about how the data should be structured to support the analysis: we make it taller or wider, thus giving it shape and defined fields. Whether it's from large transaction databases, JSON files downloaded from APIs, or CSV outputs from shared data repositories, defining useful data formats requires logic that often includes understanding what the data is intended to mean.

We all know the pains of poorly shaped data. During analysis, we spend our time creating calculations, building additional outside workflows, or sacrificing depth within the analysis. We may instead rely on writing to make the connections rather than the analysis itself. The connections must then be inferred rather than made tangible in the analysis. Poorly shaped data is the dresser that wobbles and ultimately breaks down. It is the chest of drawers where you slam your fingers over and over again and can't pinpoint why.

While preparation is invisible to those consuming visualizations, a well-shaped and cleaned dataset makes all the difference in *analyzing* the data. Data preparation is the back of the dresser and the interior supports. It holds everything together. A well-made dresser is stable, and the drawers slide out smoothly. The most elegant of dressers provide the right amount of tension in the rollers, so the drawer feels lightweight but doesn't fly out from the chest or crunch fingers. Data that is well prepared makes the analysis easier and allows a deeper exploration of patterns. It helps the analyst sift through the data with less friction. Data that is well crafted holds up to rigorous analysis and presentation. It removes the wall between us and the data and allows us to see the patterns.

Well-shaped data isn't only functional, it's also aesthetic. The fields are logically named. The dates are well formatted. The data itself is clean with nulls clearly understood. When the data is pulled into analysis tools, it is easy to create meaningful groupings. It leverages semantics to make data meaningful by following a system that is logical and natural to follow. In short, it is built to be functionally aesthetic from all angles.

Hairy Dates

One of the most common data preparation tasks users perform is parsing date strings into date representations. Dates can be constructed in a myriad of ways—March 9, 2021; 9 Mar 2021; 3/9/21; and 2021-3-9 to name a few. There can also be ambiguity in these representations as 3/9/21 could be either March 9, 2021, or September 3, 2021, as we discussed with these different endian formats in Chapter 5.

Many data preparation and visual analysis tools provide users with date parsing calculations to recast columns of strings or integers as dates or datetimes. A few months after Tableau released the DATEPARSE calculation to parse dates, the research team found that 15 percent of the user-authored date format strings that were extracted from Tableau Public were invalid (Wesley et al., 2018). Further, they found 744 distinct date and time formats that produced no errors for their associated columns in the data tables. Table 7.1 shows some examples. There are too many formats to manually check and validate. The researchers developed an automated way to cross-validate all these date formats from two different points of view: one focusing on pattern recognition while the other uses natural language grammar rules. They then applied these two complementary algorithms to the corpus of date string columns extracted from Tableau Public.

TABLE 7.1 Variations in date formats

UCU Format	Example
EEE MMM dd HH:mm:ss zzz yyyy	Fri Apr 01 02:09:27 EDT 2011
[dd/MMM/yyy:HH:mm:ss	[10/Aug/2014:09:30:40
dd-MMM-yy hh.mm.ss.SSSSS a	01-OCT-13 01.09.00.000000 PM
MM "yyyy	01 '2013
MM/dd/yyyy - HH:mm	03/09/2014 - 23:47

Dates have a semantic hierarchy of years, quarters, months, weeks, and days. We expect to be able to easily pull out these parts, along with additional tasks like identifying the day of week and time zone. Identifying these elements as dates allows greater expression of these elements.

Dates can be localized to area, showing 9 March 2021 in the UK and March 9, 2021 in the US. They can be abridged to 3/9, for example, where the year is clearly understood.

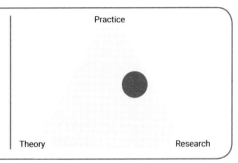

Using research techniques to automatically recognize patterns of dates that people use in practice speeds efficiency and makes dates more meaningful.

Practice

Theory   Research

Common Transformations

Date parsing represents one possible transformation. Field types, like parts of speech, classify elements into particular categories to clarify their use. Fields with clearly defined types adhere to a standard, perform efficiently when pulled into analysis tools, and provide analysts clues into how to use the data. For example, integers are a data type that can be aggregated, while text dimensions usually filter, frame the analysis, or set the level of detail. We are breaking up fields into their smallest building blocks of meaning. These building blocks create a system, allowing us greater expressivity and keeping us in the flow of analysis.

Common transformations include the following:

FIGURE 7.1 Validating uniqueness to understand shape

■ Numbering unique rows with a row ID

■ Validating uniqueness and deduplicating (see Figure 7.1)

■ Filtering data (see Figure 7.2)

■ Field formatting and typing (standardizing)

■ Splitting to different tables (topic/context)

■ Pivoting (up and down)

■ Densifying (filling in semantic gaps, such as dates)

■ Aggregating/summarizing

FIGURE 7.2 Filtering data

■ Removing nulls

■ Creating taxonomic structures or hierarchies

■ Joining (intersections, see Figure 7.3)

FIGURE 7.3 Joining

■ Unioning

■ Parsing and extracting, such as through regular expressions (see Figure 7.4)

FIGURE 7.4 Parsing

Transforming data requires understanding the shape of it. Shape is determined by the grain, or what one row represents. A row might be a transaction, a patient, or a written language. Operations such as normalization reduce the data into meaningful unique elements across several tables. Details at one grain are not repeated, but are referenced through keys. This reduces redundancy and makes storage more efficient by using lookup keys. Analysis data sources may join the tables physically together to create a single view or use logical models to establish relationships. Logical models preserve the separate tables and do joins based on the analysis.

ScriptSource (www.scriptsource.org) provides a database of writing systems, shown partially in Figure 7.5. Elements captured include the name, unique code, family, type, direction, and a number of other dimensions useful for printing and writing. Altogether, the CSV export from the database contains 20 fields. The grain of the data is one row per writing system, identified by Script Name and Script Code. Some languages have

script_name	script_code	script_type	script_family	script_status	script_direction	script_baseline	script_casing
Coptic	Copt	alphabet	European	Current	LTR	bottom	yes
Cypriot syllabary	Cprt	syllabary	European	Historical	RTL	bottom	no
Cyrillic	Cyrl	alphabet	European	Current	LTR	bottom	yes
Cyrillic (Old Church Slavonic	Cyrs	alphabet	European	Historical	LTR	bottom	no
Devanagari	Deva	abugida	Indic	Current	LTR	hanging	no
Deseret (Mormon)	Dsrt	alphabet	American	Historical	LTR	bottom	yes
Egyptian demotic	Egyd	logo-syllabary	African	Historical	RTL	bottom	no
Egyptian hieratic	Egyh	logo-syllabary	African	Historical	LTR	bottom	no
Egyptian	Egyp	logo-syllabary	African	Historical	LTR	centered	no
Ethiopic (GeÊ»ez)	Ethi	abugida	African	Current	LTR	bottom	no
Khutsuri (Asomtavruli and	Geok	alphabet	European	Current	LTR	bottom	yes
Georgian (Mkhedruli and	Geor	alphabet	European	Current	LTR	bottom	no
Glagolitic	Glag	alphabet	European	Historical	LTR	bottom	yes
Gothic	Goth	alphabet	European	Historical	LTR	bottom	[unknown]
Greek	Grek	alphabet	European	Current	LTR	bottom	yes
Gujarati	Gujr	abugida	Indic	Current	LTR	hanging	no
Gurmukhi	Guru	abugida	Indic	Current	LTR	hanging	no
Hangul (HangÂ-l or Hangeul)	Hang	featural	East Asian	Current	vertical (RTL) and horizontal (LTR)	centered	no

FIGURE 7.5 Partial view of ScriptSource data

more than one writing system and some scripts cover a vast number of languages. Script Code represents an optimal primary key, as it is unique, short, and sustainable when new rows get added. It is also useful for other tables we create.

Other details include direction of writing. A quick scan down the sample shows many LTR (left-to-right), writing systems with a few RTL (right-to-left) systems. Languages also can be written sometimes in multiple directions, which is documented in Script Direction with "and" separating the options. Hangul, Korea's writing system discussed in Chapter 6, located on the bottom row, can be written either vertically right to left or horizontally left to right. If we want to count the different allowable directions, this shape does not help us achieve that task. We'll want to create a separate table of writing directions that has one row for each writing direction for each language.

As we scan this data with an eye toward reshaping for analysis, we are searching for patterns in the data where reshaping will extend our analytical capabilities. Figure 7.6 shows an abbreviated abstraction of this process. Script Family creates a hierarchy related to language (first two tan boxes). We might sort the data in different ways or reorder columns to detect what elements repeat (yellow boxes in the third column). We might find data that needs to be parsed, split, and transformed to additional columns, such as writing direction (blue and dark brown). Columns such as Baseline, Complex Positioning, and four other columns contain Yes/No

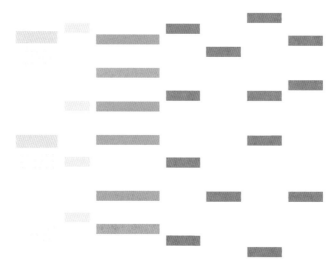

FIGURE 7.6 Abstract reshaping map

answers and may be more useful in a pivoted format (highlighted in rose pink).

As we find the areas to transform, we start planning the rough shape we need and some of the transformations that we will need to do. We identify columns to select and shape separately, shown in Figure 7.7. ScriptSource also has a data dictionary online. Many of these columns contain information that clarifies abstract writing concepts or items that seem similar by field name (such as Baseline versus Complex Positioning). We can use the field definitions within the visualizations to provide greater clarity. Additional details on demand may help us with our analysis as well as help those who view it later.

Preparing data is an exercise in expression. We are moving data from a stored state from the database to an active one for analysis. It requires understanding how the analysis tool best works with data to achieve a given intent. The natural hierarchies and relationships within the data create allowable combinations. From the exercise earlier, we can see that data shape is quite malleable. As we begin shaping, we will want to preserve accuracy and support ease of understanding.

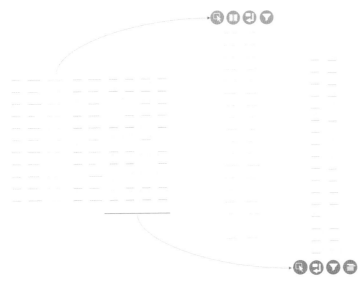

FIGURE 7.7 Abstracted data shaping diagram

Clarity in Conversation

While data values are concrete, the ways in which we shape for analysis increase the chances of vague table constructs. ScriptSource, for example, provides the output with one row per script. Understanding what one row represents in this model is reasonably clear. Our planned transformations add complexity:

- One table with 272 logged scripts
- One table with writing direction, adding an extra row to some scripts
- One table with up to 1,632 rows (6 feature types × 272 scripts)

While this arrangement allows certain analytical tasks to happen, it requires greater detail into what each table represents.

Shaping can be done in either a tangible manner or an abstract one. Excel allows reshaping to progressively happen through the analysis by creation of additional sheets, pivot tables, LOOKUPs, and other formulas. Each row of the data in Excel can clearly be seen. We could reshape the ScriptSource data by creating pivot tables and additional columns and even manually adding rows. Tools like Tableau Prep (www.tableau.com/products/prep) work to balance abstraction with multiple panes for tasks. The first pane provides a highly abstract layer for joins, unions, and pivots. The data profile pane allows for direct member editing, the creation of calculations, or other premade cleaning tasks. Programs like Alteryx (www.alteryx.com) are highly abstract but very visual. Users can program a variety of tasks using visual commands. Writing Structured Query Language (SQL) is the most abstract and relies on fluency to complete shaping and modeling.

Fields provide the basis for the analysis. We can take one field in the database and refactor it into seven fields that act as Boolean flags. As we decide what one row represents, we are structuring the types of conversations analysts and consumers can have. The fields affect what one row represents and how tall or wide the dataset is. Hierarchies and natural relationships affect the connections and layers available to clarifying, expanding, or contracting the analysis.

Field typing and renaming is a common exercise. It allows phone numbers, numerical IDs, and dates to be classified and formatted as such. Typing from preparation makes visualizing data easier and clearer. In addition to typing, clarifying field names helps those analyzing data or consuming premade visualization understand what the domain covers. If we sold 399 bottles of wine on March 9, we expect that number to hold regardless of whether we show each individual sale or aggregate the data to the types we've sold or summarized solely by day. The field type should make it clear that 399 is a count and the name of the field should lend some clue into the grain: daily_sales versus individual_sales. Some data shaping and analysis tools also allow data sources to be enriched with additional metadata, such as comments and synonyms for the field name.

Data shape affects the types of analyses that can be done. Dates across multiple columns may make it easy to count days between various events. Constructing a timeline, however, may be harder, unless all the dates are in one column. Data shape affects the types of conversations we can have with our data: it favors certain scripts and allows certain types of queries to be answered. It sets the context and defines the limits of what meaning can be extrapolated.

Shaping for Intent

The shape of the data affects what the visualization tool can reasonably interpret. The Sapir-Whorf hypothesis states, "The limits of language shape my reality" (Jannedy et al., 1994). As we work to make data both functional and aesthetic, we will keep the endpoint in mind. Good shape is defined by the analysis tool. Tableau Desktop (www.tableau.com/products/desktop), for example, allows tables to be related on a logical plane (multiple tables) in addition to being joined on a physical layer (a single view within the analysis). As we return to our ScriptSource example, we can plan for separate tables at different grains. Using Tableau's relationship model, we can have script direction exist as its own smaller table with one row per direction by script. Some languages may have several directions associated with them and have multiple rows.

A good shape for one platform may be a terrible shape for another. Certain shapes may also allow easier analysis for some tasks but increase complexity for others. Earlier, we identified high-level tasks we need for this dataset. Figure 7.8 shows a simplified data preparation workflow. It takes the main table and splits the workflow into three tables. In addition, the data dictionary is pulled in for all elements to provide additional descriptions for fields like Writing Direction, Script Type, and others. Tasks shown include selecting, splitting, joining, pivoting, filtering, calculating, and deduplicating.

FIGURE 7.8 Simplified data prep flow

The outputs are in separate tables at different grains (Figure 7.9). The main table is at the same grain as the source table. The other tables are

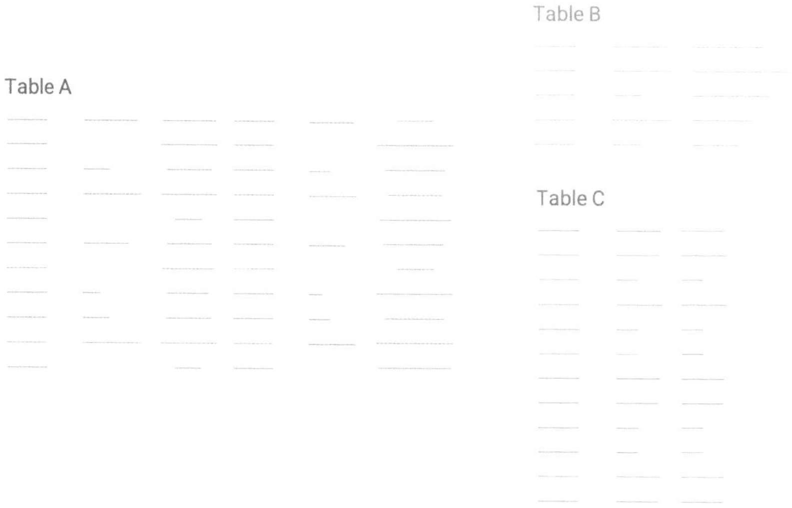

FIGURE 7.9 A relational model

at lower grains, allowing a different type of analysis to be performed. Each table has a different shape. Table A is the widest table. Table B is the shortest, while Table C is tall and skinny.

Data preparation is a time-intensive endeavor. As we look into the future, research offers insight into how data might be shaped in easier ways by leveraging semantics. Looking at common tasks, we can see what we as humans can easily parse out but that computers, until now, have struggled to achieve.

Prepping for the Future

Understanding the semantics of the data and the context in which it will be used, provides techniques to help automate the data transformations that analysts need to do for their analytical workflows. Research has explored techniques to detect whether data attributes represent known semantic concepts such as person, place, dates, and time. Having a better understanding of the data provides unique opportunities to prepare the data for the real world. In recent years, the problem of automatically determining semantic properties in data has been steadily gaining attention among visualization, NLP, and AI researchers (Caveness et al., 2020; Chen et al., 2019; Hulsebos et al., 2019; Iida et al., 2021; Zhang et al., 2020).

Let's explore three examples: semantic joins, smart sorts, and column splits.

Semantic Joins

Join is a prevalent data operator used to combine records from

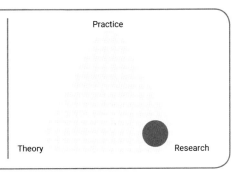

NLP and AI techniques have already begun to transform the way humans interact with computers. In practice, they bridge between the worlds of machine language and human language in the context of data analysis.

two or more tables. Traditional join processing mostly relies on checking if attribute names exactly match. With the growing demand for ad hoc data analysis, there are an increasing number of scenarios where the desired join relationship is not an equi-join (i.e., a type of join that combines tables based on matching values in specified columns). For example, in Figure 7.10, a user may want to join one table having a country-name column with another table having a country-code column. Traditional equi-join cannot handle such joins automatically and the user typically has to manually find an intermediate mapping table in order to perform the desired join.

Country	Sales	Users
BR	1,418	75,000
CN	4,995	432,000
DE	1,445	126,000
GB	1,719	41,045
IN	1,421	205,869
JP	2,535	115,000
MX	755	123,650
RU	1,370	12,533
US	9,125	235,455

Country	Internet users	Adoption rate
Brazil	99,350,744	45.20%
China	568,192,065	34.60%
Germany	56,286,824	87.74%
India	245,289,322	18.50%
Japan	100,456,980	65.10%
Nigeria	45,787,000	28.53%
Russia	65,849,001	48.00%
United Kingdom	78,572,984	89.92%
United States	289,547,750	91.30%

FIGURE 7.10 Semantic joining of country name and country code columns from two data tables

To address this problem, research has explored data-driven methods that determine the statistical correlation between two semantically related data columns (He et al., 2015). More sophisticated semantic joins have evolved over the years. For example, a user may want to join two tables, each having a currency column—USD and Euro. A semantic join can be suggested to the user where the currency in one table is converted to another based on the locale, the currency rate, and the time stamp of the data.

Smart Sorts

Another form of data transformations is smarter sorting. If you've taken a survey, you may see qualitative questions with answers ranging from "highly dissatisfied" to "highly satisfied." These are called Likert scales. A system that can detect the data type could then sensibly sort the Likert scale values in their *semantic* logical order rather than an alphabetical order on text strings. This form of sorting enables a semantically resonant divergent color palette to be associated to each of the responses, with the most negative sentiment in a red hue and the most positive one in a blue hue, shown in Figure 7.11. These defaults support color cognition as described in Chapter 1 and map the semiotic properties of the data to meaningful color associations (from Chapter 4). Smarter sorts help reduce the workload for the user by reducing manual interventions during data preparation and chart creation.

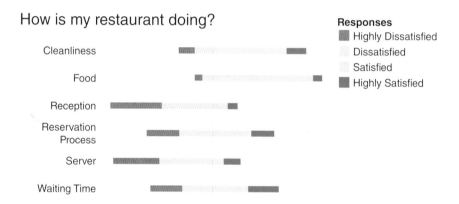

FIGURE 7.11 Automated sorting for Likert scales

Column Splits

For many data shaping recipes, a common step is to split the data from a single column into multiple columns. Data preparation tools provide various manual and semiautomatic methods for column splits based on character or pattern matching. However, knowing a bit more about the semantics of the data can enable delightful defaults in the data shaping process. Consider the example in Figure 7.12. You have a column of full names that you want to split into first and last names. A smart column

FIGURE 7.12 Column splitting

split algorithm could detect that the strings are names based on access to an external corpus such as census data. Applying a split to Full Name not only splits the columns into two but provides sensible headers to the newly split columns. Rather than being called generically as Split Column 1 and Split Column 2, they are named First Name and Last Name respectively.

Data Enrichment

Enriching data with additional semantics provides a foundation for richer analytical inquiry. One common way of enriching data is by adding synonyms and other related concepts to the attributes in the data table. Knowledge corpora like a dictionary, thesaurus, or taxonomies derived from systems like Wolfram Alpha (www.wolframalpha.com) help support data enrichment.

Let's look at Table 7.2, which shows a sample dataset of houses for sale.

TABLE 7.2 Sample housing dataset

Datetime	Price	Latitude	Longitude	area	#beds	Openhouse_time
1/4/20	600000	38.8977	77.0365	5320	3	3:00 PM
. . .	. . .	. . .	. . .	. . .	. . .	. . .

If we import this data into a natural language interface such as Tableau's Ask Data (Setlur et al., 2019), one can begin by asking a question, "What's the house *cost* in Palo Alto?" With access to a thesaurus, it would be pretty straightforward for the system to identify *cost* as a synonym for *price*. But we know that language is much more nuanced than that. We could then ask, "Show me the *expensive* houses." If the interface has access to a dictionary, it can pull up the entry for *expensive* and determine that *expensive* is a descriptor for the attribute Price (Table 7.3). Further, the value for price falls in a high range and the system might pick a reasonable numerical range as part of its response. The answer may not be perfect and would depend on the user's intent and the context of the data. Also, the range for *expensive* is different for a house when compared to a bottle of wine. Geography can also play a role in perceptions of expense as well.

> expensive (adjective): entailing great expense; **very high priced**; costly (Oxford Dictionary).

TABLE 7.3 Associating the Price attribute for defining the concept "expensive"

Datetime	Price	Latitude	Longitude	area	#beds	Openhouse_time
1/4/20	600000	38.8977	77.0365	5320	3	3:00 PM
. . .	. . .	. . .	. . .	. . .	. . .	. . .

Moving on to a more complicated example, we may want to get more specific about the types of houses that we are interested in and ask, "Now, show me the *large* ones." Looking at the definitions for *large* and one of the attributes in the table, area, there are some common concepts that are bolded in the definition for *area*.

> large (adjective): ample in dimensions, quantity, or number. Having much size or extent, capacity, scope, length, breadth etc., or relatively being of more than common measure wide, broad, spacious, great, big, or bulky.

area (noun): a **measure** of the **extent** of a surface; it is measured in square units.

Here, *large* refers to size, which can be measured as *area*, and the system can provide a reasonable response, similar to how it may handle *expensive* (Table 7.4).

TABLE 7.4 Associating the area attribute for defining the concept *large*

Datetime	Price	Latitude	Longitude	area	#beds	Openhouse_time
1/4/20	600000	38.8977	77.0365	5320	3	3:00 PM
. . .	. . .	. . .	. . .	. . .	. . .	. . .

But there are limits to this approach where abbreviations or colloquial language such as *sqft* may not be found in a dictionary or a thesaurus. Language models and knowledge graphs created from unstructured, semi-structured, and structured data sources store information about the world, including abbreviations like *sqft*. These linguistic-based approaches have evolved to better handle the richness and ambiguity of concepts and their semantics. Encapsulating the rich semantic knowledge into a structured dataset provides a better understanding of the underlying data and, consequently, the ability to reason at a more abstract level. This deeper data understanding enables more sophisticated data preparation and analysis, including natural language interfaces, entity disambiguation, and entity resolution as well as ontology-based query answering, aspects of which we will cover in Part C, "Intent."

Summary

Quite often, when we think of communicating information effectively, we focus on the representation of the data in a chart or other visual format. However, functionally aesthetic content is only as good as the data that feeds it; flawed data leads to flawed results. We hope that this chapter helps you appreciate the importance of data preparation. It is a meaning-centered activity that solidifies the foundation for analysis. Spending time preparing and enriching the data makes analysis easier. In the next chapter we will explore how meaningful data can help communicate patterns, relationships, and takeaways given the size and the context of the chart.

Scaling It Down

In the previous chapter, we discussed how you could prepare data so that it can be converted in a systematic and logical way into the visual elements that make up the final graphic. Charts can be described with a common language that captures how the data is transformed into ink on paper or pixels on the screen. Functional aesthetics concerns mapping these prepped data values into quantifiable features of the resulting graphic.

While presenting functionally aesthetic charts, size is important. Common tasks in which size is part of chart creation, involve the composition of a dashboard where multiple charts compete for space in a limited screen or when charts created on one display must then be retargeted to a different-sized one. The major challenge of developing techniques that facilitate resizing and creating multi-scale visualizations is the significant number of variations with which to represent a rescaled visualization properly. A visualization designer will typically struggle to express every detail of the visualization at a given scale while also considering every possible combination of display (or view) resolution, size, and aspect ratio.

Generalization refers to the process of abstracting the visual detail in a map to maintain the legibility of the map at any given scale (McMaster & Shea, 1992). In Chapters 1 and 2, we discussed how generalization is applied to maps to effectively convey what's important at that certain size given the context of the task at hand. Inspired by these generalization principles, this chapter explores ways we can emphasize things that matter and come up with ways to deemphasize things that may not matter for a particular context or task as we scale things down.

Generalization

General resizing techniques, such as uniform scaling and scale-and-stretch, can be used for easily resizing a visualization. Yet they tend to make the visualization more illegible and increase visual clutter at smaller scales. Notably, such resizing also does not consider semantic information that we may want to convey with data. It's crucial to support better ways to adapt visual representations so that the viewer can read data more efficiently regardless of the display size and scale.

One of the key ideas behind generalizing a chart at a particular scale or display size is determining what information is important to emphasize and what information is unimportant and should be deemphasized. Often, determining what is unimportant is the more challenging dilemma. Let's start with a line chart example, as seen in Figure 8.1. Features such as the local maxima and minima (peaks and troughs), and the first and last data values, tend to be visually prominent and continue to be emphasized as the line chart is rendered at smaller scales. Other features such as tick labels may be of lower importance, especially at smaller sizes.

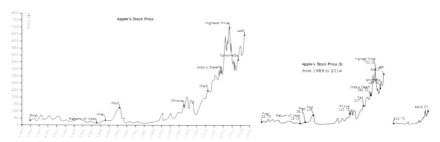

FIGURE 8.1 Line chart generalized to different display sizes

Based on visualization best practices (Kim et al., 2019), charts need to be generalized to minimize visual clutter yet still functionally convey the intended message to the reader. Research techniques (Setlur & Chung, 2021)

have identified various heuristics to help guide how one could address visual clutter while designing charts:

- **Congestion:** A chart should not include too many elements such as data points and labels rendered in a specific region. Using a visual indicator to guide a reader to zoom in to see more detail could be one effective way of addressing congestion. This indicator is a form of the demand technique where parts of the data are visualized in more detail while providing an overview of the whole informational concept.

- **Conflict:** To maintain legibility, elements such as text labels and annotations should not overlap. Each element should be easily identifiable and readable. Jittering and moving labels about their anchor points could help with overlap.

- **Semantic importance:** An element of higher importance should be more visible than less important ones. Annotations for unimportant data values and axes can be removed or made smaller, such as tiny sparkline charts used to show a trend in data.

Natural Sizes

The sizes of charts in space reflect how we convey information to a reader. In a dashboard context, the content, size, and space that the various charts occupy should reflect the form and function of the main message. As you saw with the bento box metaphor from the introduction, there needs to be deliberate thought put into the placement and size of each individual chart so that they all work together in harmony. Revisiting the bento box example, placing the individual food items just anywhere in the box or sectioning the compartments to simply fit the available space does not provide an optimal dining experience. The salads and sides need to support the main dish. Size and placement convey the relative prominence, guiding the gastronome in their dining experience.

A well-designed dashboard needs to provide a similar experience; information cannot be placed just anywhere on the dashboard. Charts that relate to one another are usually positioned close to one another. Important charts often appear larger and more visually prominent than less important ones. In other words, there are *natural sizes* for how a dashboard comprises charts based on the task and context. For example, a map chart may take up the most space in a dashboard based on its prominence in terms of both display and interaction. These natural sizes shape how the reader sees and understands the big picture and how the smaller charts piece together. Natural sizes help guide the reader to scan the dashboard in a particular order that supports that sequence of visual attention, showing where to start and where to go next. Let's explore more about natural sizes in the context of display, starting with mobile. Note that mobile also includes smart devices like a watch, but for the purpose of common examples, we consider tablets and phones in this chapter.

Fat Fingers and Small Screens

Cursors are beautiful things, and most people who use a computer nowadays are pretty good at getting their cursor over things on their screen to click or hover on. Mobile touch screens attempt to emulate this precision when the conductive material in the touch screen responds when contacted by another electrical conductor, like your bare finger. However, we often inadvertently trigger an unintended secondary action when navigating a touch screen interface. Our fingers are instinctual, but the lack of texture and minimal feedback is not—in other words, the fat finger syndrome.

When it comes to the mobile user experience, fat finger syndrome continues to cause problems. Although some might be tempted to lay blame on the user, whether for being clumsy or inattentive, the truth of the matter is that fault lies squarely with the interface. After all, isn't the job of a good design to eliminate all the factors that might confuse or frustrate the user? Common best practices when creating content for the mobile include making the touch targets large and making sure that there's enough white space around these zones.

Beyond optimizing content for the mobile, consider that the user is on the go, stealing glances at their phone (hopefully while not driving) and wanting quick information. However, dashboards are different from web pages. You click on the dashboards, filter things, and take away the key insight conveyed by the charts working together—keeping true to the whole definition of "at-a-glance insight" (Cogley, 2016, 2019). Nothing ups the ante more than the challenge of shrinking a screen and removing precision. Smaller screens not only mean less space but reconsider how the data itself is presented due to an entirely different shape—most people interact with their phone upright. When we know in advance that our dashboards need to be retargeted to the mobile, we can design for this. We can select large bar charts as filters and limit our use of scatter-plots (try picking a point on a touch screen!). We may limit filters and use items that allow comparison and contrast to avoid certain mental loads. We can also be friendly to retinas.

Figure 8.2 shows adaptive design at work. A darker background picked as a mobile screen in general, seems wickedly bright and reflective, especially in a bright white background. Individual charts are rearranged when viewed in portrait mode, along with some text box changes to be conducive for both mobile viewing and interactivity. The small screen forces us to reconsider what's important. This example treats the key performance indicator (KPI) numbers as one reading element. For both the desktop and mobile, they spread across a single line at the top, while the mobile version splits them up into two rows. The map and bar charts are closer together, using negative space to divide them from the prominent multiples of area charts. The bar charts are labeled, making it easier to get exact numbers quickly.

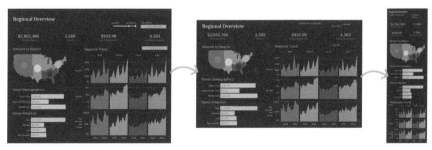

FIGURE 8.2 Retargeting dashboards to different mobile display sizes

The larger dashboard in Figure 8.2 looks great on a desktop, and parts of it seem conducive for a mobile screen. However, when we look at these two charts side by side, we get an idea of how much smaller the mobile truly is. On the left, we have a large screen. On the right, we have a much

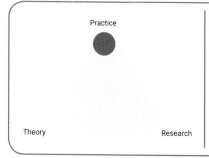

When we discuss mobile design, we think about the eyes and users but not the hands interacting with the charts. Views need to keep true to "at-a-glance insight", yet preserve the ability to click on marks and filter values.

smaller vertical screen. Additional optimizations would include building in finger landing zones to allow easier scrolling and exploring what parts of interactivity need to change. While on a desktop screen, the map and even the bar charts can act as filters, the smaller screen and scrolling require rethinking how charts are filtered across the piece. With so much out of sight at a time, filters and even flyout overlays can provide powerful alternatives.

As you start to think about designing for the phone, here are some considerations:

- **Plan for the worst.** Your dashboard will be used in a restroom, in a dark bedroom, or in a car (with someone else driving). Reduce the brightness of the background and review all your interactions.

- **Defeat distraction.** Make navigating your dashboard easy. Use icons to help people navigate or remember certain concepts.

- **Translate to the form factor as much as possible.** Include more mobile-native gestures, such as swiping, stretching (two-finger expand), and dragging. While tooltips make for great supplemental information on desktop dashboards, they often add complexity to touch-centric experiences. Move to actions so you can control their location or consider a screen jump for items that need greater clarity. New button experiences also make the interactions easier.

- **Use new features.** Sheet transparency makes it so much easier to swap backgrounds. If you format at the dashboard level using the layout pane, you can conditionally change colors. Throw a blank zone or text box in the background if the charts are floating.

- **Create "finger-safe" landing zones.** Determine how mark size and white space can handle the case of the fat finger without frustrating the user.

■ **Think of the mobile dashboard as an app.** Look at some of the apps on your phone that you use daily. Compare them to their desktop counterparts when possible. Look at the colors they use. What have they changed about the interaction? Bring these design and interaction patterns to your dashboard.

Color as a Function of Size

The form factor and context play a role as we think about the design and placement of charts on a device screen. As we design with color for digital applications, we need to consider various sizes of the targets.

There is a well-understood premise that the appearance of color varies significantly with size. Size also impacts shape recognition when the marks become small (Stone, 2012). How often have you agonized about how a paint color looks in real life on a wall based on a 2-inch chip in a color deck? We spend hours trying to figure out the undertones and other color nuances, trying to visualize the color on the walls. Some chips will appear to be identical, even though you know they aren't. When it comes to choosing a paint color, small color chips can only give you a starting point. They can help narrow down your options, but they are of no use when you need to make a final decision. Larger paint color swatches on the actual walls, with actual light, give a much better idea of the differences between all the hues you are considering.

The ability to distinguish different colors is especially important in data visualization where the color indicates a property of the data. Take a look at Figure 8.3. The bar colors indicate product categories and are easy to distinguish. But when the same colors are used in smaller scatterplot marks, you may have to squint and stare hard to see the differences. Various researchers have explored this problem of color discriminability at various sizes. Stone et al. (2014) came up with an actual engineering model that computes color differences between two samples as a function of size. The work explored color hues at different sizes in a 3D color space called CIELAB that is device independent and enables accurate measurement and comparison of all perceivable colors. Here, numerical differences between color values roughly correspond to the amount of change humans see between colors. The model computed the minimum step in CIELAB needed to make two colors visibly different at a given size. Measuring this color-size phenomenon under more realistic circumstances helps figure out how to automate these practical design choices in tools when creating charts for various target sizes.

FIGURE 8.3 Colors that are distinct in bars are more difficult to distinguish in scatterplot marks.

Thumbnails and Visual Summaries

Finally, given the topic of creating functionally aesthetic charts at smaller sizes, thumbnails are yet another way of showing pictographic representations of the underlying information. Thumbnails are effective artifacts to help users quickly browse and find images. On your desktop or phone, you have probably perused through a gallery of image thumbnails, using the scaled-down images as visual cues to find the content that you are looking for. In addition to their use for image search, thumbnails often accompany news articles to attract the readers' attention and providing previews to aid in the decision of which article to dive into. Semantically relevant thumbnails help people locate information of interest, especially when accompanied with informative contextual text.

Recognizing objects in an image is critical in these retrieval tasks, but merely shrinking the original image often renders the objects in the image illegible. The web search community started using thumbnails as a meaningful depiction in the sensemaking process by leveraging the unique advantages of spatial memory. For instance, Woodruff et al. (2001) created textually enhanced web page thumbnails where the appearance of salient HTML elements such as "recipe" and "pound cake" are made as visually recognizable as possible (see Figure 8.4). Visual snippets shown in Figure 8.5 composite a salient image, title, and logo from each web page to create thumbnails for easy browsing (Teevan et al., 2009). Visual puns combine two or more symbols (picture and/or text) to form a new meaning. Semanticons are automatically generated icons that better reveal the semantics of desktop file contents (Setlur et al., 2005). Figure 8.6 shows four alternative icons for the filename `JapaneseVGA_Driver.exe`. While the algorithm does not return a specific image for the phrase *Japanese VGA Driver*, it composites images that depict the individual terms *Japanese* and *Driver* with sushi and a car, respectively. A viewer would need to mentally elaborate on these visual connections to interpret this metaphorical relationship. That cognitive exercise arguably makes these representations more memorable.

> *Physical distinctiveness* means that the thumbnails must be visually distinguishable. *Perceptual distinctiveness* refers to the viewer's understanding of what the thumbnails represent, or what we refer to as the semantics of the thumbnail.

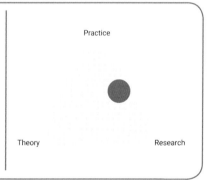

Many of these design choices can be applied to visualization thumbnails and show what's important in the view. In Figure 8.7, the original dashboard has three views. With uniform scaling, the contents of the thumbnail can be somewhat distinguished, but you would need to squint hard to read the title and the annotation on the line. Applying semantic resizing, that is, preserving the recognizability of what's important in the

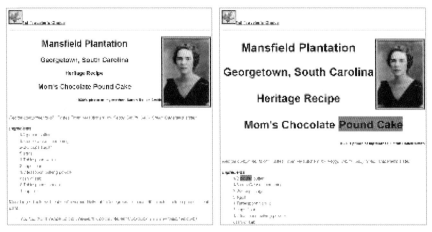

FIGURE 8.4 Left: Original. Right: Enhanced web thumbnail.

FIGURE 8.5 Bottom: Original web pages. Top: Corresponding visual snippets.

FIGURE 8.6 Semanticons for the file `Japanese_VGA_Driver.exe`

dashboard, can lead to more thoughtful resizing. For example, cropping the line chart to the annotation makes the chart more recognizable at a smaller scale. As with the web thumbnails, increasing the font size of the title "Sales by Week" and excluding other text information can improve success for cursory glances during browsing.

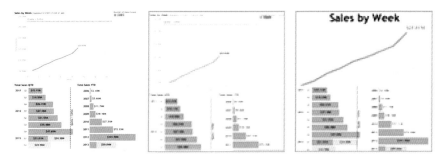

FIGURE 8.7 Left: Original dashboard. Center: Thumbnail without semantic resizing. Right: Thumbnail with semantic resizing.

But not all thumbnails are just for browsing. They can serve as effective data metaphors for information in a visualization. Figure 8.8 uses small multiples of brains and highlighted activity regions to break down the tasks associated with literacy. This allows each task and region to be seen separately relative to its location on the brain. This also helps provide an order to the events. The brain sees, recognizes the distinct patterns of ink as known words, and then processes them as words. The forms (in this example, an alphabet) are interpreted to sounds and their meanings. When broken out in this manner, the visualizations can be smaller and still preserve meaning.

With the prevalence of data journalism, the COVID charts (where we discuss "flattening the curve" in Chapter 4) have now become ubiquitous as we followed the pandemic. There is definitely an uptick in visualization summaries, thumbnails, and other ways of representing data for storytelling. Design choices include more deliberate thought put into resizing, cropping, simplifying, and enhancing information within the limited real estate. These thumbnails need to be visually interpretable, yet inviting and engaging to the audience.

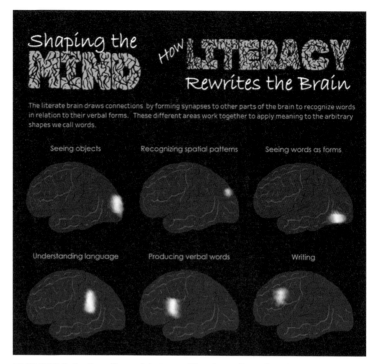

FIGURE 8.8 Small multiples of brains showing highlighted activity regions for various cognitive tasks

Summary

"The medium is the message" is a phrase coined by communication theorist Marshall McLuhan (1964) that represents the synergistic relationship between the content, that is, the message, and the medium for communicating it. Whether the medium is print or digital, its form embeds itself in the message to influence how readers perceive it. Arguably, this phrase still has meaning, even though the media has evolved over the years. With mobile devices around us and the rise in data-driven storytelling and journalism, visualizing information is happening at different scales, sizes, and contexts. In the next chapter, we take this conversation to a new level as we discuss how grammar and pragmatics shape the message in the medium through design, aesthetics, and interactivity.

CHAPTER 9

Cohesive
Data Messages

So far we've covered vagueness and abstraction, data literacy, preparation, and sizing. Let's dig deeper into the visualizations themselves and figure out how visual encodings of data make sense to their intended audience. Cohesion is achieved when parts of a message bind together, making it understandable. Ideas that stick together can build a complete unit that readily stands on its own. People interact with their data as part of a flow that we call *analytical conversation*. Analytical conversations take place in a variety of ways. They happen during the analysis as we examine the data directly. They can be scripted for others to consume. Novel approaches to analytical conversations include incorporating natural language into the process, through innovations such as Tableau's Ask Data and Microsoft's Power BI, for example. The binding characteristic is that the response aligns to our request.

Cohesion means ideas work together to build a unified whole, which helps conversation interlink in purposeful ways, and the basic parts adhere to grammar. Like language, text and visual mediums also need to be coherent to ensure clarity. Coherence is a semantic property of conversation where content stays relevant and flows from one state to another (van Dijk, 1977).

As you saw in Chapter 6, a literate culture builds commonly shared approaches to expositions so that writers and readers know what to expect. Images paired with text also have cohesion by enhancing the piece without being redundant or in opposition to the content (Serafini, 2014). We will explore the interplay of text and charts more in the next chapter.

Comics also provide a valuable framework for cohesion. As a medium between art and story, comics balance text and images to drive a story. Comics and graphic novels rely on the ability to read space, illustrations, and stylized text for additional cues. They feature both literal interactions and ones created figuratively by use of proximity. Figure 9.1 gives a sense of how visual reading plays with placement. In this example, two cats face off between a water glass. Between the nine frames, the story itself can be read a few ways. We can follow a conventional Z-reading pattern, but we are also free to read the story in a downward direction as well.

FIGURE 9.1 Sample comic drawn by author

Comics use transitions between panels to support cohesion. Most comics favor transitions around changes in actions, subjects, scenes, or even aspects like camera angles to create unity in a narrative (McCloud,1993). These mechanisms are intermixed. A few panes may set the scene by showing aspects first, then switching to subjects and action in a single page. If you were to look at a comic, you'd see empty space between the panels that contain the illustrations and the dialog. In the comics world, this space is known as the *gutter*. The gutter provides breathing space between conversation chunks to support coherence and for closure to happen. McCloud describes closure as "observing the parts, but perceiving the whole." This idea is important because comics are a static medium where real-time actions don't happen. Rather, the author needs to convey the passage of time and movement through the comic. If you'd like to learn more about the various transition techniques that comic authors apply, it would be worthwhile to read McCloud's book. Visualizations also use techniques similar to comics to expose information and drive the interaction.

Cohesion in Designing Visualizations

Because they are scripted conversations, designing data visualizations for others to consume parallels comics and writing. Unlike a printed medium, digital charts can filter others, expand or contract, and animate to show changes. They can recolor data points, reorder sorts, and highlight various marks. As charts become a primary means for interpreting information through increased graphicacy skills, cohesion demands between them increase. This new medium provides novel ways to associate charts *semantically*.

We've seen this phenomenon play out with the rise of COVID-19 tracking dashboards. To communicate public health at scale, governments for countries, states, counties, and even cities have designed numerous tools to help the broader public understand various facets of the novel disease (Patino, 2021). The analytical dashboard is now mainstream.

Despite the new reach of data visualization, creating effective visualizations still remains a challenge for people designing the interactions. A scripted conversation requires effective prediction of the most relevant questions to ask the data. It demands building a composition that is well put together and guides users through the conversation without feeling unduly restrictive.

A semantic approach to visualization focuses on the interplay between charts, not just the selection of charts themselves. The approach unites the structural content of charts with the context and knowledge of those interacting with the composition. It avoids undue and excessive repetition by instead using referential devices, such as filtering or providing detail-on-demand. A cohesive analytical conversation also builds guardrails to keep users from derailing from the conversation or finding themselves lost without context. Functional aesthetics around color, sequence, style, use of space, alignment, framing, and other visual encodings can affect how users follow the script.

Color

Practitioners often find color to be one of the hardest attributes in a visualization. Color can make or break an otherwise stellar composition. Common advice encourages "getting it right in black and white" (Stone, 2006). Using monochrome design can help identify points of breakdown where color can clarify or identify the focus. We can see two versions of the same dashboard in Figure 9.2. The first cut is in gray. The first two charts at the top are legible without color. The bottom is where meaning starts to break down. With color, the message becomes clearer.

Semantic use of color supports the understanding of what the visualization is conveying. When color is used for a specific paradigm, those using the visualization can follow that paradigm. One paradigm might be using a specific color to highlight selections on an otherwise monochrome visualization. In others, color may be categorical but match associations with the time of day, such as in Kelly Martin's work shown in Figure 9.3.

Color can also help direct attention to differences in the data. In Figure 9.4, color highlights specific metrics, such as blue for sales, teal for profit, and gray for amounts. While never overtly stated, the dashboard subtly supports the consumer during the analysis.

Sequence

As we saw in comics, placement and design elements affect the interpretation of sequence. To create cohesion, charts should add or refine the idea in mind. Literate societies create common exposition styles.

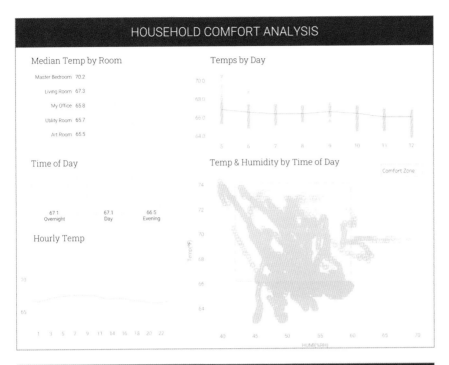

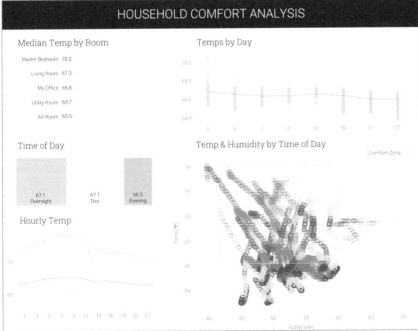

FIGURE 9.2 Identifying where color clarifies

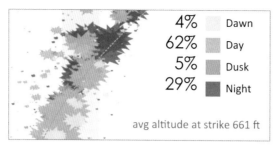

FIGURE 9.3 Semantic color use in Kelly Martin's visualization

FIGURE 9.4 Semantic color use around metrics

Practitioner and Tableau Hall of Fame Visionary Adam McCann (2019) identifies five types of dashboards commonly used in practice:

- Key performance indicator (KPI), or a baseball card style with repeating assets for various metrics

- Question and answer (Q&A), a style driven by various questions that may not be cohesive as a piece

- Top down, a cohesive narrative that starts at a high level and becomes more granular

- Bottom up, a narrative that starts with the details and contextualizes them to a greater whole

- One big chart with nuance from filters

These different exposition styles are patterns for the order in which we expose information. As we enter into certain types of analytical conversations, we expect the conversations to flow in a predictable and cohesive manner. A KPI dashboard, for example, uses redundant structures across specific dimensions or measures to convey information. A dashboard with a top-down exposition style provides high-level information first and clarifies downward, while a bottom-up dashboard starts with the details and clarifies them against the larger picture. Other exposition styles also exist, and some may blend across some of these categories.

Figure 9.5 provides an example of a top-down dashboard that doesn't follow the expected narrative formula. While the map drives the interaction, some higher-level details are at the bottom of the reading order. The details are exposed first, but the higher level doesn't add context. It feels out of place, despite the interaction at the top.

FIGURE 9.5 A non-cohesive sequence

When we redirect the sequence of this example, we get a higher-level view first. Figure 9.6 corrects the errors in sequence. The map still drives the interaction, but the sequence also helps reference what was seen before. By moving the interaction lower, we first set the tone and then allow the interaction to further nuance the information.

FIGURE 9.6 A cohesive sequence

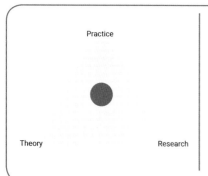

Beyond the design of individual charts, the sequence of data visualizations creates grammar within the exposition. Cohesive visualizations follow common narrative structures to fully express their message. Order matters.

Visual Supports and Style

We cue users with visual supports and style. A style guide is a common practice for practitioners. It's the organization of elements such as titles, headers, and body text into a hierarchy of styles. These styles create unity and help the consumer navigate the visualization. Consistency improves learnability and establishes context. Style tiles provide a quick view of branding in a singular visual pane, like the one shown in Figure 9.7. They are one way of communicating a standardized look-and-feel. Style tiles can set the fonts, gridlines, colors, and assets. They are easy to wrap into an existing analysis so that other analysts can leverage them.

FIGURE 9.7 Simplified style tile

Do lines at zero have a particular style or color? Are gridlines brought forward or should they be nonexistent for chart types? These stylistic elements tell those interacting with the charts where to focus as they dig deeper into the interaction. Are charts treated as separate elements of meaning or, by drawing gridlines across to all, are they one cohesive unit like small multiples? In comics, the style includes what features are exaggerated versus what are realistic. With charts, we can exaggerate the emphasis on the data ink or draw the focus from the data ink to either a broader picture (several charts) or the data ink in context.

In addition to style tiles, framed layouts are another means of creating and applying style. Figure 9.8 shows two layouts. The first is the frame used for Figure 2.9 earlier in this book. The second is an outline view of how the dashboard in Figure 2.9 was used. While proportionally similar, the frame likely guides toward a different design process due to the design elements.

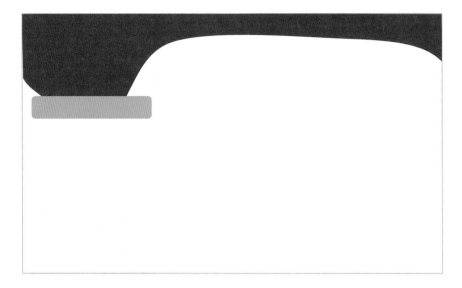

FIGURE 9.8 Frames differentiated by design elements

These frames are semantic. They help create a visual prioritization for reading, acting as syntax or a way of discerning reading order. The first frame encourages a down and over (N) reading style, while the second frame is more open to a Z-reading pattern. Multimodal reading allows the designer to encourage a reading style that best fits the message.

Like multimodal reading, data literacy relies on both primary literacy skills and numeracy skills to truly make sense of the third layer: reading and understanding graphs. Charts codify numbers visually into parameters, using stylized marks to embed additional layers of meaning and space to provide quantitative relationships. Beyond the individual chart, data visualizations create ensembles of charts. Various bento box layouts help guide the design process and cue the end user on how to read the chart, as we've discussed in earlier chapters.

Interactivity and text play a role as visual supports. We will further explore the interplay of text with charts in the next chapter. Interactivity allows a visualization to be explored as one layout visually. Interacting changes what we see, encouraging us to reexplore. Transitions can help provide context to how the data has shifted with the interaction.

Use of Space (Shape)

Charts create form through both positive and negative space use. The shapes of the data can draw attention to specific areas by creating either a positive or negative space. In comics, negative space can be used starkly to draw attention to the focal point. In Figure 9.9, a man stretches out his arm beyond the pane's view. There are two blank panes and then finally, there's the arm. Visually, it plays with the semantics of how we read comics and teases the viewer.

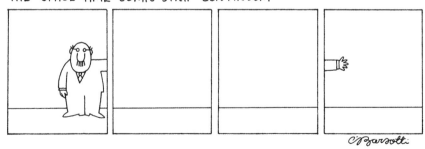

FIGURE 9.9 A comic using negative space to make a point
Charles Barsotti/CartoonStock Ltd

Positive and negative space help create balance, but they also draw interest. In Kelly's composition (modified in Figure 9.10), several shapes attract attention. We have the prominent use of the US map. Icons at the top clarify animals, while in-chart icons clarify direction of the plane. The scatterplot itself uses a distinct "crash" shape and creates a larger shape around the arced trend line. The use of space draws the eye through the visualization and creates a sense of movement.

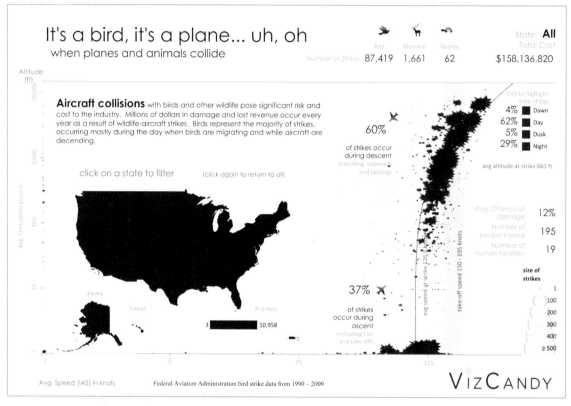

FIGURE 9.10 Kelly Martin's viz modified to draw emphasis to use of space

Chart choices can also create weight within the entire composition. Presenting information as a comprehensive visualization, such as in a dashboard, requires thinking beyond individual charts. In writing, we not only craft sentences, but write the composition as an entire piece. Certain sentences may drive the writing more, but all sentences play a role in conveying the message. In Kelly's visualization, the map may be the largest piece, but the clincher is the scatterplot.

FIGURE 9.11 Effects of chart design on negative space

Crafting the broader narrative and shape may affect individual chart choices. In the visualization in Figure 9.11, parameters around alignment are used to convey relationships. To do this, the chart itself was changed from an unsynchronized axis to one that was synchronized to focus on the relationship in context to sales.

Use of space can help guide users to areas of interaction by making the interacted item larger. Shape may also be created by using other parameters to design layouts that weigh focuses differently.

Alignment

The alignment of charts builds cohesion by communicating relationships. Alignment paradigms may be based around outside borders, titles, and axes but also the data ink itself. Figure 9.12 shows Kelly Martin's exceptional craft around using alignment to build balance. Lines drawn around key areas of emphasis highlight the alignment paradigms at play in this work.

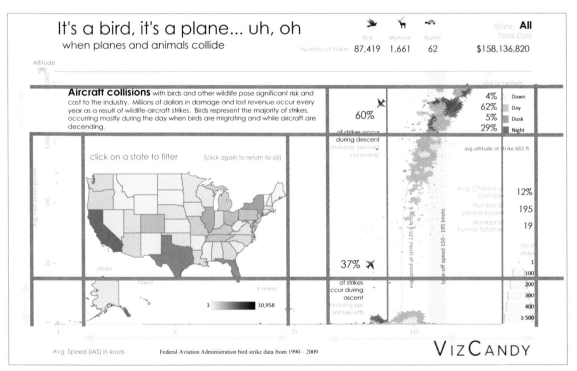

FIGURE 9.12 Kelly Martin's visual poetry

Aligning on data ink can be a powerful way to build relationships across charts. It can be used to obscure the lines between charts, making the composition feel more seamless. Kelly uses this effect to make the scatterplot not only a focal point but also the canvas on which other elements are added.

Alignment paradigms can also influence the layout design needed. In Figure 9.13, the shaded boxes are specifically designed to create ink and reinforce the relationship to the other items. The layout added to the alignment further supports this relationship.

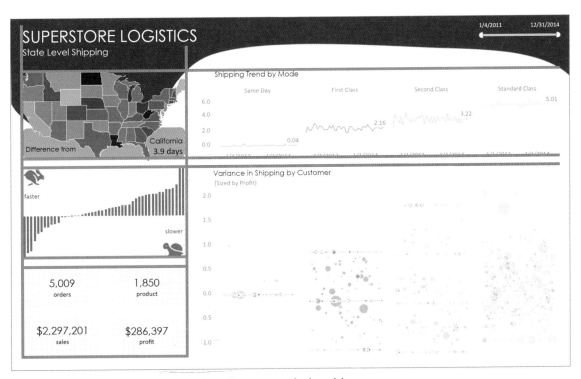

FIGURE 9.13 Coral highlighting the alignment relationships

Disrupting alignment across points alters the proposed reading flow. Comics make use of this concept throughout the story in different patterns. Some reading patterns within comics can be open or even ambiguous by design. Note how the comic at the beginning of this chapter (Figure 9.1) uses alignment.

Figure 9.13 also shows how the charts outside the layout container don't align on data ink to the charts inside. This helps further reiterate that these are different charts. Among the two charts outside the container, they align on data ink and their titles are shifted accordingly.

Register

Register determines the degree of formality, comfort with the topic, and experience reading charts that the targeted audience has. As we design dashboards as scripted conversations with data, we look at how we choose charts differently based on audience or register. Box plots are a perfect example of how charts get adapted for register. Schools, statisticians, and performance analysts may use them often. Outside of certain environments, they read like jargon. We'll explore register more in Part C as we look at visual communication in Chapter 12.

Analytical Conversation

Functionally aesthetic visualization is most effective when users can focus on the process of interacting and exploring their data, without getting bogged down by the mechanics of doing so. When we converse with other people, we try to effectively convey the main idea, often using intonation, gesture, and emotion. Let's go back to our restaurant scene in Chapter 1 where we are dining in our cozy circle at a restaurant. A waiter approaches our table and the conversation goes like this.

Waiter: *How are you folks today?*

You: *Great, really excited to try the food. What's good here?*

Waiter: *Oh, the seasonal sushi platter isn't to miss. It has seasonal vegetables with your choice of protein. A lot of people also enjoy our house Ramen Noodle Soup that you can see pictured there on the menu.*

Your friend: *What about something that's hot?*

Waiter: *Oh, we can adjust the spiciness on most of our menu items. If you're feeling really adventurous, you can try our Red Dragon, with tofu, avocado, jalapenos, cilantro on top with fresh, spicy albacore.*

Within the setting and context of this conversation, the waiter expects a brief tone-setting answer to decide how best to get an order. Questions like, "What's good here?" provide an opportunity for the waiter to pitch popular dishes, easy-to-miss delights, and seasonal fare. We've previously discussed the ambiguity of "hot." Based on the context and semantics of what is being asked, the waiter alludes to the notion of spice seamlessly. The conversation should flow back and forth, perhaps with lulls while eating or drinking, or during bits of inattention to look at a phone or peruse the menu. Threads should bind the conversation, with new topics or themes clearly marked by natural transitions. These common threads create coherence. So how can we take some of these nuggets and apply them to creating effective analytical conversation?

We can draw inspiration from how people communicate when thinking about designing visualizations to support users conversing with data. Specifically, we

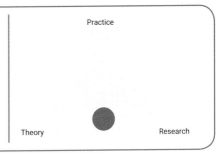

> By balancing the perception and semantics, we can encourage deeper, clearer, and better conversations with the data. Coherence in analytical conversations seeks to center the person interacting with the visualization.

explore how principles from pragmatics and cohesion can be applied to the flow of analytical conversations, specifically the notion of *centering*.

Conversational Centering

As we saw with the interaction between the diners and the waiter from the restaurant scene, conversations are more than just individual chunks of disparate dialog. We build off of what was said before, taking into consideration the context and relevance of what is currently being expressed. *Conversational centering* describes how the context of a conversation adjusts over time to maintain coherence, through transitional states that retain, shift, continue, or reset these conversational elements.

The process of conversing with data is most effective when users can focus on interacting and understanding the patterns presented and being in a state of flow. Pragmatics is particularly important for visual analysis flow, where questions often emerge from previous questions and insights. The principles of pragmatics are modeled based on the interaction behavior of a human-to-human conversation. Tory and Setlur (2019) adopted this conversational centering model to visualization flow, shown in Figure 9.14.

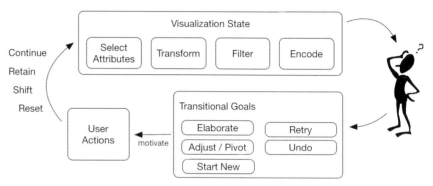

FIGURE 9.14 Conversational transitions model

A key insight of this model is that conversational transition states of continuing, retaining, and shifting apply to all parts of the visualization. Maintaining state in the visual encodings supports coherence, as abrupt changes to the visualization can be jarring and easily misinterpreted. Look at the earlier examples again and you can see effects of changing encodings. As a user interacts, they expect the results to follow a script that aligns with the original inquiry.

After interpreting a visualization (the thinking human in Figure 9.14), a user may continue their analytical conversation by formulating a new question. This analytical intent will ultimately drive a user's transitional goals (how they wish to transform the existing visualization to answer the new question), which in turn drive user actions. The research identified the following transitional goals:

- elaborate (add new data to the visualization)

- adjust / pivot (adapt aspects of the visualization)

- start new (create an altogether new visualization)

- retry (re-attempt a previous step that failed)

- undo (return to the prior state)

A key principle in visual analytics flow is the need to support interactive exploration and continue to build on the last question. A single static chart is rarely sufficient except in the simplest of investigative tasks. The user often needs to interact with their data, iteratively evolving both the questions and the visualization design. Direct manipulation is an effective interaction technique when one can easily point to the objects of interest. An icon may cue us to click. As we do, the data may shift with transitional movement helping us catch the changes. Chart marks might fade entirely or reorder. As we continue to interact, we may keep elements in mind: sales last week were around $200K, but this week they're only $120K. Elements within the chart, such as color and shape, may provide bread-crumbs of where we last clicked.

Natural language interfaces support analytical conversation, where a user can have a back-and-forth interaction with these tools. Evizeon (Hoque et al., 2018) is a system that supports pragmatics and coherence in analytical conversation. Figure 9.15 presents an example from that system.

The first query in Figure 9.15, "measles in the uk," filters to measles cases in the United Kingdom. The user then types "show me the orange spike" and the system understands that the query is a reference to the line chart and annotates the spike. In the third query, the system interprets "mumps over there" as containing a reference to the United Kingdom and a differ-ent value in the disease attribute. It retains the filter on "United Kingdom" but updates disease from "measles" to "mumps." "Epidemics here" is a reference to marks selected on the map with a mouse, so epidemic diseases in that selected region are highlighted.

Throughout this exchange, the user has been able to build on their prior queries and adapt the current state rather than starting over each time, just like how we speak with other people. Language is often incomplete or imprecise, relying on the audience to interpret using their contextual knowledge (i.e., speaker, topic, time, location, past dialog). These tenden-cies carry over into interactions with a visualization, where it is known that people use ambiguous language and may refer to items in the past. We will continue this conversation (pun intended) as we go into text and charts.

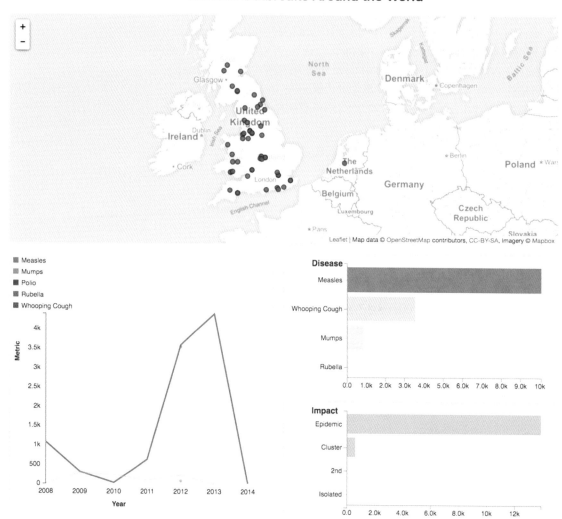

FIGURE 9.15 Example results of various forms of natural language interactions with a dashboard showing disease outbreaks in the world

"show me the orange spike"

⊗ DISEASE == Measles   ⊗ COUNTRY == United Kingdom

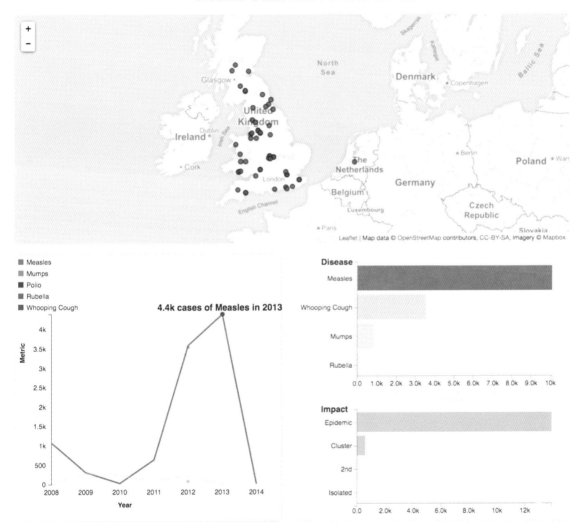

Disease Outbreaks Around the World

"mumps over there"

DISEASE == Mumps   COUNTRY == United Kingdom

Disease Outbreaks Around the World

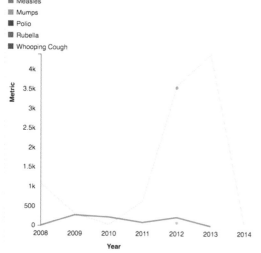

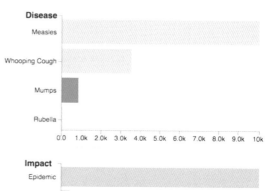

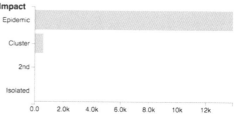

"epidemics here"

IMPACT == Epidemic   in the selected area

Disease Outbreaks Around the World

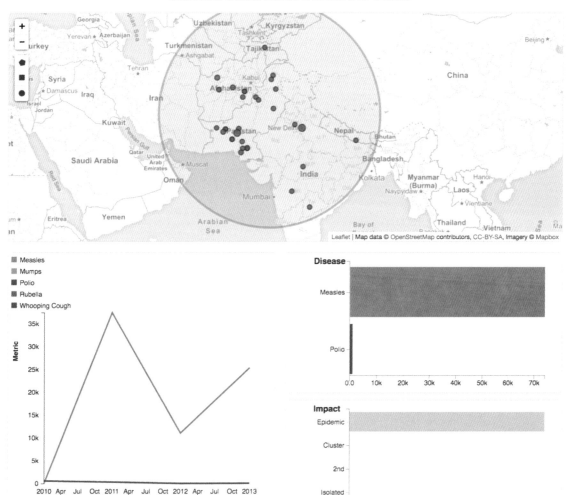

Summary

Getting one chart to flow to the next smoothly relies on a variety of techniques that create cohesion. Comics also challenge us to think beyond standard patterns. While Z-reading can be an effective technique, framing can help bind units to encourage new paths. We can free our design experiences by playing with layout, drawing tighter or looser spaces, and aligning in ways that pivot the conversation in new directions. Analytical conversations are not linear, but they rely on logical transitions to shift directions. They build in ways to repair or lend nuance to a detail. Charts work together clarifying one another, faceting a new dimension, or directing attention to how a detail fits in the whole picture. Analytical conversations require cohesion to find insight.

Text and Charts

As we come away from discussing the grammatical construction of functionally aesthetic dashboard design, we can better appreciate how data narratives can be expressed through the thoughtful placement and sequencing of charts. Text helps add additional context, guidance, and directives to imagery such as illustrations and charts. This additional information further supports the reader in developing a coherent mental representation of the information presented to them (Bransford et al., 1972). Comprehending the visual depiction of what's important in a chart, along with suitable support from the accompanying text, further enhances the reader's understanding of the meaning of that representation. This overall understanding of the representation is the product of the interaction between the chart and text along with the reader's knowledge from both prior and current interactions that they discover as the reading progresses.

In reality, when we author visualizations, we often discount the importance of textual context that accompanies these charts. Similar to the deliberate and thoughtful placement of marks with color and size encodings, we need to carefully consider the construction of language based on its intended purpose in communicating aspects of the data to the reader. When integrating written text with charts in a functionally aesthetic way, the reader should be able to find the key takeaways from the chart or dashboard, taking into account the context, constraints, and reading objectives of the overall message.

Let's unpack all of this with an example. We return to the Bird Strikes visualization we showed in Chapter 4. In Figure 10.1, we have highlighted all the text and numbers. We can now see how much text supports the overall composition and all the areas where annotation is subtly embedded throughout the composition. With all the text called out, we can see how much of a presence it has. As we progress through this chapter, we will further dissect the roles text plays in providing clarity and user support.

FIGURE 10.1 Bird Strikes dashboard with text and numbers highlighted

Data visualization opens the channel of communication between the authors who create the visualization and the people who act upon it. As we think about ways to transform complex data into a format that is both visually appealing and universally accessible to a wider audience, we need to also think of the medium that the visualization is part of.

Medium Being the Message

The Internet is quickly changing how we read. Articles rely more and more on a reading experience that combines text, graphics, and various design elements. Yet this book and many others showcase another change happening with literacy: that words alone are rarely enough to fully make a point. Going a bit meta here, many points within this book rely on graphics or design elements to highlight or clarify the details within them. Additionally, we are using triangles both for quick reference and to be clear about our understanding of where an idea lands. Even the colored strip at the bottom provides information about the part of the book being read. It would be much harder to express these concepts in words alone. Multimodal reading requires being able to read the entire ensemble: the text, the visuals, and additional design elements that provide cues about the whole piece. We work to understand the entire ensemble as a cohesive unit of meaning presented in different ways. Together, they ideally clarify and frame the message (Serafini, 2014).

As we discussed in Chapter 9, comics artfully combine multimodal reading within frames. Deciding how to tell the story between text and pictures requires balancing intent with semantics and perception. Visually, the comic can be presented at a faster or slower pace or convey other things about the event by balancing text with the pictures. By themselves, the pictures can only say so much, relying on text to set the tone, introduce ideas, and provide perspective into the thoughts and actions of what's occurring within the comic frame. Data visualization, like comics, can expose information through charts. It relies on a balance of text to pace the exposition and set the tone.

Newspapers are using more visuals than ever, partly because digital media offset the cost of a full-color print, and because the graphic often communicates far more effectively. Academic papers and scientific journals use charts as an anchor to communicate a data-driven point of view or to invite critical discourse. Look at some of the pictures in this book and how they affect your attention or emotions as you read through a chapter. As data visualization expands into broader circles, graphicacy, or the ability to draw meaning from charts, is key.

Types of Text

Balancing the types of text used allows users to navigate our visualizations effectively. While charts are our primary medium, text provides the support and framing to fully support them and foster multimodal reading.

The words we choose can set the tone, clarify, and fill in gaps. Done well, text solidifies the understanding, providing language to both the insight and visual.

The following types of text are shown in Figure 10.2:

- Titles
- Quantifiers
- Qualifiers
- Annotations
- Narrative text
- Captions
- Caveats, disclosures, and warnings

FIGURE 10.2 Different types of text highlighted and boxed

These text elements work together to build a whole that is stronger than its individual parts. This example blurs the line between where one chart ends and another begins through layering. This premise is also reflected in how text is paired and placed.

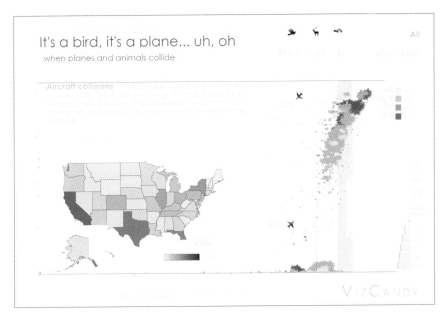

FIGURE 10.3 Boxed text shows titles.

Titles set the tone of the visualization and also start the reader on the journey to figuring out what the visually encoded data means. In the composition shown in Figure 10.3, the title relies on a familiar phrase to invoke some of its playfulness: "It's a bird, it's a plane . . . it's Superman!" indicating the visually encoded data is about birds and planes. The subtitle helps pull toward the heart of the story and answers the question, How likely is a plane going to hit an animal during the flight? The tone of the title and the visual presentation match. The scatterplot leverages a "crash-effect" jagged icon to represent events, while icons provide clarity and match the tone. Data encodings like the fill coloring in this map view do not convey the meaning of the data without the "balance of text." Charts themselves are not titled; instead, the semantics of the visualizations and layered effect create a whole unit under the primary title. Most visualizations use titles to frame charts in addition to the entire composition.

Quantifiers form the backbone of any visualization. They allow the visual pattern to be articulated into quantities and mathematically understood as well as visually. They also allow us to take the information we're seeing and compare it to other statistics, such as the likelihood of similar accidents while driving rather than flying. Beyond what we see, quantifying allows us to assess our world. Figure 10.4 shows the quantifiers in the dashboard providing numerical information that supports the data story about bird strikes.

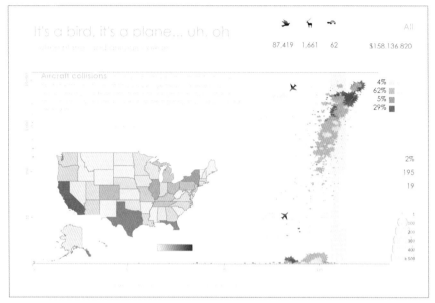

FIGURE 10.4 Quantifiers are highlighted in sea green.

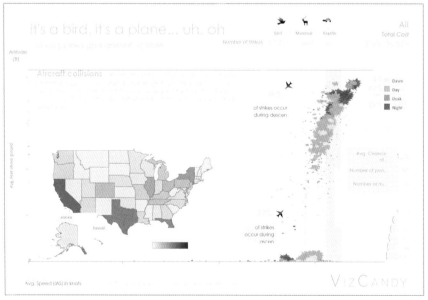

FIGURE 10.5 Qualifiers are highlighted in peach.

Qualifiers are words and fragments anchored to quantifiers that provide context to the number within the visualization. They label axes, serve as legends, segment measures as dimensions, and format large numbers with stylization and units. This visualization uses a variety of techniques: pairing legends with numbers, clarifiers (such as state names), and dimensional faceting (such as species types and statistics about strikes at the right). Several techniques overlap, creating clarity that compounds understanding. For example, legends in the graphic in Figure 10.5 are accompanied by numbers providing additional depth to the topic.

Annotations are in-chart clarifiers. They identify salient points within the visualization using placement as a primary attribute in their understanding. They call out peaks, averages, or notable reference points. Figure 10.6 shows how annotations provide contextual support to the individual chart elements, such as the marks in the scatterplot and the color legend.

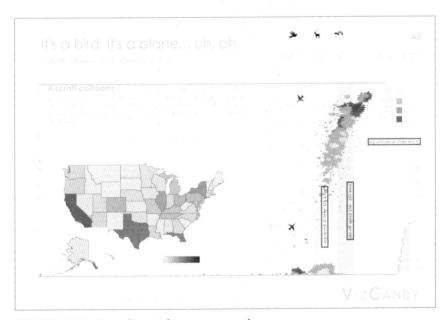

FIGURE 10.6 Boxed text shows annotations.

Framing text includes sentences that are captions, narratives, and other callouts outside the visualization. They set the angle, reiterate salient findings, and expose other contextual information. Framing text can be a sentence or multiple paragraphs designed to further expose what is both displayed and not displayed in the chart. Figure 10.7 shows a caption that provides additional narrative for the charts by making a point about the risk of aircraft collisions with birds and other wildlife.

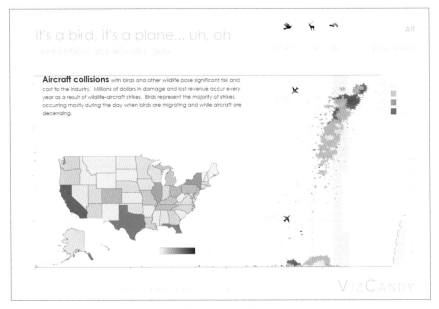

FIGURE 10.7 Framing text is highlighted in grey.

Functional text provides those consuming the visualization, the necessary information to use or evaluate the limits of the visualization. Here, the visualization discloses its data source, the time limitations of the data, and what filters are applied. Caveats around qualifiers include nuance around what is included in a given category. Functional text can also include interactive features, such as drop-down filters. Figure 10.8 shows how functional text provides directives to the reader about the interactive aspects of the dashboard, such as "click on a state to filter."

While there is a definite utility of text to help add additional semantics to the data, too much can actually do harm. It's a common design problem—when to include information versus when not in the quest to communi-

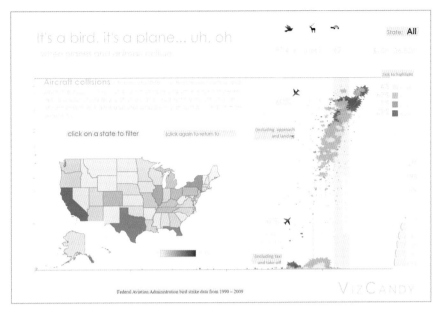

FIGURE 10.8 Functional text is highlighted in Lilac.

cate clearly. Text with charts is no exception, especially when the data is both abundant and thought-provoking. So how does one avoid the pitfall of overtexting?

Balancing Text with Charts

Data visualization is a medium requiring multimodal literacy skills (Serafini, 2014). Drawn on paper or displayed interactively, the visualization combines the balance of numbers and text with the language of charts to convey information. Additional elements, such as interactivity and animation, can affect both the delivery of the message and its understanding. Balancing between these elements relies on the interplay of perception, semantics, and intent. In working with these visual patterns, the goal is to relax the eye so that the visualization can be read "at a glance," allowing the visual aspect to come forward. Thinking of the words as being in a field, or white space, will help you see the different aspects of the visual pattern. Recurrence and predictability are the basis of this pattern. This includes words, phrases, and sentences that can be easily scanned and seen.

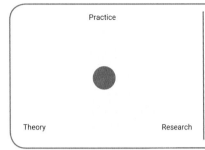

Practice

Text should be treated as a first-class citizen, just like any chart type. The thoughtful placement of text along with its encodings of shape and color determine the visualization's layout, structure, and flow.

Theory

Research

Figure 10.9 shows an example of where text is not balanced with the visual. The visual accompanies the text rather than the text amplifying the visual. Many of the points are told rather than shown. In a static medium such as this book, finding the referenced points is even harder. The top chart showing the running count of visualizations is only effective for seeing the hockey stick shift in the trend, while the bottom daily count provides perhaps the most insight due to some annotation.

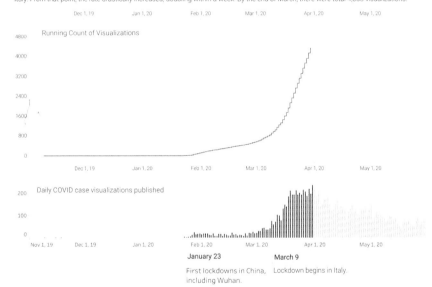

Clear-Cut Case Visualizations

The following visualization shows data pulled from Tableau Public API using terms "COVID" and "Coronavirus" and filtered to include terms that highlight cases. Between November 1, 2019 and January 22, 2020, only 3 visualizations were made. On January 23, 7 unique visualizations were made, coinciding with the first lockdown in China. March 9 was another tipping point, also lining up with a lockdown in Italy. From that point, the rate drastically increased, doubling within a week. By the end of March, there were total 4,333 visualizations.

FIGURE 10.9 Text is not balanced with the visual.

As we move some of the information from the paragraph to the chart (Figure 10.10), we can see that the number of visualizations from March 8 to March 16 nearly doubled. Four days later, the number is almost triple our first number. The annotations work within the chart to call out a pattern that is nearly undetectable in the first example.

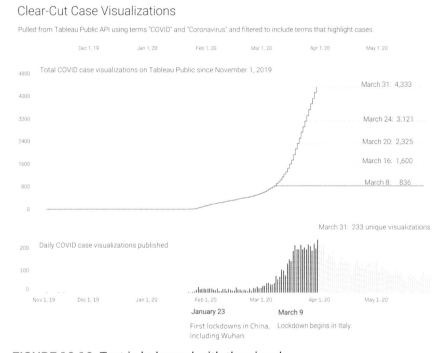

Clear-Cut Case Visualizations

Pulled from Tableau Public API using terms "COVID" and "Coronavirus" and filtered to include terms that highlight cases.

FIGURE 10.10 Text is balanced with the visual.

Adapting this visualization for the print medium requires thinking through what information is salient for those viewing it. Without the ability to hover, selecting dates for emphasis becomes critical. The dates give the closest times to which visualizations on Tableau Public multiplied from March 8. The intent of this composition is to highlight the relationship between lockdowns and publications to Tableau Public.

Chart and Text Agreement

Charts are used to communicate information about data to a reader. Authors often add text such as captions along with charts to provide additional context and clarification to help with their message to the intended audience. But what makes for a good caption? And how does the caption interact with the chart?

While charts can draw a reader's attention to various visual features such as outliers and trends, it's unclear what the reader takes away from both text and charts together.

Take a look at this line chart in Figure 10.11. What do you think are the main visual features of the chart, and what are your key takeaways?

FIGURE 10.11 Line chart example

Now, consider each of the following caption possibilities with the chart. How do your takeaways change with each one?

1. The chart shows the 30-year fixed mortgage rate between 1970 and 2018.

2. The 30-year fixed mortgage rate increased slightly from 1997 to 1999.

3. The 30-year fixed mortgage rate reached its peak of 18.45% in 1981.

4. The 30-year fixed mortgage rate reached its peak of 18.45% in 1981 due to runaway inflation.

The first caption simply describes the attributes graphed in the chart and only provides redundant information that could be read from the axis labels.

Many of the automated caption generation tools create captions of this form. The next three each emphasize aspects of the data corresponding to a visual feature of the chart, such as a peak or an upward trend. However, there are differences. The second caption emphasizes a feature of low visual prominence—a relatively local and small rise in the chart between 1997 and 1999. The third caption describes the most visually prominent feature of the chart—the tallest peak that occurs in 1981. The fourth caption also describes this most visually prominent feature but adds external information not presented in the chart and provides context for the data.

So, how do each of these different captions, when accompanied with a chart, affect readers' takeaways?

Kim et al. (2021) explored this question using a set of 43 line charts. Findings from their study showed that users described the feature doubly emphasized by both the chart and caption in their takeaways when they both provided a coherent message. However, when the chart and caption diverged in terms of the feature that they were emphasizing, participants were less likely to use information from the caption in their takeaways.

Going back to our initial line chart example shown in Figure 10.11, when the caption mentions the most visually prominent feature as in the third caption (i.e., the peak in 1981), readers will probably take away information from that feature. When the caption mentions a less prominent feature as in the second caption (i.e., the increase from 1997 to 1999), there is a mismatch in the message between the chart and the caption. Readers will have a strong tendency to go with the message conveyed in *both* the chart and the caption when they mention the most prominent feature. Revisiting the chart and the third caption from Figure 10.11, the portions of the chart and caption highlighted in blue (shown in Figure 10.12) agree with each other. Finally, the external information about the peak value present in the fourth caption will further reinforce the message in the caption and the readers will more likely take away information about the peak.

The work shows how charts and text relate to one another when they occur together. Findings from the study bring up an important aspect of functionally aesthetic charts with text. Authors should effectively convey their message to readers by ensuring that *both* charts and captions

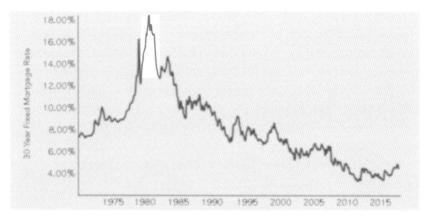

FIGURE 10.12 **The 30-year fixed mortgage rate** reached its peak of 18% **in 1981.**

emphasize the same set of features. For example, authors could make visual features that are related to their key message more prominent through visual cues (e.g., highlighting, zooming, or adding annotations) or include external information to further emphasize the feature described in the caption. Visualization authoring tools can provide guidelines for authors when they craft charts and captions together so that the intended takeaways are effectively communicated to the reader.

Text in Analytical Conversation

With the proliferation of smarter and more interactive visual analysis systems such as natural language interfaces, text is a useful mechanism for the system to converse with the human, explaining the system's behavior to the human, or providing additional context to the system's response. A well-accepted principle in visual analytics is the need to support interactive exploration and iterative view refine-ment. A single static visualization is rarely sufficient except in the simplest of

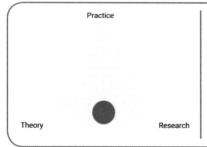

Text and visuals together can help support an analytical conversation that is cooperative and interactive. Just like conversation among people, there needs to be both visual and linguistic coherence between the charts and the text.

investigative tasks. The user often needs to interact with their data, itera-tively evolving both the questions and the visualization design. Natural language interaction (NLI) is a complementary input modality to traditional mouse- and touch-based interaction for visual analytics.

Let's walk through a few examples of how text can be used to support an analytical conversation between a human and a computer.

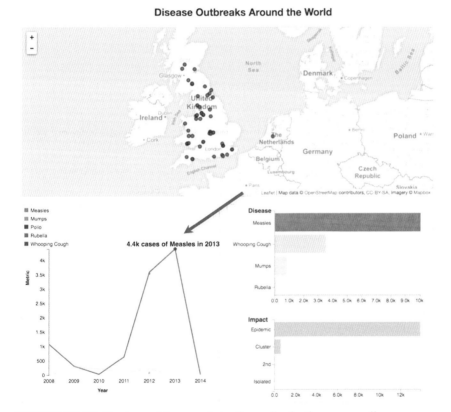

FIGURE 10.13 Text used to annotate the spike in the orange line

The first example, in Figure 10.13, shows an NLI using a conversational approach, where the user has a back-and-forth exchange with a system called Evizeon (Hoque et al., 2018). The user types "show me the orange spike", and the system understands that this is a reference to the visual properties of the line chart and dynamically adds a text annotation to the spike in the line. The display of the annotation serves two goals:

1. It shows to the user that Evizeon understands that the phrase "orange spike" is a reference to the visual properties of the line chart.

2. The detail in the text provides contextual information about that spike, supporting the intent of the question.

The second example describes how text can help clarify ambiguity during an analytical conversation. NLI often involves the use of vague subjective modifiers in utterances such as "show me the sectors that are *performing*" and "where is a *good* neighborhood to buy a house?" Interpreting these vague modifiers is often difficult for these tools because their meanings lack clear semantics and are in part defined by context and personal user preferences, a concept we discussed in Chapter 5. Sentifiers (Setlur & Kumar, 2020) was a research prototype that explores ways to handle these vague concepts in users' input queries. The algorithm employs word co-occurrence and sentiment analysis to determine which data attributes and filter ranges to associate with the vague predicates. The provenance results from the algorithm are exposed to the user as interactive text that can be repaired and refined. Figure 10.14 shows how the system interprets the vague concept "struggling" in the input query "which countries are *struggling*?" The red hue shows a negative sentiment mapped to the attributes "income per capita" and "life expectancy." The system maps values to lower ranges for each of these attributes, given the negative sentiment. Clicking on a numerical value shows a slider, encouraging the user to play with it, as the corresponding scatterplot below updates.

Making Data More Accessible

Alt text, a contraction of *alternative text*, is a concise description of an image when it can't be viewed. Effective alt text helps more people understand the content. Assistive technology like screen readers reads the alt text out loud for people with certain visual and cognitive impairments. Alt text is also displayed in place of the image in web

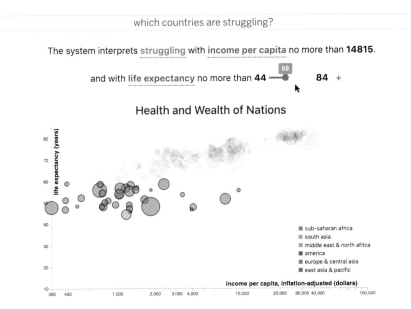

FIGURE 10.14 The Sentifiers system shows interactive text as a response.

browsers if the image file is taking a while to load, for example. This text can be read by search engines or be used to later determine the content of the image from page context alone.

So, how do you write something concisely that conveys the essence of a visualization? Given the precedence of alt text for images, the World Wide Web Consortium (W3C) offers guidelines for alt text for complex images (2021), but it can be difficult to interpret how to apply the guidelines to data visualization. While those guidelines don't completely transfer to charts, there are some helpful pointers (Cesal, 2020):

- Keep the alt text concise. There is no point in describing information that only makes sense visually. Rather, pick key insights and takeaways. Also, alt text tends to be read linearly by screen readers, meaning that people can't go back a word if they missed something.

- Supplement the chart with a link to the raw data so that readers can access the data in their own preferred program.

- For the benefit of people with partial sight or for people who have a good sense of space, including the chart type may be helpful to add some context to the key insights described in the al text.

- Finally, multimodal interaction that includes haptic feedback and sonification could be used with text to speech when describing aspects of the chart.

Text can also be used to generate summaries about data insights. Natural Language Generation (NLG), a subcategory of Natural Language Processing (NLP), is a software process that automatically transforms structured data into human-readable text. NLG tools such as Narrative Science (Figure 10.15) and Automated Insights automatically analyze data, interpret it, identify the most significant parts, and generate written reports in plain English (or localized to other languages).

FIGURE 10.15 Narrative Science NLG plug-in for Tableau
Narrative Science

Text for Supporting Reading Fluency

Lastly, fluency is a complex reading skill that is crucial in the understanding of text. The cognitive process of reading creates changes in the visual cortex of our brain, which is the area that receives, integrates, and processes visual information relayed from our retinas. This is where we visualize images of individual letters and the patterns of letters strung together. So why is reading fluency important?

Cognitive neuroscientist and child development expert Maryanne Wolf (2007) states that reading fluency is an important skill as it provides the extra time for the brain to infer, understand, predict, and interpret the meaning of the information when processing words. When text is used effectively with visuals, we get a preview of what lies ahead as we read, making it easier to understand what follows. As we continue to explore the role of text with charts in effective takeaways and reading comprehension, it is important to consider whether the juxtaposition of text with imagery interrupts the flow of reading or aids in further understanding. As we have seen with text in the flow of analytical conversation, it is also important that we identify ways in which text can be combined with updates to charts for adding context and reasoning to the interface. As we see an increase in the presence of charts and text coexisting together, we need to consider how the structure and placement of words and imagery affect layout and fluency at various levels of granularity, ranging from sentence to document levels.

Summary

We close out this chapter and Part B by discussing how text is just as important as the visualizations themselves, supporting data semantics when used effectively. While we can explore different ways to present data that is meaningful, how do we know if the intended message by the author matches that of the reader? As we enter Part C, we will explore that very question. Data, visual depiction, and language help map the author's mental model to the intended audience. Functionally aesthetic visualization that conveys intent effectively can be a useful scaffold for helping people make relevance judgments and aid in sensemaking. So, let's continue our journey.

Maui coastline
Photo by Vidya Setlur

Intent

Flow in a conversation feels effortless. There is no sense of anxiety or awkwardness; you're able to respond and listen to the other person as if the conversation were a well-choreographed dance.

Max Weiss, an American scholar and translator says,

Let the conversation flow at its own pace, don't try to rush it or control it.
You need to let go and be part of the conversation.

According to psychologist Mihaly Csik-szentmihalyi (1991), the mental state of flow is "being completely involved in an activity for its own sake. Every action, movement, and thought follows inevitably from the previous one. Your whole being is involved, and you're using your skills to the utmost." There is a sense of intentionality built into the conversational flow as we communicate, share ideas, and converse with others, at times forgetting the minutes and hours slip by as we completely immerse in this delightful experience.

Understanding the purpose, or in other words, intent of the conversation is rather organic and unscripted. Just like the river that often meanders around, adjusting its path along the way, we often need to clarify with one another, going beyond the shortest path of communication efficiency. With the world inundated with mobile devices, ads, social media, and various forms of multi-tasking, much of our lives consist of endless interruptions, hindering productivity and reducing our ability to simply enjoy the moment. In visual analysis, these interruptions can often hinder a user from having a fluid conversation with their data and exploring answers to questions they may have along the way.

Interactive visual analysis is most productive when users can focus on answering the questions they have about their data rather than focusing on how to operate the interface. Visualizations that support flow create a strong sense of place. So, how do we get attention in an already attention-starved world? As we move into Part C, we will explore this very question of intent and flow. The next set of chapters draws inspiration from our experiences around us. Calm spaces help us focus our attention: intentional harmony between components that bring a sense of purpose, using visual pauses to breathe, and that bring out the best in each artifact that occupies that very space.

CHAPTER 11

Defining and Framing

Like water, conversations flow in and around points until they reach their destination. While not always linear, these interactions achieve several purposes. Parts of the conversation may be to set the tone, build relationships, or convince someone to do something. Conversations—whether person to person or with a machine—work to balance competing intents. Beyond the literal sum of the parts, intent balances meaning with goals.

Semantics explores *how* we communicate. Intent digs into *why* and dictates *what is hidden* in our communication. "What's going on?" is an abstract question that could be understood in a variety of ways. Asked in a friendly tone while approaching a group at work, it could be a means of getting an invite to the lunch table as a way to build relationships. Asked in the same way by an authority figure, the group might quickly disband. The sum of the words and tone didn't change, but the meaning behind the words did.

We leverage semantics as a tool for communicating intent. Mood, setting, tone, register, and power dynamics also play a role. Functional aesthetics uses perceptual and semantic properties of a visualization to draw the two parameters toward intent as the basis. As you saw in the preceding paragraph, semantics can be used to soften or hide intent—the speaker was able to use the same words to create different effects. We, too, can use charts in semantically meaningful ways for different goals while balancing perceptual needs. Figure 11.1 shows how intent completes the functional aesthetics paradigm.

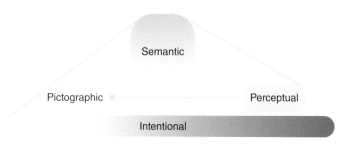

FIGURE 11.1 Functional aesthetics—completing the cycle with intent supporting the other parameters

Functionally aesthetic charts are created with the intention not only to satisfy the aesthetic criteria of the author but also to provide utility and practical function to the reader. This combination gives rise to the important issue of how intent can be conveyed through thoughtful data representation and interaction. Let's explore further with some defining and framing.

Analytical Intent

We define *analytical intent* to be the goal that a consumer or analyst focuses on when performing either targeted or more open-ended data exploration and discovery. Analytical intent is expressed as part of a conversation between the user and a visualization interface. A user can express their analytical intent in a variety of ways:

- They can explicitly pick a few attributes and choose a chart type, as you see in Figure 11.2. Here, the user picks a histogram with the Wine Points attribute, indicating their analytical intent to see the distribution of wine points in the data source. Note that multiple charts could satisfy the same analytical intent in this example, like a clustered scatterplot.

- Analytical intent can also be expressed through natural language. In Figure 11.3, the user types in Tableau's Ask Data interface. "show me the life expectancy by location." As you saw in Chapter 5, vagueness and ambiguity are common when users express their intent through language, and it's up to the system to try to make sense of what the user is intending, providing reasonable responses. Here, the system infers that "location" maps to a geospatial attribute, thus showing a map of life expectancy colored by county, with darker colors indicating higher life expectancies.

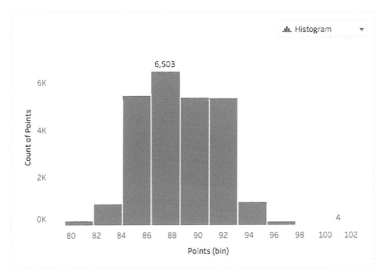

FIGURE 11.2 A histogram addressing the user's analytical intent for seeing the distribution of wine points

FIGURE 11.3 A map shown in response to the user's query, "show me the life expectancy by location"

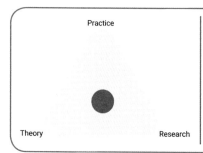

Practice

Theory

Research

Charts need to support ways for users to express intent continuously during their analytical workflows. Data semantics, context, and interaction are useful ways of understanding user intent during data exploration.

The different ways of expressing analytical intent is only part of the conversational picture. How does one create an ambience to support the feeling of engagement and inclusion, inviting people to contribute to that conversation? There are several pieces of that puzzle, of which register is one.

Register

How we communicate tells others that they are invited into the discussion or sends signals to keep them out of the conversation. The term *register* communicates the degree of formality and familiarity within an interaction (Joos, 1967). Through the use of setting, vocabulary, grammar, amount of clarity or precision, and topics allowed, participants understand their role and how to respond appropriately. Register occurs in all types of discourse, including writing and creating visualizations. For example, friends having a dialog use an intimate register as a means of keeping others out of the conversation. They have little distance between them but create a large "keep out" sign for others. By using vague references to shared events ("what happened last night"), the friends can freely discuss their thoughts and opinions without others having any insight into the event or being invited to engage. The register makes clear the goals of the interaction to the parties interacting as well as those outside the conversation.

As we build visualizations, we create a register for the interaction. Is it a one-way interaction or are we invited to engage and, if so, in what ways? Moving charts from static visualizations to interactive compositions enables greater freedom in conversation if those authoring the analysis provide it. When we directly converse with our data, we may have a conversation as close friends would, each successive chart telling us more and more about the data at hand. By the time we create the dashboard to share with others, we have to change our register to invite others into the conversation. We'll examine register more in depth in the next chapter and how it affects both charts and the broader composition.

Visualizations are compositions where individuals conversing with the data can make limited requests for clarification. Detail-on-demand techniques can clarify charts that by themselves might be at a higher register, but interactivity allows the chart to clarify down to a lower register. Reducing the register democratizes information and provides guardrails to keep consumers on track. Newer natural language processing tools, such as the ones shown in Ask Data, allow consumers to expand a scripted analysis into one where they ask the questions through repair and refinement.

Repair and Refinement

In conversation analysis, *repair* is the process by which a person recognizes an error in what was conveyed and repeats what has been communicated with some sort of correction or *refinement* (Franklin, 1971). The need for clarification is an important part of the construct of language and is often based on the underlying grammar, vocabulary, and discourse style that are appropriate to the context of that conversation. Often these instances for repair happen when there's ambiguity in language or something is not understood. People are particularly adept at disambiguating information that they don't understand, such as asking clarification questions like, "I'm sorry, I didn't understand. Could you please explain?"

Colonomos (2015) shows the various levels of repair that exist within language interpretation. Designed for simultaneous interpretation, the Integrated Model of Interpreting focuses on preserving the original spoken or signed message (the source text) while constructing the new message (the target). The interpreter builds a feedback loop both through working memory and by monitoring the reactions of those receiving the message. A repair could be as simple as spelling a word wrong, gently signaling the mistake, and respelling—a correction that occurs in a second or two. In a more complex repair, the interpreter may notice confused expressions or get notified by a team interpreter (the feedback loop) and revert to the original composition stage to reassess the mood, context, and intent of the original and recompose it. Interrupting the conversation is typically reserved for more complex repairs.

However, the issue of handling ambiguity in language becomes more complex when a person interacts with a computer. Computers are not acculturated as humans are: everything must be expressly scripted or taught through either supervised or unsupervised learning. Computers read information as 0s and 1s. The user's mental model that encapsulates intent, cues, and context needs to be transformed to that of the computer's model. Further, the user's interactions with the computer are often vague and can get even more complicated when interacting with a visual analysis tool as their intent would need to be understood against the underlying data and analytical functions.

Bret Victor, a computer scientist and interface designer (http://worrydream.com) wrote a series of essays that explained the benefits of adding interactivity to an interface to help with repair and refinement. He states:

> *"I believe that dynamic pictures will someday be the primary medium for visual art and visual explanations. The medium is currently in its infancy —working in the medium is more about technological fumbling than artistic expression. The revolution cannot happen until there is a means for artists to draw dynamic pictures." (Victor, 2013)*

Outlets like the *New York Times*, Upshot, the *Guardian*, and Bloomberg point to movement. The idea of rich, interactive data-driven storytelling has really taken off over the years with authors using animation and interaction to communicate complex ideas. Inspired by these ideas for active engagement between the user and computer, the visualization research community has investigated techniques for storytelling using charts, widgets, and interactive text (Conlen & Heer, 2018). These ideas become even more relevant as visual analysis tools are better equipped to handle intentionality through natural language interaction and providing useful recommendations as they learn

Practice

There are no dead ends in conversation. For charts to be functionally aesthetic, there need to be affordances for repair and refinement to keep that conversation going.

Theory   Research

to adapt to the user's needs over time. We will explore these concepts in more detail as we discuss scaffolds for handling user intent in Chapter 13.

Pragmatics

A "smart" system can attempt to affect a match between the concepts in the utterances and the concepts known by the system. While follow-up repair utterances can help resolve ambiguities that a natural language interface may encounter, such systems are often constrained by the domain of the knowledge base or context in which the interaction occurs. In addition, analytical concepts may not map directly from utterances to the underlying information.

Pragmatics, a concept that originated from the linguistics community, explores how a user's intent can be interpreted in a particular context (Davis, 2019 Edition). This includes the place where something was stated, who said it, and what was already stated before. This concept carries over well into analytical conversation as the person converses with data using an interactive chart or dashboard as the medium. The user's current and past interactions, along with the context of the data support a pragmatic approach for handling their intent. In an analytical conversational flow, it is quite common for people to correct or clarify a previous utterance. Evizeon (Hoque et al., 2018) is a natural language interface that demonstrates the use of follow-up repair utterances to "repair" a potentially ambiguous utterance or to change the default behavior of how the results are presented to the user. Let's look at an example.

Figure 11.4 shows a user asking to see house sales in Green Lake, a neighborhood in Seattle. Evizeon interprets "houses" to be a single-family house, townhouse, or condo, the broadest definition commonly used. However, the user intended that "houses" refers to only the first two house types and enters a follow-up repair utterance, "remove condos." Evizeon updates the dashboard by removing the condo category.

As we've discussed, to support a conversation, charts need to provide cohesive and relevant responses to a user's intent. Sometimes the interface needs to respond by changing the visual encoding of existing charts, while in other cases, it is necessary to create a new chart to support the analytical conversation. In addition to appropriate visualization responses, it is critical to help the user understand how the system has interpreted their intent by producing appropriate feedback and allowing them to clarify if necessary. The next section looks at how these concepts can be brought into practice.

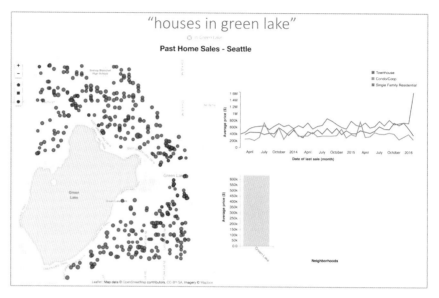

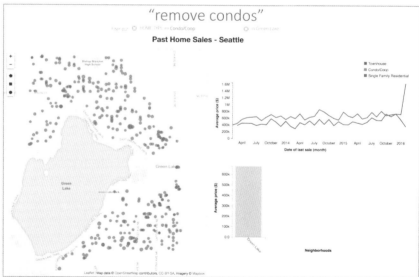

FIGURE 11.4 Evizeon uses pragmatics to support a follow-up to remove condos from the dashboard.

Practicing Intent

Moving to an intentional practice that encompasses perception and semantics requires changing how we design visualizations for others to consume. We align user goals to clearly driven tasks we semantically encode for both the brain and eye. Intent affects parameters such as order.

Figure 11.5 shows a dashboard that meets perceptual needs and some semantic ones. Perceptually, it's tidy and calm with a clear alignment strategy. The colors adhere to a semantic schema. While the charts make sense for the data they present in isolation from each other, they do not form a whole cohesive unit. Sales and Profit have no clear semantic relationship and the charts do not help the consumer navigate the dashboard. Semantically, the sequence of charts isn't clear to the consumer.

FIGURE 11.5 Assessing a visualization for intent

In assessing the visualization, we can see the seasonality in sales. Profit lacks the seasonal trends. Without some semantic relationship between these metrics —whether it's sharing an axis on dollar or time—the pattern is difficult to see. All the charts at the top are at a monthly level of detail, while the charts at the bottom represent data at day (heatmap), state (map), and year (stacked bar chart). Where should the consumer start interacting? Without someone to verbally guide, the visualization acts more like notes from a previous dialog rather than as a new conversation.

Pragmatically, we need to establish a shared context. There are not enough guardrails to set the tone as new people begin conversing with this dashboard. How do they interact and ask questions? What are ways they can refine understanding or correct a misunderstanding? We can use intent combined with semantic principles discussed in the last part to tighten this exposition.

Figure 11.6 adapts the earlier dashboard while preserving as many of the composition's original choices as possible. In light of the analytical intent, profit and sales are merged into one chart and synchronized. For both legibility and clarity, the area mark is changed to bars. The monthly profit bar chart is changed to an area graph to emphasize the overall flow and to better capture the negative value in October for Furniture. The sequence of the state map and heat map are reordered, with the interactive capabilities on the map called out with an icon. The intended conversation with this data is made clearer.

FIGURE 11.6 After evaluating intent

Redesigning this composition considers the register we seek but also provides clear ways to repair and refine understanding. In moving the map to the left, we have the one chart showing quantity separated from others. Additionally, we can click on the map to get more detail specific to the state as directed by the icon. The reordering of the heatmap puts it closer to other time-related elements while still preserving proximity to the top sales trend. This spatial relationship, along with color, reaffirms that both charts (the heatmap and top bar chart) focus on sales. The items focused on profit composition maintain their position on the right.

In altering the dashboard, we've made it clearer that the primary comparison comes from the map. Some refinements can be done via interactivity and detail-on-demand. Other means of repair may include tucking novel features into the work, such as the ability to change the chart or using natural language to ask direct questions, as we've seen earlier.

Summary

"Do what I mean, not what I say." Understanding the core principles of how we communicate with one another helps shape how we support an analytical conversation with visualizations. Analytical intent informs chart choices, interactivity, and other means of exposing information. Our charts and compositions have a register, which communicates distance in how we interact. Repair and refinement loops ensure that those in the analysis have ways to clarify and add nuance to their data conversations. The pragmatics of human language with intent and adapting to context, provides a rich space for interaction and exploration. While we may never match the nuances of human-human interaction, in the next chapter we explore promising practical and research directions to get us closer to that goal, one conversation at a time.

CHAPTER 12

Visual Communication

Without effective imagery and thought to how information is displayed, our world would be inundated with confusing instructions and a lot of text that can feel rather overwhelming. We've all seen spaces like the doors in Figure 12.1; the signs have signs. The doors have several redundant messages, such as two "Keep clear" signs, "Do not enter" in different aspect ratios, and text signs below that repeat the same verbiage. In one, *CORONAVIRUS* is written in red on green with symptoms in red italics highlighted by yellow. There is another paper above this indicating it should be read. Walls, doors, notice boards, and other communication spaces can end up being filled with alerts that no one can reasonably parse.

Let's revisit ZombieRunner Coffee, discussed in Chapter 1 and shown in Figure 12.2. The shop has two notices to communicate what's needed immediately: that only one person should enter at a time and that the area needs to be kept clear for visibility and access. Additional signs on the floor provide further information about flow and how the interaction should take place. The usage of *please* and the separation of messaging to arrows gently guide the queues as one enters the store. The setup as a whole works well as a unit to visually communicate the protocol for ordering a drink.

Imagine the same scenario with detailed verbose signage as we see in Figure 12.1 with instructions plastered all over. How would you have reacted? How would you feel at that moment while standing in line to order your beverage?

FIGURE 12.1 COVID clutter: the signs have signs.

As we think about visual communication, we need to consider not only what and how we communicate, but also *where* in the interaction this information belongs. Visual communication allows us to make use of space to pace and control how audiences take in information. Communicating a message is more than just about the message itself. It's about determining the right medium for the message based on the mood, the context, and the intended audience. In a world where attention spans are short and time is at a premium, how do we engage with our audiences more quickly, effectively, and emotionally? The premise of this chapter is to explore how imagery, specifically charts and dashboards, can interactively convey the essence of the message effectively. In other words, what are the key nuggets of visual communication through data? Let's explore some ideas.

FIGURE 12.2 Revisiting COVID arrows and signage at ZombieRunner Coffee

Do What I Mean, Not What I Say

In Chapter 9, we introduced the notion of cohesion as a way for ideas to work together so that conversation builds off the previous idea in purposeful ways to communicate the message. In the context of an analytical conversation, these ideas also need to stick together *visually*. Have you ever walked into a space that was a mishmash of styles and colors, perhaps like what you see in Figure 12.1? The experience can be rather unsettling and uncomfortable. Intentionality extends to the visual world as well. Every design choice, be it the placement of the furniture or its swatch color, for example, needs to match the intentionality of its existence. Imagine having a bunch of pure-white furniture pieces in a heavily trafficked area such as a waiting room or an odd art piece that does not match the rest of the decor in a living room and turns into an eyesore.

Functionally aesthetic charts need to support *both* the function and the aesthetics of a user's intent. As people use visual analysis tools, they expect these tools to fill in the gaps and interpret their questions in the context of the current visualization state. Having discussed some concepts and framing that support intent in Chapter 11, we can start identifying a set of characteristics for supporting how we can visually communicate information effectively. At a fundamental level, authors produce charts by encoding data properties as visual features, and readers interpret charts by decoding these properties.

Interpreting the charts involves multiple processes, including these:

- *Perceiving* and identifying important features within the chart

- Mapping those features *semantically* to the concepts they represent

- Communicating *intentionality* about the information represented in the chart and what the reader would like to explore

These processes are useful guidelines while authoring functionally aesthetic charts. As we think about visual communication in the context of an analytical conversation between the charts and the reader, the back-and-forth exchange needs to be relevant, engaging, and coherent to the topic at hand. So, let's consider how we communicate through charts and how we engage people into the conversation.

Figures 12.3, 12.4, and 12.5 show how an analytical conversation system might respond to a series of questions a user might have about a dataset with information about passengers on the ship the *Titanic*. Figure 12.3 shows a bar chart for an initial question to show all the children and adults who survived and didn't survive. In Figure 12.4, a follow-up inquiry is shown that breaks down the chart by sex and age and shows how these two data attributes are added to the original chart in a way that cohesively preserves the previous chart structure. A question to look at the correlation between age, fare, and survival in Figure 12.5 is better served with a new visualization such as a heat map to depict relationships between the data attributes %survived, Age, and Fare.

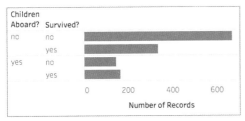

FIGURE 12.3 Analytical conversation example: The initial chart response

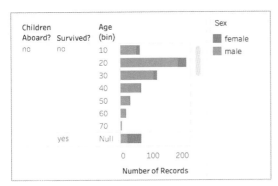

FIGURE 12.4 Analytical conversation: Expanding yet preserving original chart

Fare (bin)	Age (bin)					AGG(%survived)	
	0	10	20	30	40	0.0	100.0
$0.00	60.3	34.2	31.8	30.5	27.8		
$50.00	100.0	53.8	69.7	75.8	57.7		
$100.00	100.0	80.0	50.0	100.0	80.0		
$150.00	50.0		50.0	60.0	100.0		
$200.00		100.0	60.0	75.0	66.7		
$250.00		66.7	100.0	100.0	100.0		
$500.00				100.0			

FIGURE 12.5 Analytical conversation: Creating a new visually cohesive visualization

So how do we design interactive visualization responses that maintain visual coherence, preserving the context and structure of the conversation? In other words, we want these charts to reflect what we mean and not what we say.

Register in Charts

We introduced the concept of register in Chapter 11 as defined by Joos (1967). Joos identifies five types of register that range from very formal to highly informal:

- **Frozen:** Unchanging or ritualistic texts or recitations that are either repeated as a group or observed, such as traditional wedding vows. Interaction within a frozen text adheres to a strict script, either by reciting together or participating in a call-and-response group script. Familiarity with the script is assumed, even if no relationship exists among those in the interaction, such as singing national anthems at a sports event. Those in the stands may not know each other, but they know what performance is expected.

- **Formal:** Monologues typically feature a level of specialized vocabulary, such as religious services or college lectures. Responses generally indicate understanding or acknowledging the transmission of a message.

- **Consultative:** Dialogs within a professional setting where at least one party has expertise and questions are allowed. This is the first register with a true clarification loop that exists, allowing those involved to participate with their own goals in mind. While this type of register is less formal, the participants can be unfamiliar with each other.

- **Casual/Informal/Conversational:** Common interaction level where formality is lower and familiarity is higher.

- **Intimate:** Shorthand communication heavily reliant on familiarity.

Register will affect the pacing and presentation of a visualization. One really complex chart may suffice on its own but may need to be broken out into separate pieces when lowering the register. We saw how the conversation around *Titanic* passengers evolved in Figures 12.3 to 12.5. While the register starts at an informal level by asking a series of questions (Figures 12.3 and 12.4), the final graphic (Figure 12.5) is designed for a more consultative register. We can even see a bit of intimate register in how the labels "Children Aboard?" and "Survived?" from Figure 12.3 and Figure 12.4 pose questions in fragments; this indicates a level of comfort with what the dataset represents. In a more formal dashboard, we may change the name of the field "Children Aboard?" to "Maturity" and replace "yes/no" with "child/adult." The last chart, shown in Figure 12.5, has a more formal and psychologically distant exposition with standard labeling such as "%Survived."

Visualizations from the *New York Times* You-Draw-It series often teach those interacting with the chart how to use it first. They may include supports such as guiding a user to draw a line through key dots in a chart. Other visualizations may include a highly annotated overlay to help audiences understand the chart. Some provide several registers, allowing the information to be seen with a complex chart, or switch to a layout with a lower register and several charts. In short, they have a conversation at a lower register before presenting content at a higher register. These methods prepare the audience by engaging them and giving them the tools to understand charts that may feel like jargon otherwise.

Within the analysis, chart choices can be informed by register, taking into account the formality and familiarity of the audience. As we examine displaying amounts over time in Figure 12.6, we may find that the area chart draws undue emphasis, while the line chart is less comfortable to the audience. Blending the two lowers the register by preserving the anchor to zero while still drawing the primary emphasis to the line.

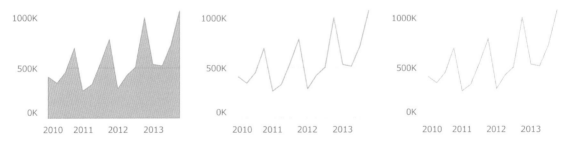

FIGURE 12.6 Adjusting the register of a chart

Our goal for the reader is to see the trend. By lowering the register, we ease access to the information by providing additional guardrails. Lines may be hard for some readers to navigate. The light shading can help introduce what the line represents while still providing a solid anchor. Within charts, we can make choices like this. We can also use the broader composition to clarify the chart.

Registers in Composition

Other ways of handling a high-register chart include leveraging techniques like detail-on-demand to make the message more readily accessible. When using the idea of register, we give ourselves as designers options for how to present the message to its intended audience.

As a whole, register impacts the ways in which we expose information. Michael Halliday, a prominent modern linguist, breaks down register by field, mode, and tenor (Lukin et al., 2011). *Field* covers the domain of the entire event or the broad topic. *Mode* includes the medium, its goal, and its narrative style. *Tenor* encompasses the social hierarchies that affect the communication, such as power dynamics and role within the setting.

In Figure 12.7, we have a dashboard where the *field* is inequality in human development. The *mode* is an interactive visualization (shown as a static one for this book) where users can hover over the individual circles to get details. Each axis is well labeled with clarifying text below to further clarify the interpretation. The relationship between income and life span is clear, and for a look at the broad theme, this visualization works well. As we dig into the *tenor*, the ability to ask questions is limited, particularly in a print medium. When presented interactively, we expect a certain tenor that allows a true conversation. In this interaction, we are limited in the types of questions we can ask by selecting filters. The tenor and register end more distant even in the interactive piece.

Online, we can hover for tooltips, but the detail is limited. This is a common story, one initially shared broadly by Hans Rosling and brilliantly reinterpreted by Lilach Manheim Laurio (2020) in Figure 12.8. Within the reinterpretation, the scatterplot is preserved. Reference lines call out the median to provide a baseline. The lines also draw you to the center, creating a quadrant and providing additional nuance. The marginal strip plots reiterate the data on each axis. The design is subtle, with these small charts falling away to the background while shaping the path for interactivity. The field and mode have not changed, but the tenor has. We are invited to participate more in the conversation as equals in the analysis.

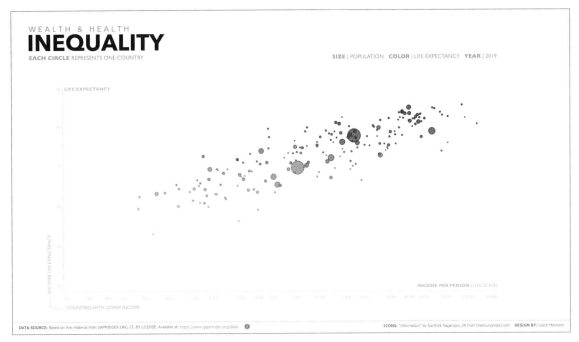

FIGURE 12.7 "Wealth and Health Inequality" re-creation by Lilach Manheim Laurio

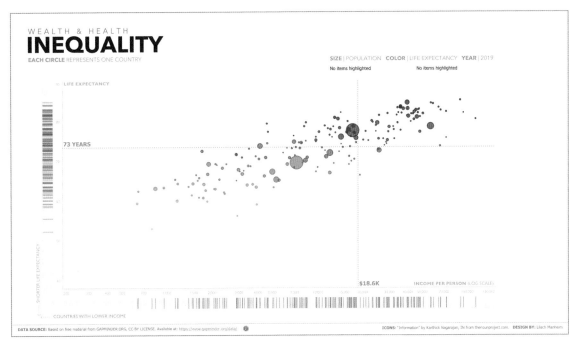

FIGURE 12.8 "Wealth and Health Inequality Deluxed" by Lilach Manheim Laurio

Manheim Laurio embraces the interactive mode to truly lower the register and improve access to the message. A reader can ask a question and get a very detailed response in an extraordinarily elegant manner. In Figure 12.9, India is selected. The original reference line fades and a second set of reference lines appear. They point to India's place on the marginal strip plots, with additional text and lines clarifying how many countries fall below that mark.

FIGURE 12.9 "Wealth and Health Inequality" by Lilach Manheim Laurio with detail-on-demand

While the primary visualization still acts as one chart (the scatterplot), the additions make parsing the country-level detail easier. A reader can begin to understand the distribution and more detail about the inequality by country. Manheim Laurio lowers the register of the scatterplot while preserving its elegance. The change in tenor makes the conversation inviting and interesting.

Mood and Metaphor

As we look at both physical places and digital spaces, they create a mood and can rely on visual metaphors. Revisit the COVID-19 signage shown earlier in this chapter. The first image (Figure 12.1) has no metaphor strategy, and the mood is at best grim. ZombieRunner Coffee (seen in Figure 12.2) makes use of a person running with coffee—we can literally follow them around the floor. Despite the seriousness, the image provides a bit of relief and eases some of the stress of navigating the pandemic requirements while providing much-needed clarification.

Figure 12.10 provides an example of metaphor and mood. Inspired by Trans-Siberian Orchestra (TSO) concerts, the visualization draws visual imagery from the lighting effects and sound systems used. The chart uses metaphor to show the two separate travel paths across the map. The changes in size and additional dots emulate laser lights as used by TSO. Both the shape and color allude to movement from lights. The light metaphor is carried over to the second chart, showing performances per day. The bar chart at the bottom uses a sound mixer's channel lights as inspiration.

The mood is designed to be playful and to draw interest toward the data. This visualization is intended for a quick glance with limited interaction. The imagery matches what the audience expects from a show: the Trans-Siberian Orchestra is known for its emphasis on lighting effects and bombastic sound.

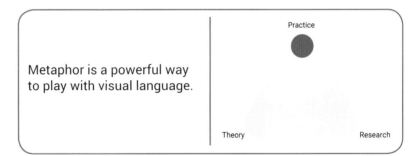

Metaphor is a powerful way to play with visual language.

Beyond Language Communication

Visuals can tell us much about the world and can leverage some of the same systems and patterns we use for language. As introduced in

Chapter 6, visual literacy—specifically graphicacy—informs how we interpret the nuanced meanings of color, sequence, visual supports, and use of space and alignment. These parameters, combined with register and the broader idea of cohesion, help us navigate what we see. They also make the difference between a door littered with signs and a friendly space with guided signage.

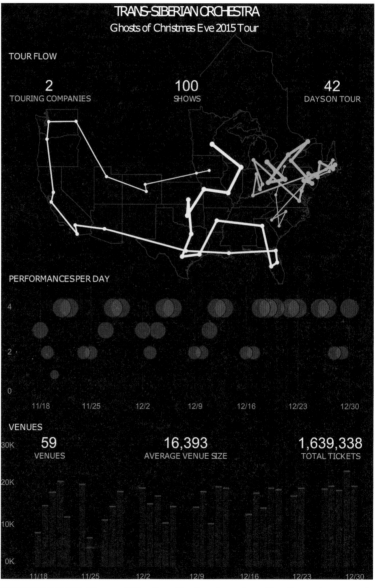

FIGURE 12.10 Trans-Siberian Orchestra visualization showcasing visual metaphors

In addition to register, design patterns can help users fall into rhythm. Common user interface conventions, such as a standard location for exiting a window, can help people appropriately respond. Ads make use of this in a hostile fashion by making the exit button hard to find. Conventional placement for exit buttons on the Web favors the upper-right corner. Learning requires time, and sometimes users select the less efficient way because it's known and more comfortable (Johnson, 2010). Familiar patterns are one way of helping users converse with visualization. The correlation in Lilach Manheim Laurio's scatterplot is well recognized among those in the social sciences and those who work with data. The words provide clarity and nuance, while the visuals depict the spirit of the message.

Deictic gestures (a concept we first introduced in Chapter 5) are part of our everyday interaction and are an effective way for exchanging information. If you are at a table dining with a group, you may use deictic communication while saying, "Please pass me *that*," while pointing to a plate of roasted Brussels sprouts. Without that deictic gesture, the other person would have difficulties in identifying what dish you actually meant. These interactions are a way to establish joint attention between two people and express where things are, how they are placed and oriented, and which spatial relations they have to each other (Diessel, 2006). In fact, deictic expressions are among the first words children learn and use (Carpenter et al., 1998), and they are present in almost every known language (Diessel, 1999).

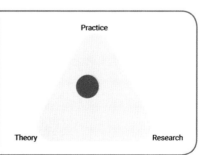

Language and pointing gestures are combined to convey meaning. We can use these deictic expressions in interactive visualizations to understand intent.

As part of visually communicating with data, modern data analysis tools enable users to directly manipulate and explore charts and dashboards. These charts use visual aids and text to help users orient themselves to click, hover, and use widgets as they interactively explore. Figure 12.11 shows the Evizeon (Hoque et al., 2018) system where a user interacts with a home sales dashboard through their mouse and speech. Selecting a bunch of points on the map while asking for "condos under 600k *here*" visually communicates the user's intent through interaction.

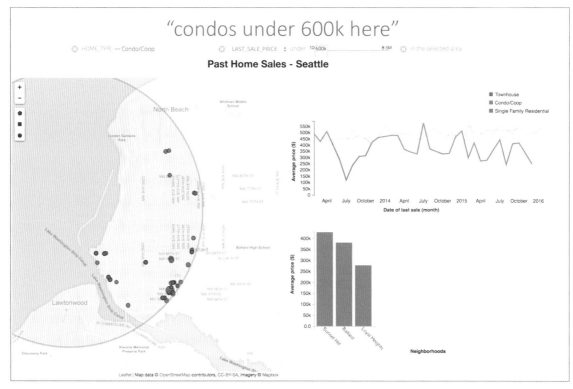

FIGURE 12.11 Deictic referencing and widget interaction in a dashboard

Deictic referencing is a means of clarifying an otherwise ambiguous statement. We visually affirm through pointing or highlighting what we want. We can also adjust messages to address cultural or knowledge differences by telling more or less about a topic.

Expansion and Contraction

Communication requires the ability to expand or contract a message based on norms within a given culture or language. *Expansion* provides more detail, sometimes adding in information that is culturally relevant or needed for the person to understand. *Contraction* preserves the same intent but discards information that isn't needed by that person. Some concepts in certain situations require greater detail than others. Consider taking a friend or relative into the office: what concepts are understood by colleagues that would need to be explained to someone outside the environment? Effective communication considers the environment but also the receiver of the message.

We've seen a few examples of messages that have been expanded (Manheim Laurio's scatterplot additions) and contracted (the final heat-map for *Titanic* survivors). Expansion and contraction can be used either to adjust a register up or down within the conversation or as a parallel discourse to bring someone up to speed. Expansion and contraction are generally done proactively. We'll see in the next chapter how they can be part of repair and refinement.

Acronyms and abbreviations are a common way of contracting information within data visualization. Key performance indicators may be better known by their acronym, KPIs. Organizations may create a layer of intimate register through the names and conventions of metrics and units. Exposing longer names through detail-on-demand techniques broadens the user base.

Summary

"You have to be in a state of play to design. If you're not in a state of play, you can't make anything." Paula Scher's quote and work embrace the idea of play as thinking (www.netflix.com/watch/80093802). Effective visual communication plays with the eye and mind to create associations. We achieve this by creating visually cohesive spaces by aligning register to where our users are and by using other systems such as pathing to help people through our visualizations. Beautiful visualization is empathetic and centered around creating understanding. Our next chapter focuses on how we repair, refine, and iterate through communication.

CHAPTER 13

Scaffolds

Let's start off by making a paper airplane. Once done, take a look at your folds and think about the process. How would you communicate the re-creation of your airplane to others? Try sketching your instructions. Now, compare your sketch to that in Figure 13.1. Are your instructions similar or different? Compare the conventions this graphic uses to yours.

This chapter is about scaffolds. While most people associate the term with building houses, we use the term as a concept of "support" when visualization authors need to help their readers build an understanding of the graphical conventions they use in their visualizations. Steve Wexler's *The Big Picture* (2021) indicates that readers often need help with building an understanding of the fundamental encodings of data, which is more than just the conventions used in a specific visualization.

Figure 13.1 relies on *scaffolding* to visually communicate the instructions. Scaffolding is a technique used in design to support the discoverability of features or functionality in a product or interface. It's also an instructional technique built around growing autonomy for its intended users. A graphical scaffold can have additional graphical elements, like building scaffolds, and have a sequential impact on the authoring, as we see in Figure 13.1. For example, step 3 in the figure teaches the turn-over convention. Sequencing is relevant to all visualization (not just instructions) because the author can use graphics and conventions to sequence the reading of visualizations. Annotations, in particular, can be used very effectively to teach conventions and to influence sequencing.

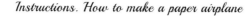

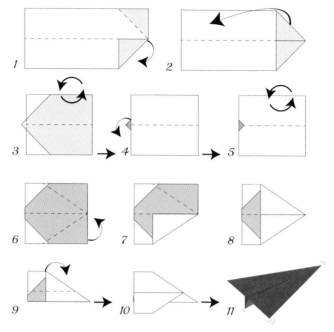

FIGURE 13.1 Instructions to help make a paper airplane
pteshka/Adobe Stock

Once you've learned the conventions of scaffolding, you can apply those scaffolding techniques to instruct how to build other plane models. For authors, the *scaffold paradigm* is about using the scaffold concept to design the graphics (both sequencing and conventions) to help their readers. When authors become more comfortable with the scaffold paradigm, they can easily skip steps. For readers, scaffolding is used to learn the specific graphical conventions used by the author of the visualization. As indicated in the book *Modern Information Retrieval* (Baeza-Yates & Ribeiro-Neto, 1999):

> *The novice user is presented with a simple interface that can be learned quickly and that provides the basic functionality of the application but is restricted in power and flexibility. Alternative interfaces are offered for more experienced users, giving them more control, more options, and more features, or potentially even entirely different interaction models. Good user interface design provides intuitive bridges between the simple and the advanced interfaces.*

These "intuitive bridges" are an intrinsic aspect of scaffolds that afford complexity and nuances, creating ease of use without oversimplifying. These bridges fill in the gaps and let those using scaffolding gain further autonomy and confidence. The North Central Regional Education Laboratory website (www.ncrel.org) describes how scaffolding fits into education and teaching:

> *Scaffolding is an instructional technique whereby the teacher models the desired learning strategy or task, then gradually shifts responsibility to the students.*

There are eight characteristics of scaffolding per McKenzie (2000):

- Provide clear directions to solve a task or interact with a physical object or software

- Clarify purpose

- Keep students on task

- Offer assessment to clarify expectations

- Point students to worthy sources

- Reduce uncertainty, surprise, and disappointment

- Deliver efficiency

- Create momentum

Chapter 1 showed how arrows, thoughtful imagery, and signage can draw a person's attention to what's important, providing active guidance to paths, direction, and relations between things. In other words, for imagery to be functionally aesthetic, the visuals need to provide appropriate cues for understanding and consuming the information they represent. These cues provide scaffolding to help set the person up for success based on the intent of what the imagery represents.

As we think about applying scaffolds to functionally aesthetic visualizations, layout, color, text, and interactive controls all play an important part in helping a user see and understand data. Let's dig deeper into ways in which these visualization scaffolds can be put into practice.

Visualization Scaffolding

As we move from tangible and familiar artifacts like paper airplanes and elevator buttons to more abstract representations of data, scaffolding plays a pivotal role in how we acclimate users to interactive visualizations and reduce friction. Visualizations should play an active part as users see, explore, and understand the data. If we just focus on instructions, they may work the first time but often detract from subsequent visits, particularly for interactive mediums. Figure 13.2 shows a visualization without styles or visual scaffolds implemented. It has a paragraph of instructions and little else to aid in its navigation.

FIGURE 13.2 Visualization without scaffolds to direct reading and interaction

Functional aesthetics created by color, alignment, sequence, text, iconography, and surrounding visual styles can create scaffolds that guide and continuously hand off greater responsibility to the consumer. Figure 13.3 takes ideas from Baeza-Yates and Ribeiro-Neto, building a world that is at a glance easy to understand but progressively introduces complexity.

From McKenzie, this dashboard creates momentum by directing attention visually to its key aspects and building in enough guardrails to keep consumers easily moving and interacting with the data. Figure 13.3 introduces a variety of scaffolding techniques:

- Clear-cut header areas

- Visual zones to support grouping of like elements

- Color for distinction (State and Shipping Class attributes)

- Call-out box for text annotation by state

- Additional text annotation (metric called out in State, speeds such as "faster," sizing for profit)

- Iconography to reiterate concepts ("faster" and "slower" labels)

- Visual emphasis around large number indicators

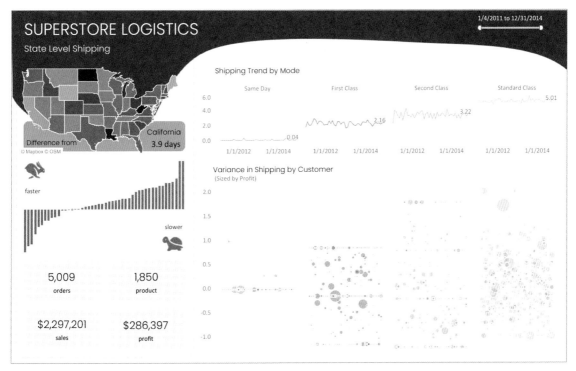

FIGURE 13.3 Dashboard using visual scaffolding techniques

Semantically, these parameters create common conventions, much like our airplane instructions. Within this template, key performance indicators like order and product counts may often live in recessed boxes. The icons may be used elsewhere in the same manner with less annotation.

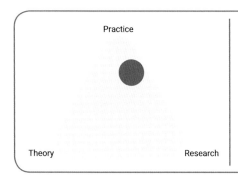

Practice

Theory

Research

Scaffolds support intent. They shape the path by rounding hard pivots and softening the turn to autonomy.

Digital spaces require additional cues to inform consumers of intent. Heavy text instructions have the challenge of referring clearly to graphical elements and fail to provide efficient support long term as users mature, seeking only intermittent reminders. Scaffolds create affordances for these jumps, allowing the consumer to take greater charge of the distances between them.

So how do we create effective scaffolds for others?

- **Balance for perception.** Chart types and formatting are informed by how they're perceived. Contrast ratios that are too low make it hard to see the information (From Chapters 1 and 2).

- **Annotate based on the medium.** Printed or static visualizations will require different scaffolding approaches than interactive mediums. Interactivity allows for greater clarification (From Chapter 3).

- **Add iconography.** Both the paper airplane instructions and the dashboard might have required you to stretch a bit the first time, but familiarity increases speed and autonomy. Leveraging familiar and consistent brand assets also helps (From Chapter 4).

- **Identify vague and ambiguous concepts.** Vague concepts, like faster and slower, benefit from additional clarification. Comparisons can help clarify and set the tone (From Chapter 5), and iconography can provide a mental image (From Chapter 4).

- **Take into account fluency with visualizations.** Fluency affects chart choices, annotation levels, and teaching tools within the visualization or outside it (From Chapter 6).

- **Trace back to familiar sources.** We alter data to fit the analysis, sometimes combining columns and check boxes into unfamiliar column names. Scaffolds can help expose the data origins as needed (From Chapter 7).

- **Use size and scale effectively for clear discernment.** Size both creates a visual hierarchy and impacts legibility (From Chapter 8).

- **Use cohesion to ease the transition.** Text, color, sequence, space, alignment, and style all create cues about the "world" that the visualization creates. For example, a control that toggles date truncation should be near the chart it affects (From Chapter 9).

- **Use appropriate register.** Scaffolds can provide nuance around register. Are your users well acquainted with interactive visualizations? Your scaffold will likely be more intimate and visual, and less comprehensive. Users with less familiarity will require a more consultative register that provides both images and text and greater expansion techniques throughout the visualization (From Chapters 11 and 12).

- **Build a language in addition to an interface.** We can use semantic techniques to start, clarify, and refine our understanding. Note how the paper airplane instruction uses different arrow styles for folding, turning, and progressing to next steps (From Chapter 12).

- **Balance emphasis to draw attention to key elements.** In the next chapter, we'll explore how to use the parameters for cohesion to draw focus to the task and intent. Guide users by indicating preferred actions. Ease complex tasks by using progressive disclosure.

Visual scaffolds pave the way toward greater consumer autonomy. Like the elevator, digital buttons and other widgets perform predictably (including responses such as pinch-to-zoom) so that authors and readers can unconsciously use them everywhere. We can leverage these scaffolds to expand creating visualizations for consumption. Additionally, the interface should predict the user's needs so that the experience is trustworthy, productive, and delightful. As readers grow more comfortable in the digital space, we can move them from directed exploration to a true conversation around data discovery.

Scaffolding Data Discovery

Search interfaces have changed how we think about information. We've become accustomed to searching for information with hints and breadcrumbs in apps and search boxes gently guiding us as we type away. Even with data exploration, a person begins with some vaguely formed question and gradually refines the search query to be more concrete to obtain the desired information. This activity can be a complex and cognitively demanding activity for this person. The onus for a successful search activity is on the searcher, who must be able to recall context from past search tasks and appropriate sense-making with the data at play.

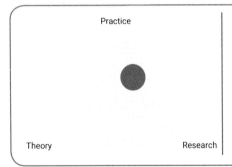

Information seeking has moved away from assuming that the information goal is well-formed; even when users are deliberately seeking information, they do not necessarily know exactly what it is they want.

Autocompletion is a useful UI feature for supporting this complex activity, displaying suggestions within proximity as searchers type their queries in the flow of their search tasks. Whether you are shopping for a new pair of shoes or searching for a good place to eat in a new city, words pop up in the search box as suggestions that help complete your query. The juxtaposition of familiar and related words, images, and surrounding information helps searchers clarify their intent. The ubiquity of autocompletion in search shows its effectiveness as a scaffold.

As Lilach Manheim Laurio (2021) explains, the first step in designing a system that helps with information seeking is to understand your audience, their tasks, and their information requirements. While information seeking in a visual analysis task bears similarities to other forms of search, there are differences. Visual analysis involves the need to understand the characteristics of the underlying data and the various domains included in the dataset (e.g., range, level of detail of the attributes), a challenge we describe in Chapter 7. Developing queries both analytically and visually requires thinking about the fields available, aggregating measures to the appropriate groups, and considering the best chart to answer the thought. One of the challenges for users in the context of visual analysis tools is having to think about the fields available, aggregating measures to the appropriate groups, and at the same time crafting a question in language form.

When users find themselves clarifying their queries again and again, it's often when their questions are too broad, too narrow, or simply not formed in a way that the system can understand. Users need guidance to understand whether they are finding new insights with the visualization they are interacting with. A lack of guidance can interfere with an accurate sense of progress toward the analytical goal. Autocompletion in these natural language systems is rather basic and tends to focus on syntactic completion of the users' queries without any suggestions or helpful previews of the data. So, is there a way that we can develop adequate scaffolds to help with autocompletion in a visual analysis context?

Sneak Pique is an interactive visual autocompletion tool developed to address this problem (Setlur et al., 2020). The goal of the tool is to help anyone, regardless of skill set, to interact with data using natural language. Sneak Pique brings the fluidity of in-situ suggestions to analytical expressions typical of visual analysis tasks. Like search, the tool leverages knowledge of common paths and behaviors to support consumers in their analytical journey. The visual autocompletion scaffolds are expressed as a set of text- and widget-based autocompletion suggestions that provide data previews of the results in the dashboard.

Figure 13.4 and Figure 13.5 show examples of autocompletion suggestions generated in Sneak Pique as a user explores a dataset of coronavirus cases around the world. In Figure 13.4, a user types the query "show me cases in" and is prompted with map and calendar autocompletion widgets providing previews of the geospatial and temporal data frequencies, respectively. "In" can reflect queries that focus on both place and time. The user clicks on China in the map. As a follow-up, the widget proceeds to find a range of cases by prompting the user to consider time with "between." In Figure 13.5, Sneak Pique displays a pair of date and numerical range widgets with corresponding histograms of data frequencies to help guide the user to pick a valid range based on the underlying data.

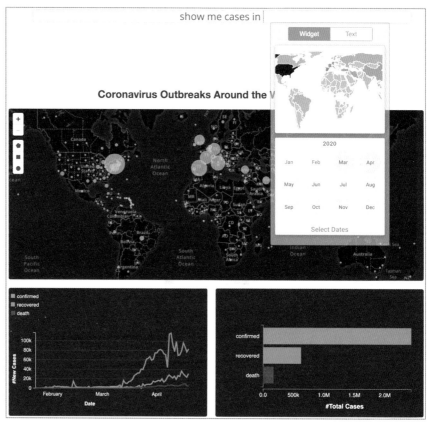

FIGURE 13.4 Sneak Pique showing map and calendar autocompletion widgets
Setlur et al.

Scaffolds such as Sneak Pique refine search and shape the path toward richer dialog. It allows users to code-switch between visual interactions and written requests, creating an interaction that is multimodal between graphs and text. As we saw in Chapter 10, text can help reaffirm and clarify what the visual shows. As we move from refining to conversations, we'll explore new ways to have conversations with data through natural language.

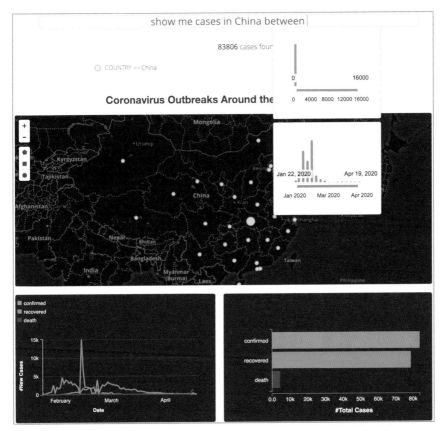

FIGURE 13.5 Sneak Pique showing a pair of date and numerical range widgets
Setlur et al.

Scaffolding Natural Language Recommendations

Popular visualization tools like Tableau, Microsoft's Power BI, and Qlik now offer ways to interact with data through natural language interaction. These interfaces make it possible for people to directly ask questions about their data and specify visualizations without having to learn the mechanics of designing visualizations. Natural language lowers the learning curve, allowing users to get answers while using a familiar language. As you saw in the preceding section, autocomplete can assist users in creating queries and provide a smooth experience.

Despite these assistive features like autocompletion, asking questions during data analysis remains a challenging task for two key reasons:

- **Cold starts and lukewarm findings**. Formulating questions requires users to know about the data domain along with potential attributes and patterns to query. You saw earlier in this chapter how to address unfamiliarity through both exploration and discovery. Asking questions can be particularly challenging when starting a new analysis or when exploring a dataset for the first time.

- **Ambiguity around natural language interaction.** Practical limitations of the interface's understanding capabilities often require users to phrase their utterances in specific ways so the underlying system can best interpret them. Without a clear understanding of a natural language interface's interpretation capabilities, users often end up "guessing" utterances, thus being more prone to system failures.

To address these challenges, a system called *Snowy* (Srinivasan & Setlur, 2021) explores the idea of generating contextual utterance recommendations during visual analysis. Snowy provides several scaffolds while a user is exploring a dataset using natural language queries. To assist with the "cold start" problem during data analysis, Snowy infers potentially interesting patterns from the underlying IMDb movies dataset and suggests analytic inquiries one may want to begin exploring the data with (Figure 13.6). Once a user types in a query or selects a recommendation, Snowy creates a visualization in the current view and suggests follow-up utterances to adjust the current view and drill down into specific data subsets (Figure 13.7). As the user selects marks in the visualization, Snowy recommends utterances that are contextually relevant to the selected points. The selection acts as a deictic reference, refining the questions to these values (Figure 13.8).

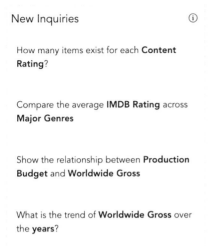

New Inquiries ⓘ

How many items exist for each **Content Rating**?

Compare the average **IMDB Rating** across **Major Genres**

Show the relationship between **Production Budget** and **Worldwide Gross**

What is the trend of **Worldwide Gross** over the **years**?

FIGURE 13.6 Example of utterance recommendations in Snowy
Srinivasan and Setlur, 2021

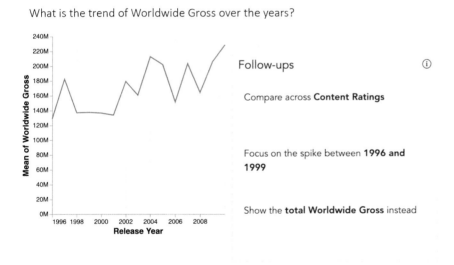

What is the trend of Worldwide Gross over the years?

Follow-ups ⓘ

Compare across **Content Ratings**

Focus on the spike between **1996 and 1999**

Show the **total Worldwide Gross** instead

FIGURE 13.7 Snowy suggests follow-up utterances based on the current chart in view
Srinivasan and Setlur, 2021

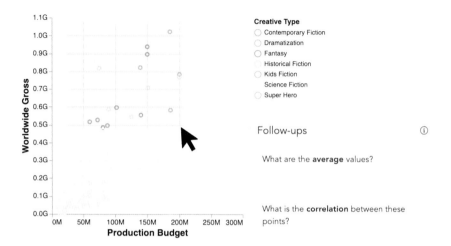

FIGURE 13.8 Snowy recommends deictic utterances when a user selects marks in the chart.
Srinivasan and Setlur, 2021

> Scaffolds can provide analytic guidance for knowing *what* to ask and *how* to phrase utterances. The two in tandem can help a user explore their data in their analytic workflows without getting bogged down by the mechanics of forming a question and determining the data to explore.

Snowy provides several scaffolds to start and move through exploring a dataset. The interface decreases the need for the user to guess how to interact with it by recommending several "scripts" one can use with it. The tool bolds key points within the utterance, allowing users to scan to the highlighted points and move quickly. Snowy uses deictic referencing to create a more conversational and intimate register in the interaction.

Natural language is one place where scaffolding can support data exploration. Let's continue exploring how scaffolding can help mediate other forms of analytical conversation.

Analytical Conversation to Repair and Refine

Smart assistants and chatbots are examples of conversational interfaces. These interfaces have become common for tasks such as simple fact-finding about the weather, making a restaurant reservation, or even doing bank transactions. However, there is profound asymmetry in analytical conversation between humans and computers, including smart assistants and chatbots. The key scaffolding for success is that the human knows the domains supported by these smart assistants and chatbots.

Human-to-human conversation takes into account the idea of register. Their constructs vary based on where they occur. Conversational interfaces have limited registers available. They know only so much about where the conversation is happening, who is engaging, and what else could come into play. Online information increased computational power, and machine learning seeks to fill in the gaps and expand both the repertoire and registers available to conversational interfaces. Whereas early augmented conversations depended on a tightly controlled script, new natural language programs can engage on more topics with explicit instructions.

Register impacts how much information is explicitly shared in an utterance versus inferred. In such conversations, there is an expectation that the information shared is relevant and that intentions are conveyed. Grice's Cooperative Principle (1975) states that participants in a conversation normally attempt to be truthful, relevant, concise, and clear. Consider this conversation snippet:

> Lizzie: Is there another carton of juice?
> Milo: I'm going to the supermarket in a few minutes!

A human who reads this conversation will easily infer that at the moment, there is no juice, and that Milo will head out to the store and buy some juice. Milo didn't ignore Lizzie but answered in an intimate register. Through closure skills or *implication*, we can infer a concise and clear answer: Milo is going to the store *because* there is no juice. This will happen soon, as Milo is headed out the door.

Examples like these prompted Grice to propose various maxims where the cooperative principle explains the implication process. Grice argued that for a conversation to support meaningful back-and-forth exchange between people, it must follow the principle "Make your conversational contribution such as is required, at the stage at which it occurs, by the accepted purpose or direction of the talk exchange in which you are engaged." Grice divided the cooperative principle into four conversational maxims:

1. **Maxim of Quantity**: Be informative. Provide all the information necessary for the purpose of the current conversational exchange. Do not make your contribution more informative than is required but ensure that the response addresses the intent in the question. For example, the conversation snippet below has just the right amount of information about the nearest store along with its opening time.

   > *human: When does the nearest grocery store open?*
   > *chatbot: The nearest grocery store is at 48 Main Street, and it opens at 8:00 a.m.*

   Violations of this maxim are either a terse chatbot response saying, "8:00 a.m." or too detailed a response such as, "There are three grocery stores located within a radius of 10 miles. The nearest store is 1.4 miles away at 48 Main Street and opens at 8:00 a.m."

2. **Maxim of Quality**: Be truthful. Avoid stating information that you believe might be wrong. If you do choose to include it, then provide a disclaimer that points to your doubts regarding this information. For example, in the conversation snippet below, the chatbot greets the human and sets the appropriate expectations regarding its capabilities of understanding the conversation.

   > *chatbot: Welcome! I'm a virtual assistant that can help you book a concert ticket. You can ask me simple questions or follow my lead. Remember that I'm not a human and can't understand everything. Shall we start?*
   > *human: Sure!*

A violation of this maxim is a chatbot greeting that simply says, "Hi! You can ask me anything about the concert." This example does not set up the conversation for success as the chatbot is not transparent about its capabilities, leading to unrealistic user expectations.

3. **Maxim of Relation**: Be relevant. Make sure that all the information you provide is relevant to the current exchange and omit irrelevant information. For example, in the conversation snippet below, even though the human did not respond to the chatbot's initial question, the chatbot provides a response relevant to the human's question. Providing a follow-up inquiry after the relevant response is a useful way of directing the human back to the original question that the chatbot posed or indicating the presence of other related tasks.

> *chatbot: Would you like to book an appointment?*
> *human: When's the next availability?*
> *chatbot: The next available appointment is at 11 a.m. on Friday. Would you like to make an appointment or modify an existing one?*

A violation of this maxim is a chatbot response, "Please answer yes or no" to the human's question, "When's the next availability?" In this case, the chatbot is not providing a relevant response to the human and continues to focus on its original intent of booking an appointment.

4. **Maxim of Manner**: Be clear and concise. Avoid obscurity of expression and ambiguous language that is difficult to understand. Ask for clarification or follow-up inquiry to support conversation turns. Unlike the previous three maxims that primarily focus on what is said during the conversational exchange, the Maxim of Manner focuses on how that exchange occurs. For example, in the conversation snippet below, the chatbot is conveying its thought process to the human clearly by sharing and requesting information in a turn-by-turn manner.

> *chatbot: Please hold while I connect you to a representative.*
> **(After 20 seconds)**
> *chatbot: Sorry, no one's available right now. Would you like me to send an email? They will respond within 24 hours.*
> *human: Yes!*

> *chatbot: "Great. To send the email, I first need some information about you. What's your first name?*

A violation of this maxim is a chatbot response that simply ends the conversation without providing a follow-up option, such as, for example, "Sorry, no one's available right now. Bye-bye!"

Gricean maxims provide a basic framework for creating conversation scaffolds. We can support cooperative conversation by making sure conversational interfaces adopt the appropriate register, provide relevant context, and evaluate utterances with a broader spectrum of knowledge applicable to the analytical conversation.

These multimodal conversations create a proliferation of new potential entry points, platforms, and styles of interaction. One emerging interaction modality is the *analytical chatbot* (Setlur & Tory, 2022), a software application that engages in a back-and-forth natural language dialog with the user about data. Like other types of chatbots, analytical chatbots are designed to simulate the way a human would act as a conversational partner and therefore need to employ natural language as both an input and output mechanism. They may additionally employ visualizations in their responses.

Figure 13.9 shows an early Slack integration entitled cha(t)bot, a gentle nod to Tableau founder Christian Chabot. We can see a data conversation evolve around Titanic data, complete with a data profile, a bar chart with text description, and a filter to help with repair and refinement. Secondary data orality enables this conversation to occur quickly and proficiently.

The promise that natural language will make visual analysis tools more approachable has led to a secondary data orality emerging. Where early conversations around data meant using written or spoken language to explain charts (as you saw in Chapter 6), secondary data orality merges *both* mediums playing a pivotal role in the conversation (Tufekci, 2021). To truly understand the conversation, one needs to be proficient in both mediums to engage. As graphicacy becomes as integral as numeracy and literacy, our technologies must shift to support the new and novel ways we will continue to interact with ourselves and future generations.

FIGURE 13.9 Scaffolds in cha(t)bot, a Slack interface
Setlur and Tory, 2022

Summary

Scaffolds allow people to scale rapidly by creating a system that feeds learning. We can create scaffolds directly in our visualizations by following practices that create cohesion and leverage semantics to support intent. Natural language promises to expand capabilities and bridge the gap between numeracy, literacy, and graphicacy by enabling conversations to occur directly in the visualization and the data. As data conversations expand to include natural language, a secondary data orality is emerging, one that intermarries other conversation skills with graphicacy. Continuing the spirit of guiding the consumer in their analytical journey, in the next chapter, we explore how emphasis can be used to draw attention to important aspects of the message through thoughtful design.

CHAPTER 14

Balancing Emphasis

While scaffolds guide and help a user to do a task, emphasis draws attention to salient points in our visualization's messaging by design. In art, we juxtapose a lone red apple against an arrangement of light green apples. The contrast draws the eye, regardless of where the red apple is located in the arrangement. In conversation, we may intone a particular word: we want *that* apple. The emphasis makes clear what the literal sum of our words do not: we're not only making a choice, but no other apple is comparable. If we shift the intonation or italics—we want that *apple*—we can expect that the apple may be among pears or other fruits. Emphasis also imparts additional meaning through semantics and intent.

Languages use a variety of techniques to shift the focus. The English language, for example, cares a lot about word order. Shifting sentences around can add some emphasis, but intonation and use of italics and underlining in print are common ways of drawing focus to a word or idea. ASL may alter the movement of the sign either by making it larger, or providing a different speed from the rest of the utterance, or by holding a particular aspect of the sign for longer than expected.

As we shift focus to emphasis in charts, we can call attention to particular data attributes and marks. Do we want to take note of the trend or distinct values? Are we highlighting a very precise number, or do we need to show-case the uncertainty of the metric? These questions will help direct not only the charts we choose but how we design and arrange them.

Individual Choices

We use emphasis in charts to highlight particular characteristics reflected in the data and to best match our analytical intent. We can use our chart choices themselves to create emphasis or the visual supports in and around the chart to draw focus. Our intent informs our choices.
Figure 14.1 shows two chart types for the same data and general pur-pose. Both bars over time (a) and line chart (b) display monthly profit over several years. As you look at these two chart choices, think about what they emphasize.

FIGURE 14.1 Chart selection affects emphasis.

At an initial glance, the bar chart makes clear what the line chart does not: that profits are quite low *frequently*. The values in a bar chart clearly have a direction-positive or negative. Even without additional emphasis, the few values above zero are clearly the exception. Is there a chart where it's easier to summarize the general pattern? The line chart, while heavily jagged, makes it easier to see where the *average* profit might fall, some-where around −500. The selection of either option will balance the chart's purpose, both individually and within the greater visualization as we also saw in Chapter 5.

The emphasis in each of these charts can be further refined. In addition to what they already display through position, we can make both the bar and line marks thicker or thinner. We can highlight the negative values through color. We can draw greater attention to the attributes that support the data marks, such as the zero line. We can modify the line chart from Figure 14.1 and adapt it slightly to draw emphasis to both the negative values by adding a line as shown in chart (a) of Figure 14.2 and calling out each negative value as shown in chart (b) of Figure 14.2.

FIGURE 14.2 Emphasis only on the zero line (a) and additional emphasis on negative values (b)

Chart (b) in Figure 14.2 balances the task of the overall trend by drawing emphasis to all the values below zero. To achieve this, we made the line itself thicker, matched the dots to the zero line, and worked carefully with the formatting options to balance where the attention went on the chart.

Collective Choices

As we move from individual charts to compositions, we have to think about the whole piece. Map generalization techniques (discussed in Chapters 1 and 8) are a good example for how important parts of a map are more emphasized than the less important ones. Focusing on points of interest and turns along the way provides a useful and delightful navigational experience. It's important to be cohesive in the way we go about guiding and communicating our message to the consumer. Amy Alberts (2017) found through her studies with eye-tracking data that people look on dashboards when the task is not clear and context is not set. Revisiting concepts from Chapter 9, we can scaffold people's visual attention by making visualizations cohesive with the following parameters:

- Color
- Sequence
- Visual supports and style
- Use of space (shape)
- Alignment

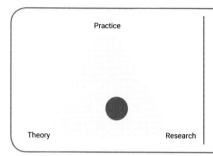

Practice

Theory

Research

Emphasis helps guide users through a visualization. How users look at a visualization at first glance versus how they scan in search of a task differs.

In Chapter 13, we used these visual attributes as parameters to create scaffolds. Now we'll revisit them to balance emphasis in our visualization's message. Let's look at a dashboard with *minimal emphasis* in Figure 14.3. Within the title, "Profit Ratio by Key Divisions," the user is cued to a control to toggle the metric used within the dashboard. It's currently set to Profit Ratio to explore food item sales for a fictional coffee and tea shop. The dashboard uses a warm brown palette to set the tone, and the charts are sequenced to draw the consumer first to the high-level categories split out by regions, then to products, and last to monthly trends. A primary analytical goal is to identify where profit and loss occur.

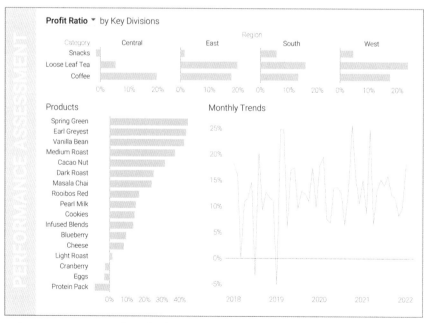

FIGURE 14.3 A starting dashboard template with minimal emphasis

Designing in this manner—where emphasis is austere—helps pinpoint what should be emphasized to support the task. Do we want those using the dashboard to focus on negative values, regional performance, or something else? We can draw attention by designing to salient points.

Most dashboards designed by analysts for consumer consumption strive to support strategic action; we want them to investigate the negative values or clearly understand regional impacts. Figure 14.4 directs the consumer's attention to all the negative values by highlighting them in yellow. Just like the red apple juxtaposed against light green apples, *strategic emphasis* draws attention to those values.

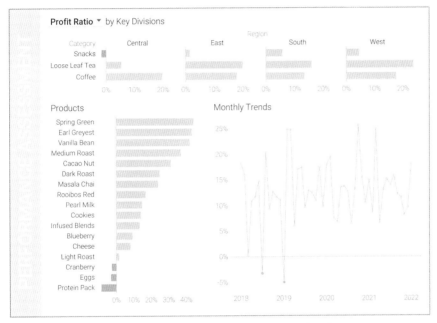

FIGURE 14.4 A small change with color alters emphasis.

Strategy supports intent. When we start with minimal emphasis, it's easier to add focus points to direct attention to the salient points. Designing with minimal emphasis requires thinking differently about the design process: rather than starting at the chart level and working to combine them at the end, we turn our attention first to getting the base elements right and seasoning the sauce as a cohesive unit. It's iterative, exploring the impacts of both small and large tweaks, and taking a step back to understand what it does to the whole piece.

Correcting Common Problems

Many data visualization tools start with the chart, which forms the basic building blocks of a visualization. From there, charts can be combined to create cohesive compositions in the form of dashboards, analytical applications, and journalistic pieces. Tension in design exists between individual parts created by charts and the greater whole. One key reason for purchasing this book could be this very problem: you've followed all of the conventional advice and something still feels off. The medium and the mode affect how the composition comes together, a topic we'll explore in greater detail in Chapter 15.

Overemphasis is a common problem. In the practitioner world, emphasizing all the points often stems from a lack of clarity, leading to a lack of results. Decisions made at the chart level become overwhelming at the composition level. Figure 14.5 shows an iteration of the Profit Ratio dashboard where decisions at the chart level become overemphasized at the composition level. In Chapter 1, we showed the Stroop effect. Colors that align with our expectations are easier to process. Coffee is colored a dark brown, tea a lighter brown, and snacks are a mustard color that align with our mental images. While the colors make sense for the first chart, they become distracting in later charts. The design choices *overemphasize* the importance of the category and don't help with understanding successive charts.

Overemphasis creates distraction and loses focus. In English, we can put text in italics to highlight *a key point*. In excess, the effect is lost. Color, in particular, can create unintended emphasis depending on the weighting and balance between colors. To correct the overemphasis on color, while preserving the original goal of using color to segment category, we'll refactor the design using the other parameters like shape, sequence, visual supports, and alignment to effectively communicate the intent of comparing categories.

Figure 14.6 separates the line chart into three panes. It preserves the original color choices but uses the other parameters to emphasize the notable differences. At a glance, consumers can clearly see that the profit ratio of snacks is lower over time continuously. The dimensions on the bar chart are swapped. Region now displays along the row, and the category splits the data across the columns. The effect of this makes the lower values of snacks more readily apparent, and the eye can travel down from the line chart to the remaining charts due to the shared color but also the strategic alignment. The final change concerns products: turning the bar chart into a scatterplot allows adding sales while reducing the size needed.

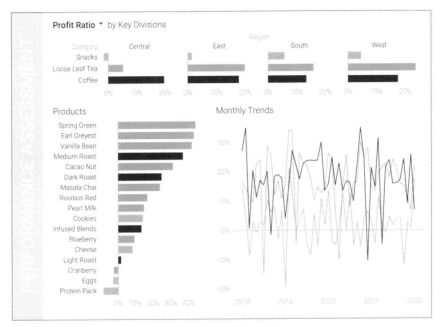

FIGURE 14.5 Overemphasis on color without using other parameters

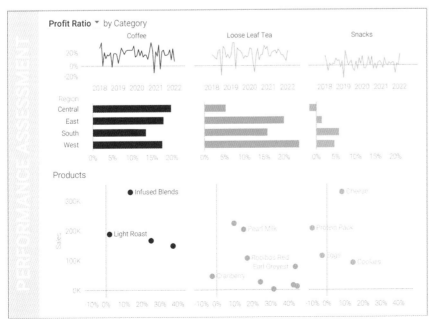

FIGURE 14.6 Corrected emphasis by altering parameters and chart selection

As a whole composition, the pieces work in isolation but leverage functional aesthetics to create clarity. A legend is not needed because the color cueing is clear and supports the eye. The analytical tasks are widened—consumers can clearly compare the categories in line with the original intent but can also spot lower profit products. The scatterplot also makes it easier to judge the scale of the problem with protein packs under snacks. Not only is the profit low, but sales are also fairly high. Where the profit losses between eggs and cranberry tea are similar, the sales are not.

Another problem in the practitioner space is the use of *ambiguous emphasis*. We want consumers to see the profit ranges and dual encode by using both the length of the bar and color. In Figure 14.7, we can see that the implementation has the opposite effect of what we desire: the positives are clearly visible and the negatives, as smaller absolute values, fade to the background. It becomes very easy to miss the problem areas of the negative values.

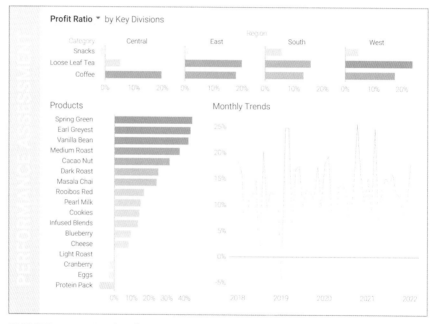

FIGURE 14.7 Emphasis created by dual encoding of charts

We can correct this issue by removing the full-color ramp and instead using only one shade of the blue and coral. Figure 14.8 shows two iterations where the ramp has been simplified. The first is to weigh the colors equally while the second lightens the blue to de-emphasize it. Notice what draws your attention.

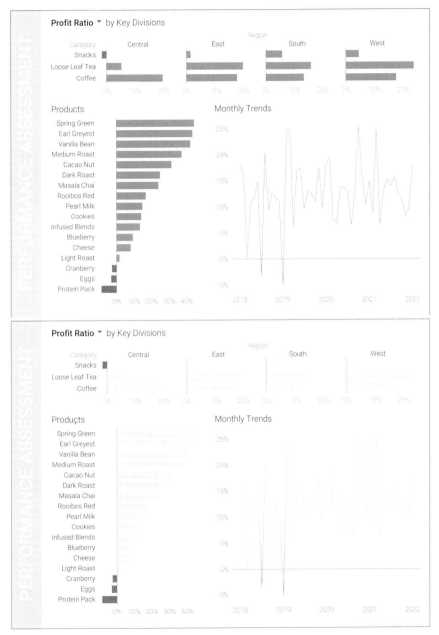

FIGURE 14.8 Iterations on strategic emphasis

Further iterations of Figure 14.8 could also get closer to the example shown in Figure 14.4. The more the positive values are de-emphasized, the more the negative values will come forward. Emphasis is a powerful way to direct attention *intentionally*. Done well, it supports the consumer in understanding the data.

When crafting visualizations, we need to be aware of what our emphasis communicates and how the message snaps together. Visual communication uses a variety of means to relay a message with graphical alignment playing a major role in understanding.

View Snapping

Graphical alignment and snapping dates back at least as far as Ivan Sutherland's Sketchpad system (1963). Using the system, Ivan Sutherland showed that computer graphics could be used for *both* artistic and technical purposes using novel human-computer interactions. A user could begin with a vague notion of what they want to draw, then collaborate with Sketchpad to layer in design constraints and iteratively refine the desired graphic. Design constraints from Sketchpad inspired several object alignment methods that are widely used in drawing programs such as PowerPoint, Photoshop, and OmniGraffle.

The premise of snapping objects together also applies to dashboards with multiple charts. However, the idea goes beyond simple graphical alignment to more of a *semantic* alignment to help the consumer see and understand the data. *View snapping* is a technique that semantically aligns charts along one or more common axes in a dashboard. When a view is placed on a canvas, it's "aligned" with the other views based on shared data properties such as common attributes, visual encodings, and axes. It's balancing the emphasis of information among views that share common semantic characteristics.

Let's go over an example. Figure 14.9 shows two sets of bar charts: one for Category and the other for Products, with Profit Ratio being the common numerical attribute. The bar chart sets are placed one above the other with the intent of being useful for comparison. However, the task is challenging with different Profit Ratio ranges on each of the x-axes. You find your eyes darting back and forth between the Category bar charts and the Products bar charts, mentally trying to compare the bar lengths, even though it's like comparing apples and oranges.

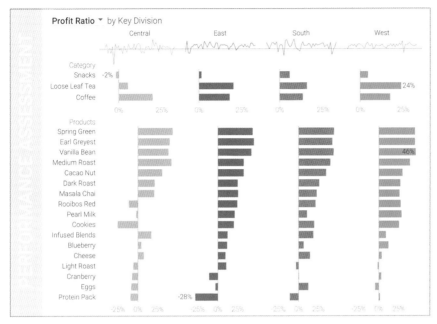

FIGURE 14.9 Dashboard without view snapping

Truthfulness in visualization is key. Depicting charts in a way that can be misinterpreted or is analytically difficult to understand goes against the principles of functional aesthetics and can even be detrimental. Figure 14.10 shows view snapping in action where the Category bar charts are snapped to Products, sharing a common readjusted x-axis. The alignment and shared colors make the dashboard cleaner and balanced, but most importantly, emphasize the focus on comparing. These charts can be read and viewed as one unit despite being two separate charts.

The challenges of mistrust and misinformation have prompted the research community to explore tools for suggesting and guiding authors to create responsible

Snapping of charts for alignment supports harmony and balance, inviting consumers to trust and converse with the information that's represented.

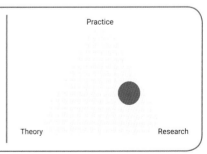

charts. Authors may not be aware of existing guidelines and lack expert design knowledge when composing multi-view visualizations. "Semantic snapping" (Kristiansen et al., 2021) is one approach for guiding the design of effective multi-view visualizations. Algorithms detect and suggest resolutions for conflicting, misleading, or ambiguous designs as well as provide suggestions for alternative presentations.

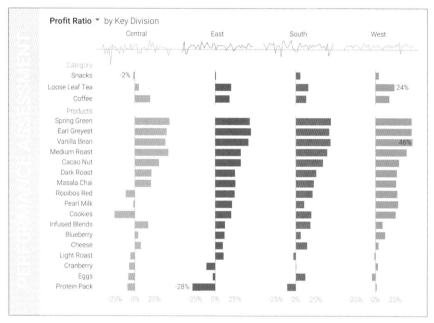

FIGURE 14.10 Dashboard with view snapping on the Profit Ratio axis

You've probably realized that there are common ties between concepts discussed in this chapter and the previous ones—we talk about the bento box in Chapter 1 and the mantelpiece design in Chapter 2. These concepts share an intrinsic appreciation for space, harmony, and proportion. There is a deliberate intent in the purpose and assemblage of the artifact, far greater than the sum of its parts.

We end this chapter with Figure 14.11, Figure 14.12, and Figure 14.13 to hopefully inspire you to think of ways to bring view snapping into skillful practice. Kelly Martin shows how text, charts, and legends can work harmoniously together as first-class citizens. The attention to detail is apparent where the legend of Cable TV consumers visually aligns with the peak in the area graph. It's an analytical work of art that takes balancing emphasis to a deeper level in the craft. We will sign off here by letting you think about ways where you can bring visual poetry into your analytical practice.

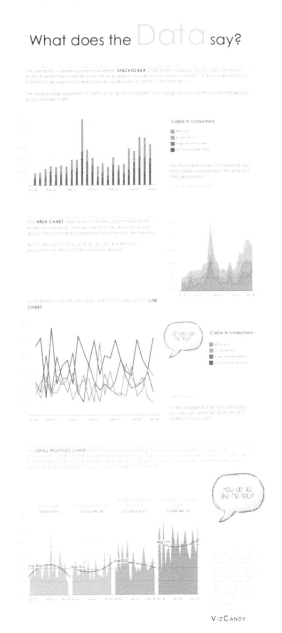

FIGURE 14.11 Kelly Martin's visual poetry as originally designed *VizCandy*

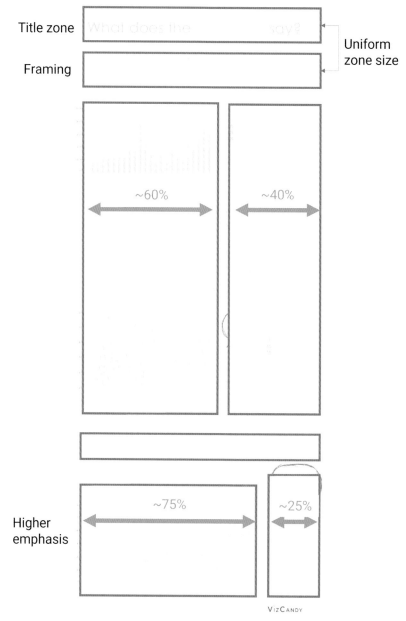

FIGURE 14.12 Kelly Martin's visual poetry by use of space
VizCandy

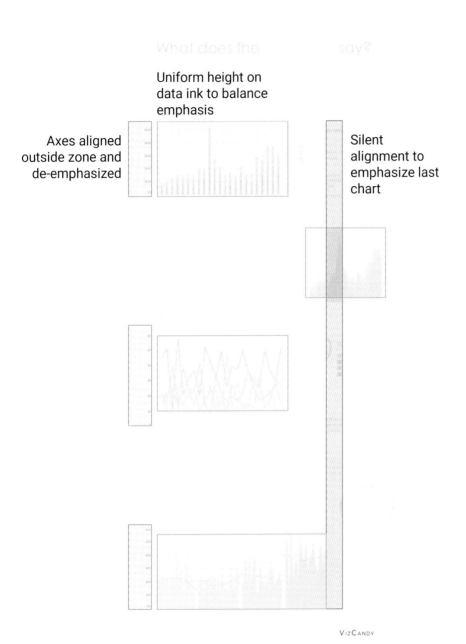

Uniform height on data ink to balance emphasis

Axes aligned outside zone and de-emphasized

Silent alignment to emphasize last chart

VizCandy

FIGURE 14.13 Kelly Martin's visual poetry with alignment
VizCandy

Summary

Emphasis is an important tool for communicating intentionality and capturing the viewer's attention. In this chapter, we discussed how we can balance the visual weights of chart elements, marks, and colors in space. Creating functionally aesthetic visualizations goes beyond the visual aspects of harmony and alignment; the semantics of the data inform the process. In the next chapter, we'll take inspiration from Marshall McLuhan and look at mode and why he says, "The medium is the message."

CHAPTER 15

Mode

How much does the medium affect the message? As TV rolled out, McLuhan et al. (1967) looked at the new way of delivering information, or the medium, and noted how it changed communication. Communication leverages the form in which it is contained. Let's revisit our restaurant and take a look at the menu. As you peruse the offerings, what medium is the menu? Is it a paper menu, a digital one on your device, or one that is multi-sensory through audio, video, and digital display?

In the age of COVID-19, menus are far more likely to be accessed digitally. The medium might be a large screen, a tablet, or a phone, but the *mode*—or the way we interact with the medium—is fairly consistent across these devices. Restaurants use QR code menus that interact with smartphones. Customers can scan the code at the table with their phones, and the menu instantly appears on their screens, as seen in Figure 15.1. Digital menus open a host of new possibilities for restaurants to display menu items in an appealing way to diners.

The mode helps us decide how we interact: whether we scroll, click, and swipe across the screen or turn pages and run our fingers along the items. Digital menus have the advantage of displaying detailed photos of plates, appetizers, and desserts, allowing us to learn more on our own without engaging the waiter. Bright displays give restaurants options to change colors, fonts, and designs around menu items. Restaurants can run promotions on a set schedule, say, based on the season, and update the menus without having to reprint. The menu on a cold rainy day could easily feature comforting ramen, while on a hot day with lots of sunshine, it may prioritize salad and sushi offerings.

FIGURE 15.1 Digital menus introduce a new mode for food ordering. *Hispanolistic/Getty Images*

Even before COVID-19, restaurants have experimented with taking the menu digital. Online menus allow diners to explore offerings and get excited about a meal beforehand. They integrate well with delivery and accessibility applications as well as novel advances in automated order taking. Experiments with ordering through voice and text chatbots allow a digital menu to adapt, showing recommended pairings or past orders. We've only just scratched the surface of what digital menus can do.

While digital menus create an interactive mode, paper menus aren't going away entirely. Restaurants often distill their whole aesthetic into a paper menu. Is the menu carefully bound into a leatherette cover, tied together with string, or quickly printed on standard copy paper? What texture does the paper have? The attributes of the menu often convey as much about price and experience as the building does. Just like books, traditional menus invite a sensory experience created by engaging touch as much as vision. The mode of paper menus is less individually customized— physical menus can show wear from use, unless frequently printed and replaced. COVID-19 sanitation requirements and contact tolerance between customers urged a faster shift to digitization.

Mode depends on the task at hand, the context, and even the local culture and norms of the target audience. Menus demonstrate this, but so do maps. We brought up maps as a strong example of functionally aesthetic visualization in Chapters 1 and 2. They are an example of how their function depends on their representation, intended purpose, audience, and context in which the map is viewed. Let's look at how the task of wayfinding brings to light the interplay between medium and mode.

Navigate Like a Local

Have you ever been lost with no clue as to where you are? Perhaps you missed that crucial turn because you couldn't read the sign in the dark, it was simply nonexistent, or it came up too fast. These are all problems that we can relate to, but navigation is especially complicated in countries where most people rely on landmarks as the de facto mode for successful navigation. India is one such country where street names are not commonly used: the typical wayfinding strategy is to simply ask someone on the street. Without road names, it's difficult to produce a set of directions that makes sense to find the dry fruit store in Old Delhi, shown in Figure 15.2.

FIGURE 15.2 A typical street scene in Old Delhi, India, where locals and tourists go about their business
Instants/Getty Images

Creating functionally aesthetic maps requires deeply understanding the target users' behaviors, their visual cues, and what makes a good landmark. In other words, we need to understand the mode of their wayfinding to provide route descriptions that are both understandable and usable. Google observed how people give and get directions in India (Unnikrishnan & Gupta, 2009). The study involved several aspects of figuring out the mode of sensemaking in a particular country. Researchers interviewed businesses, asking how to get to their stores, observed how people drew diagrams of routes to places unfamiliar to us, and even followed people around as they tried to find their way.

The study showed that using landmarks in directions in places like India helps for two simple reasons: they are easier to see than street signs and they are easier to remember than street names. Spotting a pink building on a corner or remembering to turn after a gas station is much easier than trying to recall an unfamiliar street name. Sometimes there are simply too many signs to look at and the street signs drown in the visual noise. A good landmark always stands out. It may be any object in the environment that is visually distinctive and easily recognizable (e.g., river, brightly colored building) or a well-known place (e.g., celebrity's mansion, popular restaurant), as long as its primary property is that of a point of reference (Caduff & Timpf, 2008).

There are three situations in which people resort to landmarks:

- When people need to orient themselves: for instance, they just exited a subway station and are not sure which exit to take to get to the street level.

- When people need to describe the location of a turn: for instance, "Turn right after the Starbucks."

- When people simply want to confirm that they are still on the right track and haven't missed their turn: for instance, a reassuring message stating, "Keep going for six more miles."

Even the hand-drawn route map that we introduced in Chapter 2 and show here again in Figure 15.3, embodies information that's only relevant to the attendee attending the wedding event.

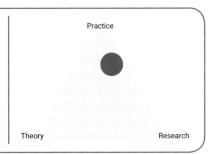

Orientation cues and breadcrumbs provide scaffolds for wayfinding. Functionally aesthetic visualizations need to provide similar scaffolds to help orient the user during data exploration.

Practice

Theory

Research

Both paper and sketching as a mode favor simplicity and allow for a bit of levity in the creation. Key highways and streets help navigate the person from the hotel to the venue. The mode is relevant to the audience, context, and mood captured by the playful sketch of the martini glass and heart on the paper medium.

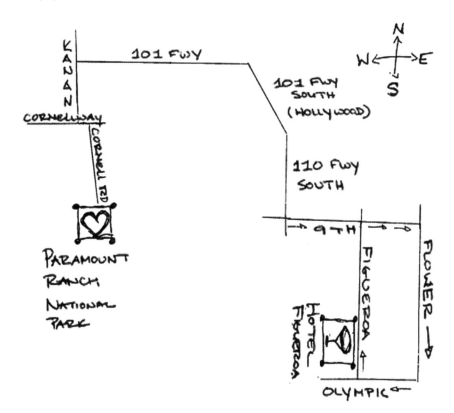

FIGURE 15.3 Hand-drawn route map to the wedding destination (revisited)

Digital wayfinding typically leverages breadcrumbs (i.e., a navigation path that shows where the user is on a website or app) as landmarks. URL construction allows people to quickly understand and verify the path chosen. Within the site, elements may move elsewhere or provide additional breadcrumbs to show the path. As shown in Figure 15.4, our site uses meaningful words from the page titles in the URL, and elements are underlined to help with wayfinding.

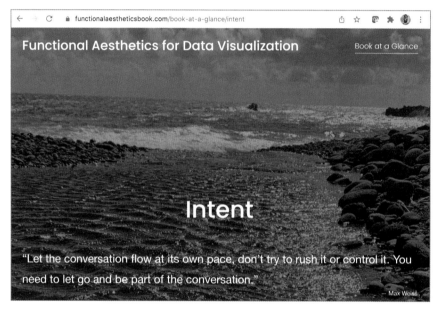

FIGURE 15.4 Digital wayfinding on websites

Landmarks in visualization help people find their way through interactivity. As consumers select marks on charts, the selections may highlight, or the non-selected marks may fade. Additional breadcrumbs provide navigational paths and scaffolds, helping users understand what filters have been applied. Figure 15.5 shows the dashboard from Chapter 14 in a non-interacted state.

As we interact with this dashboard, breadcrumbs can help users follow along with what's happening. Figure 15.6 shows a prototype of what breadcrumbs could look like with natural language integration. The selection highlights Snacks in the Central Region. Visually, the breadcrumb darkens the bar and fills the background space with a darker hue. This language helps orient people to the dashboard (Situation 1 from the

Google Map research study). Text spells out impact on downstream charts: the new comparison splits products by the Selected item (which uses preattentive attributes as a legend) and filters for the category and region (Snacks in the Central Region). Natural language in the title helps affirm what is happening: Products are now *by* select vs. rest, and monthly trends are *for* Snacks and Central Regions. This practice supports when landmarks are used for directions (Situation 2) and confirmation practices (Situation 3).

FIGURE 15.5 Dashboard before wayfinding

Just like using landmarks, balancing noise with navigation requires crafting clear cuing systems. The landmarks need to be distinct enough to find and follow while providing more clarity than clutter. Adding a second interaction to this dashboard requires a different landmark that provides distinction without creating undue overload. Figure 15.7 shows the addition of a second landmark in yellow. Careful thought around reasonable interactions means the first category chart *filters* the line chart while the product *compares* the selected attribute. The breadcrumb text first presents the filters (for Snacks and Central Region) and then the comparison (selected in yellow). In the physical world, this may translate directions that include zigzag turns close together.

FIGURE 15.6 Dashboard with both visual and natural language landmarking

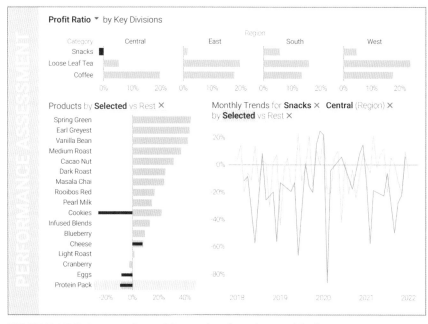

FIGURE 15.7 Interaction with two landmarks enabled

Landmark systems provide valuable scaffolds while navigating. They can be translated to the mode in which we're interacting. For paper, they may reduce details, while digital modes add clarifiers. In addition to navigation, mode takes into account the societal values that influence communication as well as impacts from the medium itself. The mode and mediums change how we communicate, or as McLuhan et al. noted, "The medium is the message." TV, chatbots, and AI assistants influence our mode of communication.

Revisiting Analytical Chatbots

The last few years have seen a lot of excitement around chatbots. They've become a prevalent way of engaging with users, especially for customer service and transactional tasks such as making a doctor's appointment or inquiring about an order. It's easy to see the appeal.

The interface, voice, and even tone of these chatbots affect mode. As discussed in Chapter 13, understanding user intent and providing relevant responses is important to any chatbot platform; the interaction and expectations can be quite different whether one is speaking to the chatbot versus typing. Clifford Nass and Youngme Moon (2000) suggested that interaction with robots activates the same social brain areas as a conversation with a fellow human. And if that's the case, adding a human touch to a chatbot's responses resonates with people better than machine-like responses. Individuals exhibited similar behaviors with televisions and computers as they did with other humans: not only did they treat the machines with respect, but they also interacted with male-sounding and female-sounding computer voices differently based on gender stereotypes.

Social heuristics are simple decision-making strategies that guide people's behavior and decisions in the social environment when time, information, or cognitive resources are scarce (Hertwig & Herzog, 2009). People often apply these social heuristics to computer interactions, focusing on cues in language, intonation, and emotions expressed by the chatbot agent. Research supports the benefits of using anthropomorphic characteristics in human-bot interactions in encouraging more conversational interaction and enhancing a person's ability to make precise assumptions on how that agent is likely to act based on its persona. There's evidence that people tend to anthropomorphize voice chatbots by addressing the interface based on their perceived gender or simply being polite and using words such as "please" and "thanks, chatbot!"

Research explored how people interacted with analytical chatbots through text and voice (Setlur & Tory, 2022). We previously showed a Slack-based text chatbot example in Chapter 13. Figure 15.8 shows the transcriptions of a human interacting with an analytical voice chatbot. Participants interacted with an Alexa Echo device through voice, and the chatbot used a popular US English–based female voice option called Joanna (https://aws.amazon.com/polly). The gray text bubbles indicate voice transcripts from the human, while the blue ones are from the voice chatbot. Follow-up questions and feedback from the chatbot encourage conversational behavior, inviting the person to continue to explore a wineries dataset. People found it helpful when chatbots clarified phrases from the question like "best wineries" with a response that included "top winery," making sure the chatbot understood them. The value of repeating validates the quality and accuracy of the system response, particularly with voice when there's nothing visual. Repair and refinement (presented in Chapter 9) is a big part of the analytical conversation experience, where the mode for being able to correct or change a system's response often depends on the medium—a follow-up question like, "Would you like to hear the next two?" when using voice or displaying widgets in a Slack interface for the user to select the next two wineries, for example.

The advancements in AI are opening up new opportunities for humans to interact with computers, such as the following:

- Simulating human voices, linguistic patterns, personalities, and appearances

- Assuming roles or tasks traditionally belonging to humans

- Conceivably, accelerating the integration of technology into everyday life

What are the best wineries?

> The top winery based on average points is the Château Cheval Blanc. Would you like to hear the next two?

Yeah

> The next two top wineries are Casanova di Neri and Dolce. What would you like to ask next?

Which wineries are in Yountville?

> Sorry, I don't understand Yountville. Mind clarifying?

Which wineries are in Napa County?

> The top winery based on average points is Hestan Vineyards? Would you like to hear more?

FIGURE 15.8 Interaction transcript with an Alexa Echo analytical chatbot

Determining the mode of interaction becomes increasingly important as functionally aesthetic visualization and the experiences built around it also get more nuanced and sophisticated.

Mode for an analytical chatbot is a careful balance between the intricacies of language pragmatics, data, and the medium. All three need to work together to support a cooperative conversation.

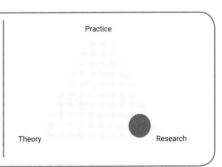

Practice

Theory

Research

Video Killed the Radio Star

Technological advances affect not only interaction but the *exposition* of information. Mode, along with literacy, affects how we frame and present information. Chatbots interact differently than humans, and we respond differently to each as well. With chatbots, we may dump word salad onto it in piecemeal bits. First, we may type "weather Columbus OH tomorrow," then we get "hourly trends," to get it to "things to do outside," whereas we may ask a person what the weather would be like and if they know of anything happening. In other words, people code-switch to "computer speak" as they interface with chatbots, quickly determining the mode of interaction to be successful. Even before the advent of intelligent computers, people found creative outlets to express their point of view in the medium that was commonly available at that time.

Back before digitalization, people displayed information on paper by painstakingly drawing graphs, diagrams, and maps. In Chapter 3, we examined how the work of W. E. B. Du Bois, William Playfair, and Florence Nightingale showcases the variety and techniques used to display data by hand. Data started to be visualized by systems and tools with the evolution of multimedia resources and all the possibilities of the Internet. They multiplied the possibilities of combination and made the visualization of data more dynamic with animations, interactive graphics, and maps at different scales. Printed or static visualizations require a different exposition style than interactive graphics. How much of our practitioner wisdom comes from printed charts?

The changes in television provide a potential road map to the changes we can expect from interactive visualizations. As sitcoms transitioned from radio to television, they heavily catered to the ear, providing laugh tracks and a speech style still well suited for audio-only listening. As TV matured as a medium, the exposition styles changed by using the camera to drive the storytelling first and balancing the dialog. The camera setup and lighting became more elaborate, using shots, angle, and shifts in hue to provide tone and nuanced emotion.

Visualization, too, changes mode to mirror shifts in the medium. Early printed visualizations were hand-sketched, allowing artistic inspiration to literally and figuratively be drawn into the work. Software enables systemizing and developing abstractions that are useful for any visualization tool. Functionally aesthetic visualization is about constructing visual representations of data to amplify cognition. As Leland Wilkinson (2005) wrote in his seminal work *The Grammar of Graphics*, the basis for many modern-day visualization tools,

If we endeavor to develop a charting instead of a graphing program, we will accomplish two things. First, we inevitably will offer fewer charts than people want. Second, our package will have no deep structure. Our computer program will be unnecessarily complex, because we will fail to reuse objects or routines that function similarly in different charts. And we will have no way to add new charts to our system without generating complex new code. Elegant design requires us to think about a theory of graphics, not charts."

Further innovations combine artistic representations of data into densely layered unique visualization. Interactivity enables filtering, animation, the unveiling of text, and changes to the graphic as the user scrolls. New modes around augmented reality (AR) create further immersion, as well as broaden the senses one can use to access the medium. Could visualizations include sounds to nuance the data?

Beyond the Desktop

Most data today is seen through a screen. Whether through a phone, a laptop, or a large display in an office, the digitization of data visualization enables a greater spread of charts. Most business visualizations still come designed as desktop-centric dashboards. What happens when other screens take priority?

Between smaller screens and touch interaction, the phone requires a different paradigm for design than a traditional desktop. The mode requires considering both of these factors and presenting information and interactions differently. We'll leverage the dashboard from Chapter 2 (Figure 2.9) and build mobile-first. As we saw in Chapter 8, scaling down our designs requires thinking about the orientation of the screen, the colors, and also the mode. Figure 15.9 preserves the first part of the dashboard and alters the second part to make it more useful. The darker color mutes the brightness of the screen, and the bubble chart allows filtering to meet the needs of larger fingers. Figure 15.10 provides a side-to-side scroll option and similar styling for each pane.

FIGURE 15.9 Mobile-first designed lengthwise

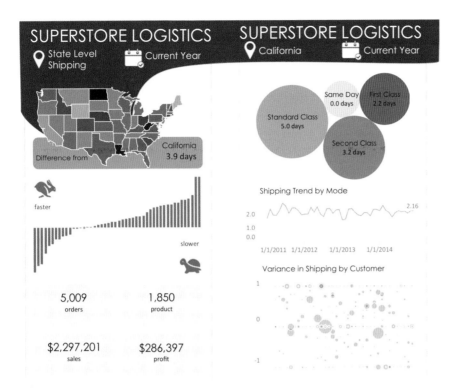

FIGURE 15.10 Side-to-side scrolling

Designing for the phone takes into account the differences in how we interact. In addition to the screen being smaller, the way in which we interact with the pixels is far less precise. Not only have we learned to become more precise with how we click with a mouse or trackpad, the operating system allows us to adjust its range, speed, and sensitivity. We can optimize how the mouse interacts with the pixels on our screen. We have a range of controls with the mouse. The cursor also helps identify— nearly down to the pixel—where exactly we're clicking. Now press a control on your smartphone or tablet. Where did you touch, and how did it identify that interaction? The preciseness of touch screen devices is still highly variable and much harder to correct as your finger is in the way of seeing the cursor. Some operating systems allow magnification slightly ajar from your finger for precise tasks.

Figure 15.11 shows interactions using the same device (Microsoft Surface) using both a mouse (top) and contact with the screen (bottom). With the mouse, the click points are closely packed within the very small circle. With the touch screen, not only do most contact points miss both the smaller and larger dot, the majority of touches land outside the data ink. The touch algorithm may address this, but finer-range tasks like selecting dots that are closer together are easy with a mouse and hard through touch. The mode requires adaptation for this chart to be useful for selection. Zoom, gestures, and even secondary charts can help increase precision.

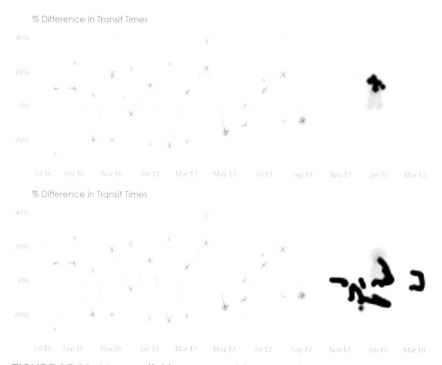

FIGURE 15.11 Mouse clicking vs. touching on points (Microsoft Surface)

Mobile screens enable greater functionality through gestures. Users can zoom into a part of the screen by drawing their thumbs and index fingers out from a C to an L. Other gestures may rotate, slide to another pane, or draw up a menu option. The semantics of gestures expands the capabilities of the medium (the smartphone) to allow the mode (mobile interactive visualization) to be more powerful.

Shrinking down isn't the only complicator. Large screens also demand a shift in how data is presented. Demographer and storyteller extraordinaire Hans Rosling is famous not only for how Gapminder (www.gapminder .org) showed data but how it was presented on the stage. Rosling would expand data points by swiping them on the screen, the bubble for the selected continent exploding into a variety of countries that dramatically moved to various places on the scatterplot. His verbal storytelling accompanied the visual, providing clarity to how the data moved. His body moved with the data as he darted from one side of the visualization to another, the distance in outcomes clearly felt in the movement.

Storytelling in literate societies demands a different narrative style than in those without literacy (as discussed in Chapter 6). Rosling allowed the visualization to be seen, then used the visual to add clarity. His audience had to see the chart to understand the nuances of his message. The audience felt the gap when Rwanda broke starkly from the median of Africa. Secondary data orality relies on an understanding of the graphicacy, of the ability to parse in Rosling's case the scatterplot for the heart of the story. Visually, his movements showcased the wide distribution patterns of income and life span. Modern data visualization competitions rely on secondary orality to clinch titles. Tool matchups like the BI Bake-Off hosted by Gartner or software-specific competitions like IronViz held during the Tableau Conference rely on contestants weaving powerful stories around the visualizations they showcase.

Future Forward

As we move toward further digitization of data visualization, the mode allows expansion into new ways of interacting with data. Going beyond the desktop to smartphones, tablets, or large displays opens new challenges that include device discovery, interaction sharing, and view management. What may start as an edge use case of one mode may quickly transform into its own mode.

Research is constantly evolving to figure out new ways to support visual sensemaking. One such technique is Visfer, which enables the sharing of visualizations using QR codes (Badam & Elmqvist, 2019). Other work explores network graph visualization and interaction between personal mobile devices in combination with a large wall display (Kister et al., 2017). Researchers developed an experience called GRaSp to allow mobile devices to quickly zoom in and provide details—a second layer of interaction made possible by AR. This allows interacting with much larger displays and moving around while exploring the data. Individuals looking at the data can use their phones and cross-compare while in a meeting easily. However, what's exciting is that these novel ways of exploring mode are making their presence known among practitioners.

Presentations involving visual displays of information are now mainstream in journalism and news outlets. Election coverage and the COVID-19 pandemic normalized the use of charts. A person often stands in front of a large touch screen using words and gestures to emote their story through data. Presenters of data cite Hans Rosling as an inspiring role model for a new generation of analysts. His performances deftly used the semantics of motion and gesture to guide the audience through data storytelling. Here are some guidelines he followed:

- Using the full screen to maximize the visualization
- Explaining the axes and the marks, including what their color and size meant
- Hovering over marks on the screen to pay special attention to certain aspects of the data
- Applying animation to show temporal changes in the data
- Describing the movement in the charts as it's happening

AR makes use of the digital screen paradigm but is rapidly becoming its own mode of interaction. The AR mode allows blending the interactivity and storytelling as demonstrated by Rosling. With AR, the visualization takes on depth and leverages metaphor in a whole new way by allowing size comparisons against real-world objects. For example, Google added support for 3D objects in its search where a medical student can search a 3D human anatomy model (https://arvr.google.com/ar). AR can provide a sense of scale and detail, with users able to see and interact with objects in a 3D view. It's one thing to read that a blue whale can be 100 feet long, but another thing to see it up close in relation to the things around you. With technology advancements and a better understanding of supporting new experiences, functionally aesthetic visualization will take new forms of display and interaction in the coming years.

Summary

Mode determines how we interact with a medium. Navigation is key, and providing landmarks and visual breadcrumbs helps guide the user. Functionally aesthetic visualization goes beyond the traditional desktop paradigm with the plethora of new platforms and devices. These new experiences provide opportunities to innovate and get the community excited about data-driven thinking. We wrap up this chapter and Part C by discussing how communicating and interacting through data can only be effective when we understand *both* the intent of the author and the audience. As we step into Part D, the last section of the book, we'll discuss how perception, semantics, and intent come together as a whole. After all, the sky's the limit.

The sun sets dramatically on the Atlantic Ocean.
Photo by Bridget Cogley

Putting It All Together

Clouds appear, move across the sky, and disappear. The clouds are not the sky. There is no concrete connection between sky and clouds, yet the sky is not separate from the clouds.

Sheng Yen

The earth dances around the sun, creating the familiar patterns of days, months, and years. We anticipate the cycles of the moon, the patterns clear and consistent. While parts of the sky are unchanging, which we know from proven science, others surprise us daily. No two skies are alike. The clouds swirl across the sky, painting new pictures daily.

The hues vary profoundly, from the deep purples of night, to the lustrous blues and bleak dismal grays of winter, to the vivid oranges of sunset. As the sun sets, it splashes its final light on the clouds, painting them and the endless canvas all around. The clouds shift from white cotton to colored puffs of cotton candy, taking on shades of lilac and orange. As we look at the sky in the image, the largest cloud transforms in our mind. Is that large cloud above an elephant laughing in the air?

The sky is a canvas for our imaginations. It invites us to play, to revel in ever-shifting beauty, and to celebrate the passing moments. The clouds are not the sky, but they play a pivotal role in how we relate to the canvas above us. It is indicative of time and timeless. The colors can at times beguile our senses. Artists, astronomers, and photographers alike have chased the sky for years, attempting to capture and understand its essence.

We, too, attempt to capture the essence of our data in a manner similar to how the sky paints a picture. Functional aesthetics balances the science we know with the harmony we seek. As we bring all the pieces together—charts, text, design elements, and interactivity—the beauty is in the unified whole. Just as with the sky, the parts may stand out more, but the entire composition creates that magical experience. Visualizations are not mere charts but an ecosystem that encompasses the text, non-chart graphics, and the ways in which everything is brought together. This last section explores how a visualization becomes whole, just like the sky.

Bringing Everything Together

We return to our restaurant scene with this chapter, spoons ready for dessert. To truly transport us, we're diving into a delightful bowl of Indonesian black rice pudding, such as the one shown in Figure 16.1. Warm, soft rice swirled with the heady delights of coconut milk awaits. We take a bite. It's lightly sweet and slightly chewy with the faintest trace of salt. The richness of the coconut milk provides weight without overwhelming or coating the tongue: it is both heavy and light simultaneously. The flavors of black rice and coconut gently fade as we take our last bite.

Like our dessert, functional aesthetics relies on the interplay of ideas that blend distinct flavors to create a unique but cohesive experience. When we take these ideas, we not only move from a pictographic mode to a perceptual one, we also move to a paradigm that allows us to support all consumers by including semantics and intent. As we see in Figure 16.2, semantic practice blurs the lines and explores what draws meaning while intent looks beyond the literal sum of the parts to the hidden goals that drive analytical work and supports the whole paradigm.

Throughout this book, we've left breadcrumbs in the form of triangles. This book blends research, practice, and theory to create a culinary journey of ideas. These triangles add spice to build better, more impactful visualizations that guide a wider array of consumers through analytical conversations. This is not a design book for charts, but a way to serve charts together delightfully for consumption.

FIGURE 16.1 A lovely dessert to end a meal
Hendra Su/Getty Images

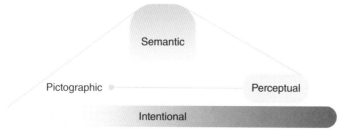

FIGURE 16.2 Functional aesthetics paradigm

Addressing the Paper Towel Problem

As we create experiences for others, we have to broaden our lens and look at the whole picture. Throughout this book, we've explored an extraordinary dining experience with a small problem

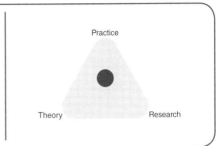

Beyond the design of individual charts, the sequence of data visualizations creates grammar within the exposition. Cohesive visualizations follow common narrative structures to fully express their message. Order matters. (From Chapter 9)

with paper towels in the restroom. In the scheme of things, not having towels is a small problem. We wipe our hands on what we're wearing and continue with our meal. Yet, in the moment, it leaves wet clothes, and a lackluster experience is what is otherwise a fond memory. The same can be applied to visualizations, where a tangential negative experience can disrupt flow.

We eliminate the paper towel problem by looking at intent and the design principles that cause that intent to fail. For visualizations, *semantics* is that subsystem. As with paper towel dispensers, we expect semantics to work in predictable ways. The towels should roll out when we wave our hand in front of the sensor and consumers should be able to interpret these charts together. However, reality shows that intents in interaction often compete. The dispenser should be able to control waste while serving paper towels. These charts in conjunction with each other should be able to meet the requirements listed or inferred from the consumers.

We'll return to the dashboard we introduced in Chapter 3, shown in Figure 16.3, and apply the various principles of functional aesthetics to elevate it. To start, we'll reexamine the goals for this dashboard through a lightweight design brief that takes into account our goals to iterate on existing work.

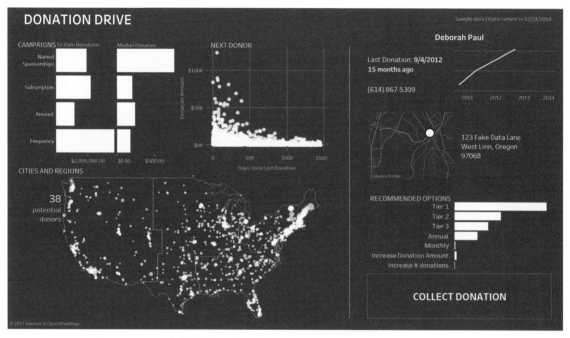

FIGURE 16.3 The perceptual dashboard started in Chapter 3

Our sample design brief may look like this:

Dataset: Donations for the last four years with cohorts already created.

Work to date: Visualization already exists.

Goal: Adapt existing work to increase either the donation frequency or amount, with both being the ideal.

Intended audience(s): Members of the nonprofit will be using this dashboard while dialing for dollars.

Intended use(s):

1. Based on the campaign, identify people overdue for contact.

2. Provide enough information for the caller to solicit an appropriate donation amount and potential frequency.

3. Allow secondary tracks to pick out the location by region to allow door-to-door requests.

Current challenges with existing work:

- Not enough direction or guidance: it's hard to find the "right" donor, it's easy to lose track of what charts are selected, and wayfinding is sometimes hard.
- Callers find it hard to remember the right script when on a call, which is based on the campaign.
- While accurate and clean, the dashboard feels "boring" and it's hard to remember what's filtered.
- It's too easy to miss the button.

Current successes with existing work:

- Charts are clear and intelligible.
- Donor profile on the right is helpful.
- Button embeds the donor portal for easy access.

We'll evaluate the charts on the visualization for the following:

- **Task**: Identify   , Compare   , or Summarize

   (Munzner, 2015; discussed in Chapter 2)

- **Exposition role**: Context, Theme, or Details (Chapter 6)

- **Efficiency**: Precision to generation scale
   (Cleveland & McGill, 1984; discussed in Chapter 2)

We'll also document features such as filters or note edits that we should consider. Figure 16.4 shows a map of how each of these items is evaluated.

As we break down the roles that charts play in the visualization, we can assess the narrative structure of the visualization. The chart evaluations are in lemon yellow, while additional annotations are off-white.

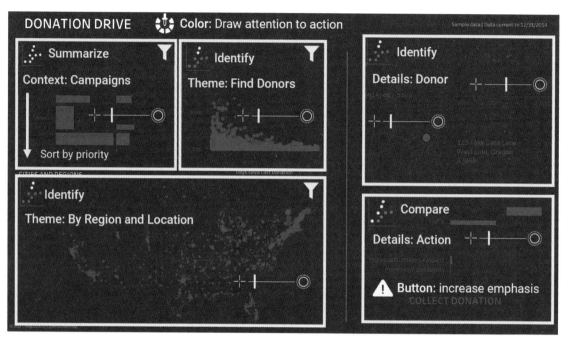

FIGURE 16.4 Mapping our evaluation

The exposition of this dashboard mirrors that of literate expositions, as discussed in Chapter 6. We want to keep the flow while adding elements that improve semantic and intentional cues. Our users are likely to work on one campaign type at a time to make going through the script easier. Campaigns set the context of this visualization and can be used as a single-select filter to reduce complexity. From our quick design brief, we know that users are sometimes struggling to remember which script to use while on the call. In addition, users want more color without trading intelligibility. Campaigns would be the perfect place to add more color and emphasize them throughout to provide additional cues for script usage. We also want to add a few more design elements that facilitate reading. Lastly, we know the button needs more emphasis so that it can be more discoverable.

To further elevate this dashboard, we'll consider semantic tactics we can use as scaffolds, as well as what aspects of the data we want to emphasize to drive action. Users need help deciding where to go. They want breadcrumbs to improve wayfinding, and they want useful flair. We can employ useful iconography and visual emphasis to help support actions. We need to provide linkages from chart to chart through color, icons, and design elements.

Figure 16.5 and Figure 16.6 show the adapted dashboard and the effects of interactivity. The entire dashboard is filtered to one campaign at a time. All the data and key design elements change to the selected color, helping to create a meaningful association. The additional banner text also calls out which campaign is selected, which provides a landmark to all users as well as accessibility to users who are colorblind. Additional design elements further break up the space and draw emphasis to the button.

These enhancements center delight. We've made minimal changes to the charts themselves, instead focusing on the aspects within the broader visualization. The colors provide elegance and direction.

Crafting Recipes for Functional Aesthetics

Much of this book centers on concepts rather than tactics. Moving from conversing about ideas to designing in a whole new way requires formulating the recipe to building something new. How do you build better visualizations with these ideas in mind?

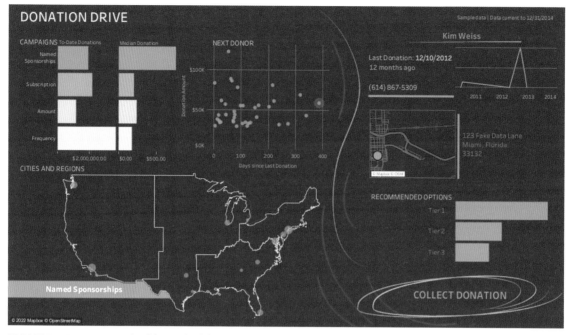

FIGURE 16.5 Donor dashboard with Named Sponsorships selected

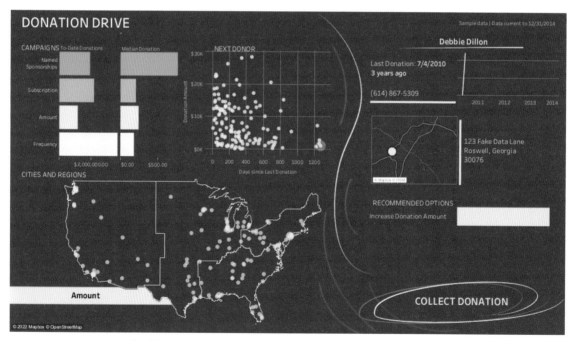

FIGURE 16.6 Donor dashboard with Amount selected

We've crafted two tools to end this chapter. The first provides a checklist to evaluate individual works. The second, a higher-level matrix, allows a broader assessment of several visualizations at once to get a sense of overall maturity. While not all criteria may fit a visualization, each point comes from parts of the book and may encourage you to adapt your work.

Individual Evaluation

Within the first evaluation tool, all questions can be answered with yes or no. If desired, you can add up all the applicable ones and "score" your visualization. Yesses align with functional aesthetics. We've marked only some items as not applicable.

Perception

Ch	Focus	Question	Answers	
1	Contrast	Do the important elements have enough contrast to be appropriately perceived?	✗	✓
		Does contrast meet or exceed WCAG guidelines (e.g., testing through accessible-colors.com)?	✗	✓
		Are there paths for accessibility (e.g., contrast toggles, screen reader accessibility, color-blind-friendly palettes, or modes)?	✗	✓

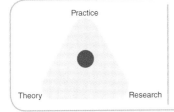

Generalization principles—Emphasize the most important elements and deemphasize the less important one.

Ch	Focus	Question	Answers		
2	Task (Munzner, 2015)	Does a selected chart clearly identify, compare, or summarize a particular aspect of the data?		✕	✓
		Does the chart's task represent the intended user goal?		✕	✓

Practice

Theory   Research

Selecting charts may include effectiveness, user comfort, surrounding charts, text, software complexities of making the chart, how the data fits the chart, and what to expect if the chart continues to update on its own.

Ch	Focus	Question	Answers		
	Relative judgments (Cleveland & McGill, 1984)	Do most charts typically support a more precise judgment?		✕	✓
		When generalized assessments are used, are they helpful?		✕	✓
	Layout	Does the layout use space in a visually pleasing or recognizable manner at first glance?		✕	✓
		Are there visual elements to frame or guide salient information?		✕	✓
3	Domain-specific presentations	Are certain chart types better for the audience or industry (e.g., control charts or box plots)?	⊘	✕	✓
		If printed, are the charts understandable with sufficient text annotation to draw conclusions?	⊘	✕	✓
		If the chart is interactive, are details available in a clear way?	⊘	✕	✓

Ch	Focus	Question	Answers
	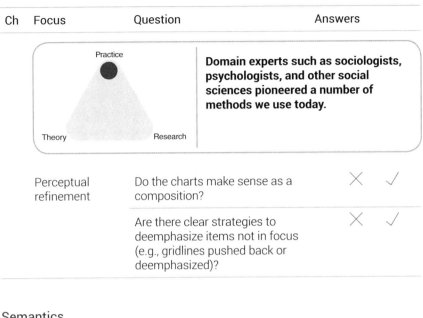		**Domain experts such as sociologists, psychologists, and other social sciences pioneered a number of methods we use today.**
	Perceptual refinement	Do the charts make sense as a composition?	✕ ✓
		Are there clear strategies to deemphasize items not in focus (e.g., gridlines pushed back or deemphasized)?	✕ ✓

Semantics

Ch	Focus	Question	Answers
4	Symbols and other relevant iconography	Are icons used? (If not, what opportunities exist to add icons to clarify meaning?)	✕ ✓
		Are they semantically resonant of the information they represent (e.g., showing an action like "click here" or some attribute of the data)?	✕ ✓

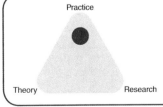

Using symbols is one common way of applying semantics to help make sense of the world.

		⊘	✕	✓
Chart clusters	Are charts layered or otherwise combined to create new meaningful depictions?	⊘	✕	✓
	Do these novelties add delight or enhance the message in some way?	⊘	✕	✓
Semiotics	Is meaning changed by modifying a component's visual characteristics (e.g., changing a plane icon's location and direction for arrival vs. departure)?	⊘	✕	✓
	Do properties like shape, color, and position in iconography help clarify or support the message?	⊘	✕	✓

Practice

Theory

Research

The effective depiction of an icon often depends on how semantically resonant the image is to the information it represents.

5	Identification of vague concepts	Are vague concepts clarified if they exist within the data (e.g., tall)?	⊘	✕	✓
		Are there opportunities to adjust the selected definition (e.g., tall is defined as 6'0" but can it be adjusted)? If not, what opportunities could be added?		✕	✓
		Are date formats clear to the region(s) viewing them?		✕	✓

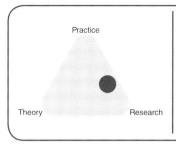

Understanding the context and the domain of the data is important to help disambiguate concepts. While reasonable defaults can be used when creating a visualization, there should be no dead ends. Provide affordances for a user to understand, repair, and refine.

| Iconicity of representation | Is iconicity used as a tool to support newer users? | ✕ ✓ |

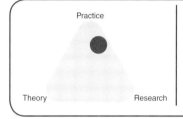

By making the patterns in the representation surface more meaningful to the reader, the chart becomes less abstract.

6	Navigating data literacy	Is the source of the data clear or readily apparent?	✕ ✓
		Are the definitions commonly shared or clearly spelled out (e.g., avoiding acronym use where possible and logical)?	✕ ✓
		Does the analysis use appropriate aggregations (e.g., median vs. average)?	✕ ✓
	Ethical representations	Does the visualization disclose biases within the data?	✕ ✓
		Is the information framed appropriately?	✕ ✓
		Do the conclusions match what the charts show?	✕ ✓

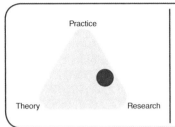

Research explores the fallacies of misconstrued information. Approaches involve assisting analysts to help them tackle questions they couldn't ask before but do so responsibly: in a way that promotes safe, ethical, and well-supported conclusions from the data.

Exposition	Can the exposition style be named (e.g., top down, bottom up [McCann])?	✕	✓
	Is there a clear breakout of context, theme, and detail within the analysis?	✕	✓
Data literacy democratization	Are we helping users learn to read the visualization within the work itself (e.g., tooltips, overlays, etc.)?	✕	✓

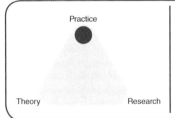

Schools are progressively teaching students to read charts and figures early. There's a new generation of data-literate students who can make data-driven decisions to think critically while solving problems of the world.

7	Data preparation	Is the data source tidy for other authors or editors who may modify the work?	✕	✓
		Are key transformations noted or clear to follow in the workflow?	✕	✓
		Does the shape of the data support the intent of the analysis?	✕	✓

8	Generaliza-tion practices	When sizing smaller, are relevant details, labels, and other items reduced or removed to reflect the smaller size (e.g., labels reduced to only the most salient details)?		✕	✓
		Are elements of the highest importance preserved?		✕	✓
	Designing for mobile	Is enough important insight visible within the screen without scrolling?	⊘	✕	✓
		Does the design consider the size, lighting, and potential use cases of the screen?	⊘	✕	✓
		Is the visualization adapted to work with fingers interacting rather than cursors?	⊘	✕	✓

Practice

Theory   Research

Mobile views need to keep true to "at a glance insight" yet preserve the ability to click on marks and filter values.

	Size and color	Is color easy to distinguish in all sizes of marks (e.g., data marks as well as text)?		✕	✓
		Are there opportunities to clarify what color represents beyond the color itself (e.g., highlighting with interactivity)?		✕	✓
	Visual summaries	When visual summaries are used, such as for small multiples, are the most salient points emphasized?		✕	✓

9	Color	Does the color support a logical or meaningful relationship with the data?	✕	✓
		Do legends clarify and support without being excessive?	✕	✓
		Do colors avoid conflicting use?	✕	✓
		Do color associations line up as expected? (Stroop, Ch. 1)	✕	✓
	Sequence	Are the charts arranged in a sequence that follows a logical narrative structure?	✕	✓
		Does arrangement affect how interactivity works (e.g., charts only filter down through the sequence)?	✕	✓

Practice

Theory   Research

Beyond the design of individual charts, the sequence of data visualizations creates grammar within the exposition. Order matters.

	Visual supports and style	Is there a clear style tile for elements such as titles, axes, lines, and colors?	✕	✓
		Are there consistent rules for the formatting of elements such as gridlines, borders, and supporting ink elements?	✕	✓
		Does any type of framing exist?	✕	✓
		Do visual elements help identify the author's intended reading order(s)?	✕	✓

Use of space/shape	Does the positive space (data ink) create any type of meaningful shape?		✕	✓
	Is negative space used to convey appropriate relationships?		✕	✓
Alignment	Is there a clear alignment paradigm (e.g., on data ink)?		✕	✓
	Using alignment to create lines, is there visual poetry?		✕	✓
Analytical conversation	Are there opportunities to continue, retain, or shift parts of the analytical conversation?		✕	✓
	Are transitional goals like elaborating or pivoting clearly achievable?		✕	✓

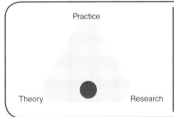

Practice

Theory

Research

> **By balancing the perception and semantics, we can encourage deeper, clearer, and better conversations with the data. Coherence in analytical conversations seeks to center the person interacting with the visualization.**

10	Text levels	Are titles used?		✕	✓
		Are quantifiers used?		✕	✓
		Are qualifiers used?		✕	✓
		Are annotations used?	⊘	✕	✓
		Is narrative text used?	⊘	✕	✓
		Are captions used?	⊘	✕	✓
		Does the visualization contain functional text, such as caveats, disclosures, warnings, tooltips, and other interactive text?		✕	✓

Text	Is the text balanced?		✗	✓
	If not, is there an opportunity to rearrange where the text is located, such as to an annotation layer?		✗	✓
	Does the text agree with the most salient points of what the visual shows?		✗	✓

Practice

Theory   Research

Text should be treated as a first-class citizen, just like any chart type.

Natural language interaction (NLI)	Do NL interfaces answer the relevant questions, including those with vague references to attributes of the data?	⊘	✗	✓
	Does it help the consumer understand through additional referencing, such as layered annotation or highlighted interactivity?	⊘	✗	✓
Alt text	Does the alt text explain the takeaway?		✗	✓
	Can consumers with screen readers access equivalent insights as those accessing the information visually in a concise and logical manner?		✗	✓

Intent

11	Analytical intent	Does the visualization allow both targeted and open-ended exploration?	✕	✓
		If there is only one option, are there ways to enable both targeted and open-ended exploration?	✕	✓
	Repair and refinement	Are dead ends mitigated or redirected?	✕	✓
		Are there ways to get clarification in an analytical conversation? (e.g., defining house types when shopping for homes)?	✕	✓
	Practicing intent	Does the visualization work as a whole to answer the targeted questions?	✕	✓
		Are tasks able to be achieved with minimal friction?	✕	✓
		If there's friction, is it to create pause or to humanize the data?	✕	✓
		Do starting points for interactivity align with user experience and expectations (e.g., not creating a U shape where interactions fall)?	✕	✓

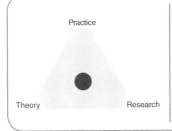

Practice

Theory   Research

Charts need to support ways for users to express intent continuously during their analytical workflows. Data semantics, context, and interaction are useful ways of understanding user intent during data exploration.

12	Intentionality	Does the visualization support both the form and function needed for consuming the analysis?		✕	✓
		Does the interactivity on the charts make sense (e.g., proportional brushing on bars on selection)?		✕	✓
		Are charts effectively consolidated and expanded where it makes sense?		✕	✓
	Register	Does the register fit the setting in which the visualization will be used?		✕	✓
		Can consumers get clarification or reduce the register if needed (e.g., additional guardrails for complex charts)?		✕	✓
		Do additional details on demand support the intended message?		✕	✓
	Metaphor	Is metaphor used?	⊘	✕	✓
		Does the metaphor resonate?	⊘	✕	✓
		Can the metaphor be clarified if not fully clear?	⊘	✕	✓

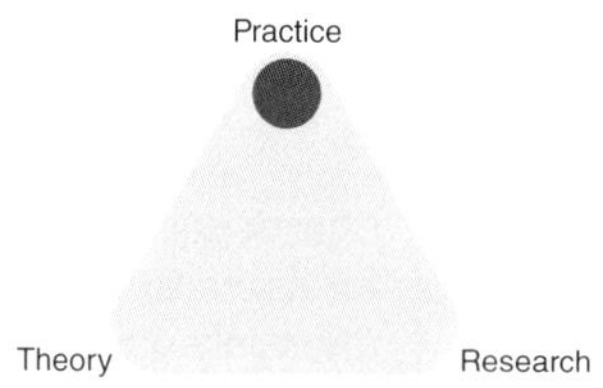

Practice

Theory   Research

Metaphor is a powerful way to play with visual language.

	Deictic referencing	Can deictic references such as clicks be used (e.g., "here" on a map)?	⊘ ✕ ✓
		Do deictic references allow clarifying or easy next steps?	⊘ ✕ ✓
13	Visualization scaffolding	Do the visual systems in place (e.g., style tile) create momentum in understanding the analysis?	✕ ✓
		Does iconography support or potentially replace repetitive text directives?	✕ ✓
		Are conventions such as icons used in a way that teach and support greater user autonomy?	✕ ✓

Practice · Theory · Research

Scaffolds support intent. They shape the path by rounding hard pivots and softening the turn to autonomy.

| | Scaffolding data discovery | Do micro-charts help to clarify filters where relevant? | ⊘ ✕ ✓ |
| | | Can tactics like auto-complete clarify or redirect vague search queries? | ⊘ ✕ ✓ |

Information-seeking has moved away from assuming that the information goal is well-formed; even when users are deliberately seeking information, they do not necessarily know exactly what it is they want.

14 Emphasis

Can the emphasis strategy be defined in a succinctly stated goal? ✕ ✓

Is emphasis strategic at first glance? ✕ ✓

As the visualization is used, do you interact with the pieces that are emphasized? ✕ ✓

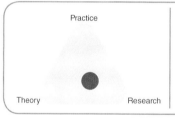

Emphasis helps guide users through a visualization. How users look at a visualization at first glance versus how they scan in search of a task differs.

Axis snapping

When axes are presented near each other on a related measure, are they snapped to the same values?

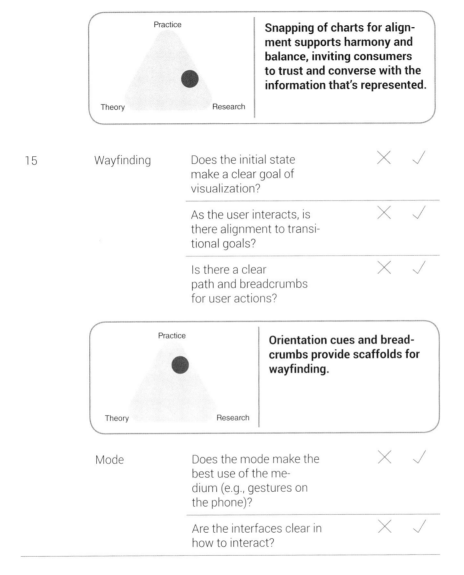

15	Wayfinding	Does the initial state make a clear goal of visualization?	✕ ✓
		As the user interacts, is there alignment to transitional goals?	✕ ✓
		Is there a clear path and breadcrumbs for user actions?	✕ ✓

> Orientation cues and breadcrumbs provide scaffolds for wayfinding.

	Mode	Does the mode make the best use of the medium (e.g., gestures on the phone)?	✕ ✓
		Are the interfaces clear in how to interact?	✕ ✓

Maturity Matrix

In addition to the detailed evaluation tool, the matrix in Table 16.1 can be used to assess visualizations at a high level if evaluating a large number of visualizations. This matrix can provide insight into an overall view of maturity, such as for organizations evaluating their overall practice.

TABLE 16.1 Maturity matrix

	Pictographic	Perceptual	Semantic	Intentional
Chart selection	Representation is not always appropriate. Chart chooser may help.	Accurate display or representation, variety may be limited.	Accurate, varied appropriately chart clusters may be used to create semantic units.	Accurate, varied clusters are logical, emphasis is controlled, may feel like one unit.
Titles	Inconsistent practice. Titles are unhelpful (e.g., naming by chart type).	Formulaic structure (e.g., trends by year).	Some formulaic with some inclusion of emphasis.	Structures balance formulaic and emphasis well. Easy to follow.
Annotation	Wall of text/ over-annotated.	None.	Some items called out appropriately.	Annotations match what chart shows.
Color use	Undefined. Logic unclear. Heavy reliance on legends.	Monochromatic. Minimal use of color. Color use might overlap.	Color use avoids semantic overlap.	Semantic color use helps support understanding and directs action.
Use of space	Single chart. Wall of charts with no clear negative space paradigm.	Negative space lines are visible. Clear boundaries. May use frame to place (no overlap).	Space used to highlight chart clusters.	Space supports eye flow. Author controls reading style.
Visual alignment	No clear alignment strategy.	Alignment may be based off worksheet location or template.	Alignment on data ink or related semantic structure.	Clear alignment strategy on ink, semantic structure or other—lines can clearly be drawn.
Visual supports (lines)	Lines, borders, grids, etc. are everywhere and inconsistent.	Lines, borders, grids, etc. pushed back and reduced. Strategy at the chart level. Some odd borders may exist.	Lines, borders, grids, etc. pushed back but may be used to integrate chart clusters.	Lines, borders, grids, etc. pushed back, integrated with chart clusters, items may be used for emphasis.
Visual supports (icons)	Logos, icons, etc. have no strategy. May also not be used at all.	Minimal icons may even not exist. Limited color on icon (flat). Used for info.	Logos, icons, etc. used semantically to facilitate understanding. May be part of filtering.	Icons are used semantically, and the strategy is clear. May also be balanced in weight. Looks like a product.

	Pictographic	Perceptual	Semantic	Intentional
Chart order (syntax)	Charts can be read or used in any order. Charts are not related.	Size may play a role in order. Charts may go in order of five whys.*	Charts are likely in order of five whys or with logical flow that can be articulated.	Charts have clear rationale for order and interactivity supports order.
Interactivity	Nonexistent or strategy unclear. High risk of overlaps and user confusion. Drop-down filters are key filtering mechanism.	Interactivity may be global. Drop-downs still play a key role—may be collapsible. Highlighting may be used.	Interactivity highlights semantic units and filters according to syntax. Drop-down use may be constrained or implemented in novel ways.	Various interactions support the relationships. High semantic practices that support the overall strategy.
Interface design	Heavy colors. Excessive lines. No clear paradigm. Changed from Tableau defaults without strategy. Color clashing. Logic not carried through dashboards.	Minimal, reduced Tableau defaults. Some stylistic elements. May use outside tools to create UI/UX structures.	Interface has clear logic that could be stated as CSS (e.g., heading style vs. sub). May be programmatic or include outside tools to create structures.	Semantic practices. Design helps learn the experience. Elements support understanding and provide guardrails to users.
User supports	Limited and not consistent. May be part of a separate document or teaching program.	Icons and or flyout may help learnability. May also include written instructions.	Icons and other elements help learnability.	Viz teaches users how to use it via the use of parameters such as color, icons, space, layout, and other techniques.
Complex charts	Not implemented or used wrongly.	Implemented minimally, may have toggle options.	Implemented with semantic supports to facilitate reading.	Implemented with semantic supports to facilitate reading, may also expose upon interaction (e.g., hover).

*Analytical technique to find the root cause by asking why five times.

Summary

Bringing together perception, semantics, and intent requires analyzing our techniques as much as the data itself. This chapter revisits the various triangles from the previous chapters and compiles key takeaways. The evaluation tool and maturity matrix enable us to assess our work and find ways to enhance our designs. Think of these tools as akin to recipes. They can encourage us to cook and help us get more comfortable in the kitchen. As we gain more fluency with the utensils and the recipes, we reach a higher level of comfort and creativity. We may need to try out different techniques until we master the craft, like baking those perfect cookies that melt in your mouth. So, let's play.

CHAPTER 17

Close

We've arrived at the end of the book after covering three parts: perception, semantics, and intent. This triad forms the basis for functionally aesthetic data visualization. Each of the parts, along with this closing chapter, introduces four visuals representing land, fire, water, and air, shown together in Figure 17.1. These choices are deliberate as they can be experienced with our senses and are directly connected with the world around us. The elements, in a way, address the realization of the artifacts and objects that we build and consume, the alchemic process that turns concepts into material.

Throughout the book, we focus on the various aspects of research and practice that provide guidelines and examples of how semantics and intent inform the meaningful visual depiction of data to the intended audience. At the core, functionally aesthetic visualizations emphasize what is important for a particular dataset, in a particular context, and to a particular audience. However, visual analytics has evolved over the years. With higher computing power, maturing AI algorithms, and the capability of being able to house large amounts of complex data in the cloud, effective ways of visualizing data have become even more important. At the same time, sensors and connectivity provide an excellent opportunity to see patterns that may otherwise remain hidden in the objects and events around us. Let's delve into this some more.

FIGURE 17.1 Revisiting the four elements that introduced each book part
Csondy/Getty Images and Hritik/Adobe Stock

Data in Everything and Everywhere

The *Internet of Things* (*IoT*) is the network of objects or "things" in our environment that are embedded with sensors and technology with the goal of connecting and exchanging data with other devices over the Internet. These devices range from ordinary household objects like a Nest thermostat and a washing machine to more sophisticated applications such as smart power grids and factories (Figure 17.2).

FIGURE 17.2 Visualizing IoT data in a factory setting
NanoStockk/Getty images

IoT provides opportunities for acquiring different types of data from the real-world environment for a range of complex and heterogeneous things. IoT data provides all sorts of useful information that can be used by context-aware applications to improve people's daily lives. We are able to control the temperature in our living room before we head home from work, get the sprinklers to turn on if they detect no precipitation in the air, or check which appliances are running in our kitchen, as seen in Figure 17.3. As raw data from these sensors is combined with contextual information (e.g., time, location, status), IoT turns into a rich yet voluminous source for data analysis tasks.

With the proliferation of IoT data come new challenges for thinking of functionally aesthetic visualizations, tools, and applications that are useful across a variety of applications:

- Find ways to identify subsets and patterns of interest and surface them to the consumer at the right time to take action.

- Adapt the mode to fit a variety of displays, adapting the perspectives and details to fit the medium.

■ Own responsibility for making black-box AI techniques more transparent and explainable as they often amplify systemic racism and other biases that manifest in the data. It's important to both visualize the results of these techniques and communicate the way they work for the consumer.

FIGURE 17.3 Accessing smart appliance data from a mobile device
hakule/Getty images

Consumers of IoT use devices in the field ranging from large displays to tablets and mobile devices. The challenge is determining how the medium affects the mode to support automated analysis and human interaction for decision making, which involves viewing data through different perspectives and focusing on details of interest. Finally, machine learning and AI methods are even more relevant as they automatically extract patterns from data and make predictions. We need to be responsible for making these black-box techniques more transparent and explainable, visualizing both their results and the way they work to the consumer.

Let's walk through an actual scenario where IoT and AI data have made a difference. As you might have noticed by now, food is a running theme of this book. It's visceral and relatable, making it easy to weave data narratives into situations that we often find familiar. Now, imagine that you ordered curbside food pickup from your favorite restaurant. You come home ready to eat and, alas, find that your spring roll order is missing. Or you wait in line at the ice cream store only to find that your favorite brown butter almond brittle ice cream ran out. The disappointment is insurmountable.

The restaurant business is tough, often fraught with labor challenges, food quality issues, and management of supply and demand. Beyond the dining experience in the restaurant, patrons order carryout via a number of channels, including the phone, apps, and third-party couriers. Global events such as the coronavirus pandemic forced restaurateurs to close in-store dining rooms, further shifting to an omni-channel model for delivery, drive-thru pickup, and takeout formats. As restaurant owners consider how to best attract wary guests back to their stores, they also must figure out how to offset the challenges of off-premise operations.

Computer vision, AI, and analytics are revolutionizing the restaurant industry as COVID-19 accelerates the pivot to greater digitization. The intelligent restaurant movement has begun to embrace technology, starting with QR-enabled menus mentioned in Chapter 15. IoTs have become a game-changer, starting from monitoring food refrigeration and progressing to enabling more sophisticated production control, food ordering sequences, and management of workers. After all, customer loyalty is so important with all the different options of restaurants to choose from.

One example of digitization being applied can be seen at Vistry (vistry.ai), which allows restaurants to use computer vision with edge computing to spot food that has sat too long. The dashboard in Figure 17.4 shows how data generated by Vistry can be used to explore the drive-thru experience at a fictional quick-serve restaurant, Los Pollos Hermanos. At first glance, you can get a sense of the average wait time by day, with the mornings being the shortest, peaking at noon, and tapering off a bit by evening. The wait times are also spatially shown by zones, starting from the pre-menu area where folks are lining up as they head to the menu board to the final pickup area. In addition to events that are consumer focused, the data shows patterns in events that are at the heart of the house (HOH), tracking food preparation from the time orders are sent to completion. Space and time are linked together with computer vision and IoT data mapping zones to metrics that change and flow. Selecting a time of day highlights problem zones, whether it's delays at the order board in the morning or long lines at the ingress for lunch.

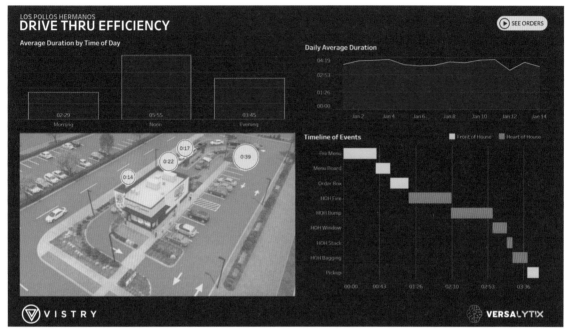

FIGURE 17.4 Dashboard showing wait times in mm:ss at a quick-serve restaurant

In addition to looking at this overview as consumers from the outside, let's now move toward the kitchen and understand what's going on inside. Figure 17.5 shows a dashboard with volumes of purchases and average wait times. The text above the bar chart shows the colors for the meeting and missing wait times. We can dig deeper into the events themselves and see individual consumer journeys. Hovering over the zones set up in the kitchen for different foods shows their effects on the ordered items, indicated by the bars. The data shown in the dashboard gives us an indication of where the restaurant is missing and meeting its goals. The inside of the kitchen provides a snapshot of what the consumer journey on the outside looks like to identify problems where orders are taking longer than expected.

Clicking on an individual order item shows the trays of ingredients in the kitchen, indicating when they were last refilled (Figure 17.6). Functionally aesthetic visualizations provide useful scaffolds for problem solving, understanding the bottlenecks and how they affect things downstream. We can get an understanding of how long the guacamole has been in the tray as well as, based on current orders, when it would be best to refill.

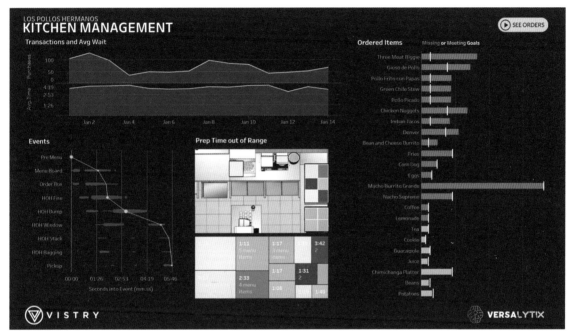

FIGURE 17.5 A dashboard showing the wait times and events inside the restaurant's kitchen

As we saw with the restaurant example, IoT has become an intrinsic part of our economy—be it traffic management, smart homes, electric grid maintenance, and factory

Functionally aesthetic visualizations play an even more important role in this new world of data ubiquity, supporting complex data-driven decisions and automation.

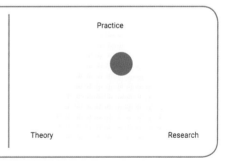

operations, to name a few. Vast quantities of continuously streaming data are filled with new insights just waiting to be discovered. There's even a bigger role for creating functionally aesthetic visualizations to help humans comprehend the volume, velocity, and variety of IoT data. At the heart of all of this is identifying and applying techniques for effectively conveying these insights to the reader.

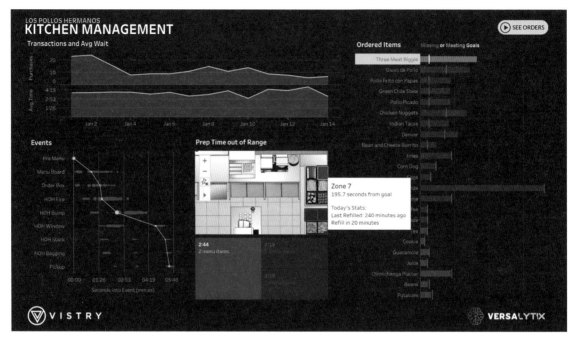

FIGURE 17.6 Interacting with the dashboard shows the stats for the various trays for the Three Meat Biggie order.

These changes will continue to challenge how we think about the world and the ways in which we work to incorporate fairness. Practicing ethical decision making as we expand technologies will demand a continuous investigation into how technology further codifies the social systems in place. We'll need to improve the ways in which we disclose how technology is used, what information is collected, and the ways we correct bias in the data.

Data democratization will enable anybody to use data at any time to make decisions with new experiences for consuming and sharing that data. Given there will always be the use case for a consumer to garner insights on their computer, we will also see mobile devices and the physical environment play a greater role in how we think about sharing and acting upon that information. In the next section, let's see how new devices and the new environment influence the types of tools and experiences they afford in how we think about visualizing data.

New Tools and New Experiences

In Chapter 15, we touched upon future-forward ideas in the space of mobile, natural language, and augmented reality (AR)—aspects of which already exist today. Visualization is now prevalent in a multitude of gadgets and settings; smartphones, tablets, wearable devices, refrigerators, cars, and wall displays show the versatility of data consumption, whether it's accessing the local weather or watching a news reporter describing and presenting the election results. While we surround ourselves with an ensemble of digital devices with high computation and rendering capabilities, there are opportunities for data sensemaking anytime and anywhere. Each of these devices and technologies also helps explore unique ways in which data can be made more accessible to the reader.

The research community has been actively exploring how these ubiquitous analytical experiences can be realized and the types of scenarios that they enable. The current challenges for making these experiences worthwhile to a consumer include the need for fast and efficient methods for device discovery, view management, and interaction. Often, one way to make progress in such a vast, open area is to focus on a specific domain or type of visualization. For instance, GRaSP (Kister et al., 2017), shown in Figure 17.7, explores these challenges with graph visualization and interaction. The system combines spatially-aware mobile interactions with large displays using gestures and touch input.

Interactive wall-sized displays enable the presentation of large amounts of data and visualization views. Systems that employ these large displays typically use natural language, gestural, and direct touch interactions with these displays as traditional mouse and keyboard modalities become unwieldy (Srinivasan & Stasko, 2018; Lee et al., 2012). One common experience involves exploring the concept of multiple coordinated views, taking advantage of the increased screen real estate (Langner et al., 2018). Smartphones have great wireless connectivity and sensors that provide information about their surroundings. With problems like the climate crisis, many groups of people can freely move and walk around these views and effectively explore data by touching the display directly and interacting from a distance using the touch screens on their phones.

FIGURE 17.7 The GRaSP system showing interaction between mobile devices and wall-sized displays
Courtesy of the Interactive Media Lab Dresden

As we explore these novel possibilities, we shift away from the technical limitations of scalability imposed by traditional desktop displays to augmenting the human, giving them superpowers. Shared spaces where people can come together and explore insights and patterns in data facilitate new levels of collaboration and creativity.

In addition to new displays and devices, we now see applications of data overlaid in our physical environments through AR or where data is projected into the visual reality. Some of the early technology advances are unsurprisingly related to navigation applications. After all, maps have been the trailblazer in terms of innovation. These AR experiences show custom landmarks and traffic information on a graphical overlay that's perceived through a transparent surface, like a car windshield.

> The potential for new forms of data exploration is only realized by understanding how perception, visualization design, interaction techniques, and display technology work together to benefit the consumer.

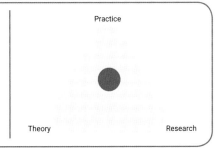

Though it's still early, AR (and possibly VR) could fundamentally change the way we interact with and interpret data. With the right tools and use cases, there could be compelling applications in the near future. People will glean insights, but they will also be able to act—both in the world, supported by the data, and in the data, informed by the world. Multi-person settings could support discussions and group interaction in industries like factory assembly and healthcare. While innovation is currently constrained to research and proofs of concept, as we better understand how this technology can support analytical tasks and exploration, we could be inventing an exciting future.

Sign-off

We hope our book has provided you with a better lens for bringing functional aesthetics into your visualization practice. Delightfully crafted visualizations can provide evocative and persuasive narratives and stories. While we head into more technology advancements, we should keep in mind that at the fundamental level, the human visual and cognitive systems are truly remarkable. At the same time, we are all intrinsically curious creatures. This combination of traits provides us with the necessary tools to problem-solve and invent, informed by data. It's our responsibility to determine ways in which computing machines can cooperate and augment our skills as we create and consume these visualizations. Along with better and more powerful AI algorithms to crunch large amounts of data comes the added responsibility to understand biases when we communicate insights to an audience. Research and practice can be a symbiotic way of thoughtfully honing and developing good examples and knowledge to further the discipline in innovative ways. As computer scientist Alan Kay (https://en.wikipedia.org/wiki/Alan_Kay) states, "The best way to predict the future is to create it." We hope this book empowers *you* to create your vision. Perhaps some inspiration from a bite of your very own bento box.

Technical Glossary

ambiguity   The concept that the interpretation of some entity varies by context, person, place, etc. (Chapter 5)

analytical conversation   The ability to converse with data interactively. (Chapter 5)

analytical intent   The goal that a consumer or analyst focuses on when performing either targeted or more open-ended data exploration and discovery. (Chapter 11)

annotation   An in-chart clarifier that identifies salient points such as peaks and troughs within the visualization. (Chapter 10)

artificial intelligence (AI)   The ability of computers to perform tasks that normally require human intelligence, such as visual perception, speech recognition, decision making, and object recognition. (Chapter 17)

augmented reality (AR)   Technology that superimposes a computer-generated image onto a user's view of the real world. (Chapter 15)

breadcrumb   A navigation path that shows where the user is on a website or app. (Chapter 15)

clarification   The act of asking follow-up questions if we do not understand what someone is saying. (Chapter 5)

closure   A sense of completion of a narrative in a conversation. (Chapter 9)

coherence (in conversation)   The way participants cooperate to maintain a reasonably focused thread of conversation. (Chapter 9)

cohesion (in conversation)   When parts of a message bind together, making it understandable to the participants. (Chapter 9)

Colonomos model (Integrated Model of Interpreting) The model focuses on the cognitive processes and decision making an interpreter experiences while interpreting the meaning and intent behind a speaker's message. (Chapter 5)

contraction The act of preserving the same intent but discarding unneeded information. (Chapter 12)

conversational centering The context of a conversation adjusts over time to maintain coherence through transitional states that retain, shift, continue, or reset these conversational elements. (Chapter 9)

data dictionary A set of information describing the contents, format, and structure of data. (Chapter 7)

data preparation A meaning-centered exercise to prepare, clean, and curate data. (Chapter 7)

data shaping The building of hierarchical relationships between two or more entities in a dataset. (Chapter 7)

deictic reference The use of gestures or other means of pointing to specify a concept, such as pointing at a place on a map and saying "here." (Chapter 5)

emphasis The act of drawing attention to salient points in a visual. (Chapter 14)

endianness The bytes in computer memory are read in a certain order. It's commonly used to express date formats. (Chapter 5)

expansion The act of providing more detail, sometimes adding in information that is culturally relevant or needed for the person to understand. (Chapter 12)

framing A technique of surrounding charts with design elements, often with visual outlines for placing charts. (Chapter 3)

framing text Text or sentences that are captions, narratives, and other callouts outside the visualization. (Chapter 10)

functional aesthetics The concept of combining perception, semantics, and intent to function together as a whole, creating beauty in meaningful design.

functional text   Text that provides those consuming a visualization with the necessary information to use or evaluate the limits of the visualization. (Chapter 10)

generalization   The process of simplifying or eliminating less semantically important features and exaggerating more important ones. (Chapter 1)

Gestalt Principles   These principles help reason why the human mind has the natural compulsion to find order in disorder. (Chapter 1)

graphicacy   The ability to understand and present information visually in the form of images, sketches, diagrams, charts, and other non-textual formats. (Chapter 6)

Grice's Cooperative Principle   A principle that states that participants in a conversation normally attempt to be truthful, relevant, concise, and clear. (Chapter 13)

icon   A pictorial representation or imagery of a concept or thing (e.g., a shopping cart icon). (Chapter 5)

intent   A goal or task in mind that a person or computer plans to achieve. (Chapter 5)

Internet of Things (IoT)   The network of objects, or "things," in our environment that are embedded with sensors and technology with the goal of connecting and exchanging data with other objects, or "things" (for example, devices). (Chapter 17)

join   The process of combining data tables based on a common data attribute. (Chapter 7)

key performance indicator (KPI)   A quantifiable measure of performance over time for a specific objective. Informally, charts using large numbers may be referred to as KPI (charts). (Chapter 2)

literacy (data literacy)   The ability to read, write, and communicate data in context. (Chapter 6)

medium   The channel or system through which communications are conveyed. (Chapter 10)

metaphor (visual metaphor)   A representation of a noun through a visual image that indicates an association between them. (Chapter 12)

mode   The means of communicating. (Chapter 10)

multimodal (reading)   Where meaning is communicated through combinations of written language; spoken language; and visual, audio, gestural, tactile, and spatial forms. (Chapter 9)

Natural Language Generation (NLG)   A software process that automatically transforms structured data into human-readable text. It is a subcategory of NLP. (Chapter 10)

Natural Language Interaction / Interface (NLI)   The act of applying various NLP techniques to enable people to interact with a computer. (Chapter 10)

Natural Language Processing (NLP)   A subfield of linguistics, computer science, and artificial intelligence concerned with the interactions between computers and human language. (Chapter 10)

natural size   The size of a chart that clearly reflects its intended form and function of its message to the reader. (Chapter 8)

numeracy   The ability to understand and work with numbers. (Chapter 6)

orality (data orality)   Where the use of charts serves as supplemental to the exposition of data. (Chapter 6)

perception   The ability to see, hear, and become aware of our environment through the senses. (Chapter 1)

pivot   The process of summarizing and reorganizing data stored in a table, preserving the data values. (Chapter 7)

pragmatics   A branch of linguistics and semiotics that deals with the relationship of symbols and linguistic expressions based on the context where they occur. (Chapter 9)

proportional brushing   A technique where a proportion of the selected data is shown in relation to all the values rather than just filtering to the selection. (Chapter 4)

qualifier   Text anchored to a quantifier that provides context to the number within the visualization. (Chapter 10)

quantifier   Text where the visual pattern in a chart is articulated into quantities and mathematically understood. (Chapter 10)

recursive proportions   The generative approach to architectural design that assembles parts based on established proportions. (Chapter 2)

refinement (conversational refinement)   An iterative process of updating a response by a series of clarifications and repairs. (Chapter 5)

register   The degree of formality and familiarity communicated within a visualization or an interaction. (Chapter 5)

repair (conversational repair)   The process people and computers use to detect and resolve problems of speaking, hearing, and understanding. (Chapter 5)

scaffold   One or more visual and interactive elements that help with the discoverability of features or functionality in an interface. (Chapter 13)

semantics   The study of how we draw meaning in communication. (Chapter 4)

semiotics   The study of signs and symbols and their use or interpretation. (Chapter 4)

Six Sigma   A set of techniques and tools that provide statistical benchmarks for process improvement. (Chapter 3)

Stroop effect   Our tendency to experience difficulty naming a physical color when it is used to spell the name of a different color. (Chapter 1)

symbol   Imagery that need not resemble the concept that the imagery depicts (e.g., a heart symbolizes love). (Chapter 5)

thumbnail   A very small or concise description, representation, or summary. (Chapter 8)

union   The process of combining the results of two or more queries into a single result set. (Chapter 7)

vagueness   A concept that cannot be precisely determined by clear boundaries and properties and often depends on the context. (Chapter 5)

view snapping   A technique that semantically aligns charts along one or more common axes in a dashboard. (Chapter 14)

visual communication   The practice of using visual elements to communicate information. (Chapter 12)

Index